# INDIVIDUALS IN MASS MEDIA ORGANIZATIONS

# SAGE ANNUAL REVIEWS OF COMMUNICATION RESEARCH

*Volume 10*

**SAGE ANNUAL REVIEWS OF COMMUNICATION RESEARCH**

# *Individuals in Mass Media Organizations:*
## Creativity and Constraint

**JAMES S. ETTEMA**

and

**D. CHARLES WHITNEY**

Editors

**SAGE PUBLICATIONS**
Beverly Hills / London / New Delhi

*For information address:*

SAGE Publications, Inc.
275 South Beverly Drive
Beverly Hills, California 90212

SAGE Publications India Pvt. Ltd.
C-236 Defence Colony
New Delhi 110 024, India

SAGE Publications Ltd
28 Banner Street
London EC1Y 8QE, England

Printed in the United States of America

**Library of Congress Cataloging in Publication Data**

Main entry under title:

Individuals in mass media organizations.

   (Sage annual reviews of communication research; v. 10)
   Includes bibliographies.
   1. Mass media—Addresses, essays, lectures.
2. Communication in organizations—Addresses,
essays, lectures. 3. Creation (Literary, artistic,
etc.)—Addresses, essays, lectures. I. Ettema,
James S. II. Whitney, D. Charles (David Charles),
1946-   .III. Series.
P91.C564     302.2'3     81-18437
ISBN 0-8039-1766-X     AACR2'
ISBN 0-8039-1767-7 (pbk.)

FIRST PRINTING

*Individuals in*
*Mass Media Organizations*

*To Marsha and Elizabeth*

*To Ellen*

# CONTENTS

# INTRODUCTION:
## Mass Communicators in Context

### James S. Ettema and D. Charles Whitney

THE SYMBOLS OF contemporary culture are more than anything else the products of complex organizations. To understand these symbols, it is necessary to understand among other things the organizations producing them.

These are central ideas in the recent scholarship collected in this volume. The first seven contributions seek to understand more about organizations whose symbolic products primarily entertain, the studios of Hollywood and Nashville and the television networks and publishing houses of New York. The remaining six seek to understand more about organizations whose products primarily inform, the newsrooms of the United States and Great Britain. More fundamentally, however, all are about the same thing: the way symbol-producing organizations shape the form, content and meaning of their products. All recognize that individual communicators work within the context of organizational structures and processes. These structures and processes in turn operate within the contexts of the economic, political, legal, ideological and other institutional arrangements of society.

A number of the contributions are of value for their rich description of these contexts. Ryan and Peterson, for example, review the process by which the country music establishment winnows out a few songs from among the many submitted by writers. Powell discusses recent economic trends which have prompted large publishers to concentrate on the "blockbuster bestseller" at the expense of the "middle-size" book. And Peters and Cantor survey the screen acting profession in which a few workers receive most of the rewards thanks to the structure of the film industry and the ideology of the workers themselves. Each of these chapters thus describes an entertainment industry structure or process in which a few products, whether hit songs, bestsellers, or Hollywood stars, are selected for public consumption from among the many possibilities.

Similarly, a number of the chapters on news organizations seek to describe structures and processes accounting for what becomes news and what does not. Two chapters, for example, focus on election news. Gurevitch and Blumler describe how BBC general election coverage is structured by a host of considerations ranging from the logistics of broadcast newsgathering, to sometimes competing journalistic norms of objectivity and balance, to attempts by their news sources, the major political parties, to control coverage by controlling availability of news. In their study of American congressional elections, Clarke and Evans do not so much describe as analytically demonstrate that such news coverage is shaped by individual and organizational forces within American newspapers.

Moving beyond description, all of the contributions recognize that individual work cannot be understood apart from its various contexts because it is powerfully shaped and constrained by them. If there is, in fact, a single theme to this volume, it is constraint. Ryan and Peterson, for example, find the writing of country music to be constrained by a "product image" of songs currently popular. Fishman argues that journalists' attempts to make sense of events are enclosed by the "phase structures" of those events which provide ready-made though highly circumscribed definitions of what an "event" is, and whether it is newsworthy. Becker suggests that organizational and technological differences between newspapers and broadcast organizations mold the news products of those two realms differently, and Powell finds book editors to be constrained by the strategies for marketing their products.

The view of constraint as a powerful, and often destructive, limitation imposed by organizations upon the professional autonomy or creative freedom of individuals is the dominant view here. But it is not the only view. In his pioneering work, *Administrative Behavior,* Herbert Simon argues that organizations constrain individual activity, but in an important sense, they also enhance it. Organizations do not, of course, increase the intelligence or skill of individuals, but through division of labor and coordination of effort they harness individual abilities and direct them toward the organization's tasks. Mass communicated creativity, for example, can only be effected in an organizational context.

Several of the chapters in this volume take this more positive view of the relationship between individuals and organizations. Newcomb and Alley show how a television producer has assembled an organization which is able to realize his vision of quality television and portray his view of the world, all within the constraints of the commercial television industry. Ettema offers the most radical interpretation of this relationship between individual and organization in his case study of a public television producer. He argues that the demands of television production routines and the necessary compromises in organizational politics did not so much compromise as energize the producer's creative activities. The constraints on the design of the programs were pieces of a puzzle which the producer as creator was called upon to solve. Newcomb and Alley and Ettema thus find the opportunity for individual creativity and control within the bounds of complex media organizations and they focus on how individuals use these opportunities.

Chapters by Turow and Pekurny complement those of Newcomb and Alley and Ettema by focusing on how opportunities for individual control emerge from the television industry in the first place. Turow argues that an opportunity for innovation in commercial television occurs when a network in ratings trouble and thus receptive to something new comes together with a producer who is only marginally involved in television production and thus has little to lose by taking a chance. Pekurny's essay is an ironic counterpoint: while Turow argues that innovation represents a successful organization response to certain conditions, Pekurny argues that innovation represents, in a sense, organizational failure. Innovation is possible because the television industry is not, and cannot be, fully rationalized through such devices as ratings and reliance on track-record producers. Because the tasks of television production are not completely routinized, some individual creativity is necessary and innovation is at least a possibility.

Interestingly, all the authors who focus on the opportunities for and exercise of individual control within media organizations are writing about entertainment industries. Perhaps this need not be the case, but as Ryan and Peterson suggest, it may well be that the production of entertainment as compared to the production of information is in fact less routine and allows the individual workers more control. Peters and Cantor, however, are quick to remind that this control is not shared by all workers. At the same time, the authors writing about entertainment organizations are focusing on somewhat different aspects of the relationship between individuals and organizations as compared with those writing about information organizations. While all of the authors share an interest in the organizational and institutional determinants of symbol production, those writing about information organizations do not let those determinants slip from central focus. Those writing about entertainment organizations, on the other hand, are more willing first to stipulate the importance of these determinants and then to shift focus to how individuals, in the words of Newcomb and Alley, "work within, around and through (them) to achieve creative goals."

In briefest overview, these have been some of the conceptual threads which weave together the diverse chapters of this volume. In terms of both theoretical perspective and research method, the editors sought variety: the volume offers chapters grounded in structural-functional theories of organization and others which rely primarily on work drawn directly from the evolving specialty of mass communication; still others depart from both of these. Peters and Cantor, for example, begin from a macro-sociological perspective while Fishman begins from an interpretive sociology grounded in phenomenology. At the same time, the volume offers chapters diverse in method, from case studies and historical accounts, participant observation and semistructured interviews, to structured surveys and quantitative and qualitative content analysis. For methodological vigor, few current examples of mass communication research match that of Clarke and Evans, combining surveys of both journalists and their audiences with content analyses of the journalists' products. Likewise, Robinson, Sahin, and Davis match interviews with television journalists with those of their audiences. Whitney concludes this volume by considering the interplay between the choice of research problems and perspectives by communication researchers and the methods which they have employed.

This theoretical and methodological diversity testifies to the richness of current scholarship in mass communication organizations. The goal of bringing together this work is to display that richness before scholars working in mass communication, the production of culture, the sociology of knowledge and other pursuits and to invite reinvestment in further research.

*Chapter 1*

# THE PRODUCT IMAGE
## The Fate of Creativity in Country Music Songwriting

### John Ryan and Richard A. Peterson

THE ROMANTIC IMAGE of the creative artist or undaunted reporter pictures an individual working alone on a piece from its conception until it is completed (Zola, 1968; Becker, 1978). More realistically, however, few creators in the fine arts, and none in the commercial media, do everything needed to complete a work (Becker, 1981; Cohen and Young, 1981). Instead, a number of skilled specialists have a part in shaping the final work as it goes through a series of stages which, superficially at least, resemble an assembly line.

The shaping of symbols by such systems of collaborative production has been focal in the production of culture perspective which has coalesced in sociology in recent years. The perspective calls attention to the influence of factors such as organization structure, technology, law, market, reward systems, industry structure, and the like, on the content of symbols in various fields ranging from the arts and popular culture to science and religion (Peterson, 1976, 1979; Butsch, 1981). Here, the perspective is brought to bear on the ways in which creativity is shaped by the day-to-day processes of production of country music.

Country music production is appropriate to our purposes for several reasons. First, in contrast to the folk music from which it derives, contemporary country music is produced and marketed through a complex system of collaborative activity (Kosser, 1976; Peterson, 1978; Baskerville, 1979; Guyon, 1981). Second, the degree of standardization in creating phono-

AUTHORS' NOTE: We gratefully acknowledge the following people who have given invaluable suggestions on an earlier draft: George Becker, Jan Belcher, Daniel Cornfield, Michael Hughs, Claire L. Peterson, Beth Rabeck, John Rumble, and Deborah Sim. We also appreciate the support of the Kennan-Venture Fund during the early stages of the project.

graph records is intermediate between the more highly routinized system of newspaper and television news production (Tuchman, 1978; Gans, 1979; Cohen and Young, 1981), and the less standardized contemporary feature film and television entertainment production (Cantor, 1980; Rosenblum and Karen, 1980). Being intermediate in standardization, song production shares characteristics with production processes in a wide range of other media. Third, the country music segment of the commercial phonograph record industry is appropriate because the division of creative labor is greater there than in the contemporary pop/rock music field. Numerous singers in the latter field write the songs they perform (Melly, 1971; Denisoff, 1975; Davis, 1975), but in country music the largest proportion of all songs which reach the popularity charts are written by nonperforming writers (Siman, 1976). In a recent study, Peterson and Ryan (forthcoming) found that professional songwriters accounted for fully 75.6 percent of the songs on a sample of 1979-1980 *Billboard* magazine country music charts. Finally, the country music field has been chosen as the focus of study because the authors, separately and together, have engaged in a number of studies of this segment of the commercial music industry over the past 12 years (see Peterson and Ryan, forthcoming, for details of the various data sources). All unattributed quotations and examples come from our interviews.

This chapter has three sections. The first traces the loosely linked decision chain a song passes through to reach the consuming public. This review shows how the musical product is shaped at each link in the chain by a number of people with differing skills and goals. The second section describes four alternative frameworks which have been used to explain how collaborative production is possible in the loosely coordinated media arts. A fifth framework, identified as "product image," is then offered as a more parsimonious explanation of how the problems of collaborative creation are solved. The final section of the article shows two alternative strategies songwriters use to accommodate to the fact that they are the first link in the long decision chain, and thus they must try to anticipate the preferences and interests of a large number of decision makers down-chain to insure that their creative efforts are presented to the consuming audience. In order to understand the dilemmas faced by the songwriter, it is necessary first to describe the decision chain.

## THE DECISION CHAIN

A large number of distinct tasks from songwriting to record promotion is required to make a hit country music record. One person might do all of these, but ordinarily the various tasks are performed by numerous specialists who do their part and pass the work to the next stage. What is more, no one specialist has artistic responsibility for or financial control over all of the stages. Consequently, the project has to be promoted and sold a number of times as a song idea evolves toward being a phonograph record.

Songs are often rewritten or reinterpreted at several points along the way, and although the developmental history of each song is unique, there are recurrent patterns. These we call the decision chain. Figure 1.1 maps in schematic outline the major decision stages through which a song must pass. We begin the discussion of the decision chain at the point where the writer presents a song to the publisher.

## PUBLISHING

Today the publishing firm derives its income not so much from selling sheet music as from the royalties it receives for the radio, television, and live performance of the songs it controls, as well as from the small percentage it earns for each recorded copy of its songs which are sold to the public. The chief function of the publisher in the contemporary music market, therefore, is to get its songs recorded and released by commercially successful performers (Siman, 1976; Baskerville, 1979; 59-93).

Much of the effort of the employees of commercially successful publishing firms is devoted to what is called "pitching" songs to recording artists or to the persons who choose songs for them. When a producer hears, or reads in one of the industry tipsheets, that an artist is recording soon, the first step is to find out what sorts of songs are needed. These requests are often of the following sort: "a positive ballad," "a honky-tonk woman song," "an answer-follow-up to the artist's latest hit." If the firm has any songs that might fit, or might be altered to fit, the publisher plays demonstration tapes (called demos in the industry) to the artist or representative.

The songs which the publisher has available are of two sorts. The first includes all those songs in the catalogue—that is, the songs, many of which have been recorded before, to which the publisher already holds publication rights. The second source includes all the songs currently being written by writers under contract to the publisher or songs by unaffiliated writers that come to the attention of the publisher. Most songs that are played for the artist are such newly written songs. With this information in hand, it is now possible to describe the decisions which the publisher makes concerning the songwriter (arrow 1 in Figure 1.1).

The publisher reviews hundreds of new songs, looking for a few to accept. The quest is not for songs that the publisher likes, or songs that are unique, or songs that coherently express the feelings of the writer, or songs

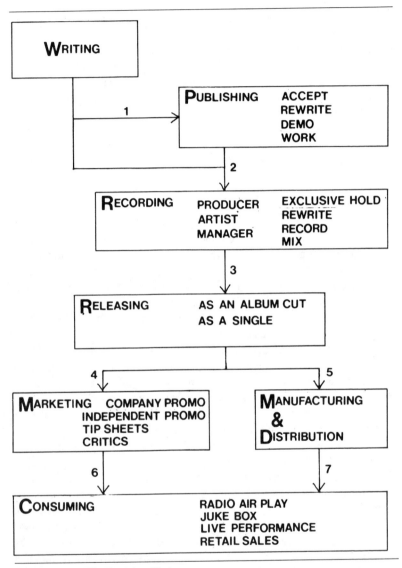

FIGURE 1.1    The Decision Chain

that portray the human condition. Although each of these descriptions is sometimes used to categorize desired songs, the songs which the publisher accepts are those which fit the publisher's image of a successful artist or type of artist. Typical judgments are as follows: "That's a perfect Barbara Mandrell song," "This will be the new 'Take This Job and Shove It' for Johnny

Paycheck," "I can hear Janie Fricke or almost any of the new girl singers doing that," or "It may be fine as a personal statement, but it's not commercial; it starts off all George Jones and ends up too intellectual."

Songs judged to contain little more than a good line or two may be accepted if the publisher believes the songwriter is able, and more importantly is willing, to take suggestions on rewriting the song to make it a more commercial product. Fred Rose, a writer-publisher who helped Hank Williams and many others with their songs, was widely known as the "song doctor" (Rumble, 1980; Flippo, 1981).

The changes may be minor, such as the substitution of a word to fit the meter of a lyric, or they may be major changes which entirely alter the meaning of the song. For example, an aspiring writer, Rick Shields, played a song called "Old Love Letters" to a publisher who thought the song should have a more positive message. To illustrate this, the publisher suggested that the lines, "Old Love Letters, like the cheapest of wine, grow bitter not sweet, with the passage of time." (copyright 1980, Rick Shields) be changed to, "Old Love Letters, like prime vintage wine, grow better and better, with the passage of time."

Nevertheless, most publishers influence writers not by rewriting songs, but rather by the selections which they make among the songs that are offered to them. The mesh of the filter at this stage is very fine. David Baskerville (1979: 74) has observed that "the ratio of material submitted to the amount accepted is almost one thousand to one."

When the publisher is satisfied with a song, a demonstration tape is made in order to pitch it to artists who might record the song (Baskerville, 1979: 48). The prime requisite of the demo tape is that the words and melody be presented in a clear and articulate manner. In the 1960s demos consisted of a singer with an acoustic guitar, but in recent years demos have become ever more complexly orchestrated, arranged, and mixed.

Demos have become more carefully produced for several reasons. Increasingly, publishers have produced demos that will appeal to a particular producer and artist. Thus, they arrange the song in ways that will reflect the style of the artist. The more polished demos will help to sell a song by making it sound better, and also by suggesting to the record producer the instrumental arrangement, tempo, and dynamic range that might be used in recording the song. Thus, the process of making a demonstration record may shape and delimit the interpretation of a song as much as the process of rewriting may change the lyrics (McNeel and Luther, 1978: 87-88).

The final step in the publisher's part of the decision chain is to "work" the song by "pitching" demo tapes to those who decide what songs will be recorded. This process is depicted as arrow 2 in Figure 1.1. The ready access of publishers to record company decision makers attracts aspiring writers to the established publishing firms, but the best known writers are not so dependent on a publisher. Based on their own successful "track record" of writing commercial songs, they can pitch their own new material themselves (Gant, 1974; Kosser, 1976; Dranov, 1980). In this way, the few most successful writers can circumvent the filtering and shaping influences of the publisher. Whether worked directly or through a publisher, all songs must travel the path depicted as arrow 2 to progress along the decision chain.

**RECORDING**

Numerous publishers and writers acting on their own compete with each other to get their songs recorded by the leading recording artists. Here again the chances of success for any one song are not great. For example, Dennis Lecorriere, lead singer of the group, claims that over 2000 songs were screened to find the 10 that fit the image and mood for a 1981 Dr. Hook album (Peterson and Ryan, forthcoming).

Ordinarily, decisions about what songs to choose are made by the recording artists' producer in conjunction with the artist (Peterson and Berger, 1971). Often the manager of the artist is involved as well. The prime question is whether the song fits the artist's established image. In the process of looking for such songs many otherwise excellent songs may get bypassed. For example, a writer explained that his boisterous "What's so great about Texas?" wouldn't be recorded because no country music singer could afford to alienate 20% of all country music fans. Another illustration is provided by a participant in a Nashville songwriters association workshop who had written a song about a blind friend. A producer told her, "No blind people songs, please!"

But the artist's image is sometimes a poor indicator of acceptability because a producer may be trying to get beyond a stereotyped image in order to broaden the artist's appeal. For example, one singer was deluged with novelty songs after he scored with several up-tempo novelties. Rejecting all these, his producer sought out story ballads to establish the singer's career as a serious artist.

If the song is a likely prospect, the producer may put it on "exclusive hold" so that the demo will not be played to another artist for a few weeks. The artist or producer may rewrite the song somewhat to make it more commercial or so that it better fits the image they want to convey. They may insist on these changes and may demand co-writer credit (and the royalties that go with it) as a condition of using the song. Although this tactic is generally frowned upon by the industry, it is not uncommon. By including the producer or artist as co-writer, the composer is essentially giving up a portion of his creative product in order to better compete in the marketplace (Williams, 1972; Wood, 1980; Peterson and Ryan, forthcoming).

Billy Sherrill, one of the leading producers of country music, who has been criticized for changing lyrics in order to ask for co-writer credit (Wood, 1980), asserts that his reasons for changing a song are "purely altrustic and commercial." Asked in an interview whether he found it necessary for writers to rewrite songs before he recorded them, he answered: "Eighty-five percent of the time, I change something or suggest some changes. Most writers are very cooperative. The only changes I ever want to make are changes that I think will help the song become a hit." He goes on to explain that he has responsibilities to people down the decision chain. "It's going to cost a record company a whole lot of money when I record a song and they're going to work on it and promote it and try their damnedest to sell it. They'll buy ads in the trades and buy time on the radio stations and send artists on promo tours and in-store appearances. In short, it's going to cost many, many thousands of dollars for me to say, 'That's a hit;' and I will do whatever I can to help that song become a hit" (McNeel and Luther, 1978: 141).

Further changes in the song are made when it is recorded. Words may be changed or whole verses cut to simplify the song or to bring the record within the three-minute time frame that is virtually required for country music songs to be played on the air (Siman, 1976). Even if words are not added, cut, or altered at this stage, the meaning of the song is inevitably shaped and interpreted by the way it is recorded. As a courtesy, songwriters are usually allowed to be present during the recording session of their songs, but the writer is not expected to make any comments on how to render it properly. The style of voice used, tempo, rhythm, recording technology, instrumental and vocal accompaniment, and the way these are mixed together in post-production editing all help to fix the interpretation of the song in ways which may or may not have been intended by the writer.

In some cases the changes are dramatic, and numerous writers complain that one or another of their songs has been ruined by a tasteless rendering. Such songs by successful writers may later be reinterpreted by another artist, but most songs are not given a second chance.

## RELEASING

Even when a song has been cut and mixed there are still questions about whether and in what form it will be released to the public. This brings us to arrow 3 in Figure 1.1. The artist and the producer are involved in deciding what will be released, but persons from the promotion and distribution departments may also be involved in the decision process with record company executives arbitrating when disputes arise.

There are no published estimates of what proportion of all the songs "in the can" are eventually released. An industry expert has estimated to us that about 70 percent of all recorded songs are released as album cuts, and 15 percent are released as the "A" side of 45 rpm records. Although the public buys more country music albums and tapes than singles, singles are the most important to the songwriter. Singles receive the lion's share of promotion; they are sent to radio programmers and to the distributors who service jukebox operators for exposure through these media. In turn, the title of a single release is often used as the title of the album in which it is found. All of these factors together mean that much more money can be earned by a hit single than can be earned by having a song on an album which sells equally well (Baskerville, 1979).

In summary, while some songs are screened out at the stage of deciding what to release, this stage is most important in determining the likelihood that the song will be released as a single and thus have the best chance of being widely played.

### MARKETING, MANUFACTURING, AND DISTRIBUTION

When a record is ready to be released, the decisions flow simultaneously along two parallel lines. The one, represented by arrows 4 and 6 of Figure 1.1, concerns the numerous marketing activities which bring the recording to the attention of consumers. The other line, arrows 5 and 7, has to do with the manufacturing and distribution of the record itself. This latter line will be discussed first because it is problematic only for the records cut by the numerous independent recording firms which together account for no more than 15 percent of the contemporary country music market (Siman, 1976; Peterson, 1982).

The term "independent company" is used in several different ways in the music business. Most commonly, it refers to those companies which have the resources to bring a record to the point of release, but which do not have the facilities to manufacture, fully promote, and rapidly distribute records to the consumer (Gillett, 1972; Baskerville, 1979: 306-309). Independents must rely on specialty companies for these services or have them performed on a contract basis by the major companies. Almost inevitably, the product of the independents is not as promptly manufactured, well distributed, and thoroughly promoted as the records of the leading performers at the large vertically-integrated firms (Denisoff, 1975). Consequently, a song released by an independent company is less likely to get the attention of consumers.

Producers for the major artists may hear and like one of these songs released on an independent label and have it recorded by one of their own artists. Such cuts are called "cover versions" or simply "covers." Covers were most conspicuous in the late 1950s when songs recorded by black rhythm and blues artists were recut by white popular music singers (Gillett, 1972), but the tactic also prevails in country music today. For example, Diane Davidson cut "Delta Dawn," and it became a cover hit for Tanya

Tucker; Don Schlitz cut "The Gambler," and it became a cover hit for Kenny Rogers. A successful cover by a major artist may hurt an aspiring singer, but it is an excellent way for an aspiring writer to become more visible. This shows that the interests of people at different points in the decision chain are often at odds. Being covered hurt Davidson's career as an artist, but Schlitz was not disappointed by the cover since he had written "The Gambler" and thus earned royalties from the sales of the hit cover version.

If the song is released by a major company, manufacturing and distribution, arrows 5 and 7, are nonproblematic because the majors have their own facilities. Marketing decisions represented by arrows 4 and 6 can, however, greatly influence the chances of a song being brought to the attention of the consumer public. The major recording firms have promotion departments with personnel across the country. Moreover, these firms may contract for additional promotional services. They may choose to put ads in the trade magazines, buy radio air time, offer record store promotional displays, plan television talk show exposure, rent roadside billboards, and underwrite the tours of artists to promote their latest records.

The effectiveness of record company promotion is widely debated in academic circles. Some critics assert that high levels of promotion can convert any song into a hit (Denisoff, 1975). Country music industry decision makers hold quite a different opinion. They believe that no amount of promotion can make a weak record into a hit, but that without extensive promotion a song has little chance of exposure to potential consumers (Siman, 1978; Peterson, 1978).

Since a large company releases many records at the same time, decisions have to be made concerning how to allocate available promotion personnel and financial resources. Ordinarily, priority is given to the new releases of the artists whose recent releases have been selling the most.

This is the safest strategy from the perspective of the promotion department for several reasons. First, the new product of "hot" artists is most likely to receive wide exposure without promotion, so the promotion campaign can easily appear to be successful. Second, it is politic to flatter hot artists by promotional attention. Third, since most promotion expenses are charged against earnings of the artist, the company knows that it can recoup expenditures from hot artists. Finally, industry officials believe that it is not wise to expend much money in promoting their older established artists who have not had hits recently. They believe that these artists have a stable following of fans who will buy their product without promotion and that active promotion will not attract many new buyers.

The case of Dottie West provides an exception which proves the rule about promotion. West began recording for RCA in 1963 and without much promotion established an image of being the often-wronged-but-wholesome woman with songs such as "Six Weeks Every Summer, Christmas Every

Other Year" and "Country Sunshine." When she switched to United Artists in 1978, she was paired with Kenny Rogers. With heavy promotion her image has been reshaped by having her wear tight pants and sing a series of sexually provocative songs (Peterson, 1979).

The fate of the song "New York Town," written by James Talley, illustrates some of the ways in which both the content and exposure of a song can be shaped by promotional considerations. As written and performed by Talley, the song recounts in somber tones the observations of a country person viewing all the exotic, fascinating, and frightening people that walk the streets of New York. Johnny Paycheck's manager decided the song would be the perfect lead song for an album that Paycheck was recording live at the Lone Star Cafe, New York's leading "urban cowboy" club. The negative or critical images were all omitted, and Paycheck sang the song in his rousing, up-tempo, honky-tonk style as a city-billy anthem of New York. While the album was called "New York Town," the promoters refused to release the song as a single, explaining to Talley that the song was used to "break the artist in New York," but that it would not be a successful single for national release because it would not be played often by radio stations outside New York.

## CONSUMING

The final act of consuming country music occurs when a person tunes in a country music radio station, views a country music television program, spends money to play the jukebox, attends a movie scored with a country music soundtrack, buys a live performance ticket, or purchases a country music record. Each of these is more likely to happen if the record marketers persuade country music programmers to play a song frequently over the air. Most of the marketing effort in the country music field, then, is focused on convincing program directors, music directors, and disc jockeys (collectively called programmers here) to play the songs that their company currently is promoting most diligently. This process is represented as arrow 6 in Figure 1.1

Most country music stations now play a short list of current releases, with a few older hits salted in from time to time (Peterson, 1978). The list is modified slightly from week to week, but each week the station receives over one hundred records and has room to add no more than half a dozen to the play list. Thus, the collective decisions of programmers around the country act as a major final filter of songs in the decision chain.

Commercial radio programmers are interested in selling air time to clients who wish to advertise a product or service. Advertisers, in turn, are interested in a large audience which has the same age, sex, income, and other demographic characteristics as the buyers of their products (Barnouw,

1970; Routt et al., 1978). These constraints on radio programming have had a major impact on the music that is played.

While more men than women, for example, are fans of country music (Peterson and Davis, 1975), most advertisers want to attract women between the ages of 25 and 49, and, as a consequence, it has become an axiom among all those in the decision chain, including programmers, marketers, producers, artists and publishers not to accept songs which portray women in a negative light (Peterson, 1978). Women are portrayed as tempted and long-suffering, but only men are played as weak, drunken, guilty bounders (Peterson, 1979; Bufwack and Oermann, 1980). Thus the interests of Proctor and Gamble, Burger King, and the local drugstore impinge directly upon the aesthetics of country music.

Although the importance of radio station programmers is difficult to discern from their daily decisions, it can be seen when a longer time perspective is taken. Peterson (1978) has shown that the remarkable shift in the nature of country music which took place between 1973-1977 was due in the first instance not to the emergence of new songwriters and artists or changing audience tastes, but rather to a series of changes taking place in the programming philosophy of radio station management. Programmers believed that they could greatly enlarge the total listenership without losing too many hard-core fans if they eliminated the farm/small town imagery and muted the hard edge of the "country" sound.

These decisions had a dramatic impact on the lyrical content of songs, on artists' careers, and on whole subgenres of music (Peterson, 1978, 1979; Ryan and Bales, 1978; Corbin, 1980). The commercial success of the older generation of songwriters was eclipsed by a rising generation of new writers uninhibited by the standard canons of the older country music genre (Kirby, 1980). Kris Kristofferson was the harbinger of this new generation of writers, and his freer writing style has been emulated by numerous full-time commercial songwriters.

This review has shown that many more songs are offered to the people at each link in the chain than they can accept and offer, in turn, to succeeding links. The review has also shown that the surviving songs are subject to modification at each link. With this example of a loosely-linked production system in mind, we are now in a position to ask how best to conceptualize the way decisions are made along the way.

## CONCEPTIONS OF COLLABORATIVE PRODUCTION

Theorists of industrial organization including Thompson (1967) and Woodward (1965) have based their models on the more stable and bureaucratic manufacturing industries which do not provide a good basis for understanding how decisions are made in the volatile consumer service industries such as the media arts. While a number of studies have been made of the collaborative production in the media arts, the focus has usually been on particular industries (Denisoff, 1975; Cantor, 1980) or particular firms in an industry (Metz, 1975; Balio, 1976; Burns, 1977). These researchers have developed ad hoc explanations which work adequately for their particular cases.

## FOUR FRAMEWORKS

While no general model has emerged, four different frameworks have been used to explain how decisions are made in the loosely-linked decision chains in the media arts. Each of these frameworks will be discussed briefly in order to highlight a fifth framework which incorporates elements of the others.

(1) *Assembly Line*. At least since Edwardian times, industrial metaphors "tune factory," "song mill," and "assembly line" have been used to describe the way commercial songs are written and processed to become hits (Pearsall, 1975). Songs, like industrial products, pass through a number of distinct stages of fabrication on the way to becoming hits, but the decision chains differ greatly from the assembly line along which an automobile is created. Assembly lines are constructed so that, insofar as possible, all skills and decisions are built into the machinery. Decisions which cannot be thus automated are specified through a set of procedural rules for machine operators and inspectors (Stinchcombe, 1959; Woodward, 1965; Thompson, 1967).

The genius of assembly-line production is economically to produce numerous products which are identical, but the goal of media arts production is cheaply to produce products *each* of which is marginally different and, it is hoped, more attractive to prospective customers. The means of doing this, as the review of the decision chain in country music has illustrated, is to produce many more items at each stage of the production process than will be accepted at, and successfully passed through, the next stage.

(2) *Craft and Entrepreneurship*. Most persons involved in media arts production would be classified as artisans rather than semiskilled assembly-line operatives (Bensman and Lilienfeld, 1973; Ritzer, 1977). They have the requisite skills and experience to perform a technical task, but they rely on their employers to tell them when, where, and in what style their work should be performed. The important role of such norms of craftsmanship has been widely noted in a range of arts and media production systems (Brown, 1968; Rosenblum, 1973; Mukerji, 1976; Lyon, 1978; Peterson and White, 1979; Kealy, 1979; Rosenblum and Karen, 1980; Becker, 1981).

But how are the efforts of the various sorts of artisans who work on making or "putting out" newspapers, television programs, movies, or phonograph records, coordinated? The emphasis seems to depend in part on the degree that each new product needs to be novel in order to have a chance of succeeding in the marketplace. When consumer tastes are changing rapidly or are difficult to judge, one person is often given charge of overseeing the efforts of artisans from the beginning to the end of the production process. Powerful movie directors, rock music producers (Peterson and Berger, 1971), and innovative ballet choreographers (Mazo, 1974) provide cases in point. Peterson and Berger (1971) call such persons entrepreneurs because, like the classical independent entrepreneur, their function is to juggle and recombine the interesting elements of production such as writers, artists, arrangers, musicians, engineers, in innovative ways in order to continually create marginally novel products.

Producers in the relatively less turbulent country music field do not often play such an entrepreneurial role. As our review of the decision chain has suggested, no one directly controls all stages of the production process. The same can be said of some other multilink media decision chains such as newspapers and television news broadcasting (Gans, 1979; Cohen and Young, 1981; Peterson, 1981).

(3) *Convention and Formula.* Becker (1976) proposed the concept "art world" to explain how many specialists in the arts and crafts are able to coordinate their activities. A "world" consists of all those people sharing common standards of evaluation of a particular "art" form and who also agree on how tasks should be done and what occupational specialist should perform them (Becker, 1976, 1981).

A number of researchers have used the concept of shared normative order to explain coordination in the arts (Bensman and Lilienfeld, 1972; Brighton and Pearson, 1978; Lyon, 1978), mass communication (Guback, 1974; Burns, 1977), intellectual discourse (Coser, 1965; Smith, 1974; Sennet, 1977), science (Kuhn, 1970), and in a wide range of work settings (Hughes, 1971; Bensman and Lillienfeld, 1973; Friedson, 1980).

The concept of "world" presumes that creative personnel are concerned with the development of the aesthetic, scientific, and so forth ideals of the field and also subscribe to the conventional norms of working toward these goals. There are a number of situations, however, in which participants subscribe fully to the technical norms but may, or may not, embrace the ideals toward which the activity is directed. Thus, for example, reporters may work for a newspaper whose editorial policy differs from their own; actors may play parts in movies they think mindless, comic book printers may produce comics they feel are immoral, and so on.

Normative theories evoke the concept "formula" to explain how collaborative production is possible in such circumstances. A formula is much like a recipe, a set of widely held prescriptions which tell workers how to combine elements in order to produce works in the genre. Much of the recent research on news media takes this tack in describing the formulae that emerge to guide the processes of news production (Seeger, 1976; Tuchman 1978; Schudson, 1978; Lester, 1980; Lee, 1980) or in describing how unusual events or classes of events such as labor news (Beharrell, 1976), the Tet offensive in Vietnam (Braestrup 1978), student radicalism (Gitlin, 1980), and the death of Elvis Presley (Gregory and Gregory, 1980) are interpreted to fit existing formulae.

(4) *Audience Image and Conflict.* Rather than posing a shared world view or set of technical norms, some researchers have sought to explain collaborative production as the outcome of a contest in which all parties argue their case in terms of what will succeed in the marketplace. Gans (1957) has put this position clearly, asserting that those involved in shaping a Hollywood film envision an image of what the audience will like and try to shape the film to fit this image.

Since movie producers, directors, script writers, and actors tend to define the audience somewhat differently, Gans (1957) argues that they will often be in conflict over filmmaking. This model suggests that collaborative production is less the result of shared norms than it is an interpersonal contest of wills, cabals, and behind-the-scene alliances in which contestants rationalize their self-interests in terms of what the audience will like. In varying degrees, this view of audience image can be seen in the work of Cantor (1971, 1980) and Gans (1979).

### THE COUNTRY MUSIC CASE

How useful are the four frameworks for understanding collaborative production in country music? The model of an aesthetic world fits the way decisions were made in the 1920s during the earliest days of the commercialization of country music. Songwriters, artists, musicians, and audiences shared a common understanding of what country music was and how to go about making it (Malone, 1968; Wolfe, 1975). Quite rapidly, the process of production became formulaic (Peterson and DiMaggio, 1973; Peterson, 1975).

In recent years, however, the changes in music have been rapid enough so that no strict formula for how to put together a hit country music record could be consolidated (Peterson, 1978). People in the decision chain sometimes make reference to what the average country music fan will like, but an audience image is evoked much less often than another sort of imagery.

(5) *The Product Image.* Within the music industry, songs are most frequently referred to by words depicting the stage in the decision process through which they are passing. Thus, a song is called "a copyright," "a

property," "a demo," "a tape," "a dub," "a transcription," "a cut," "a master," "a side," "a release," "an A side," "a pick," "a selection," and finally, "a hit" or "a dud." At all points in the decision chain, songs are regularly referred to as "product."

This distinctive product image nomenclature focuses the attention of creative people at each link in the chain on the commercial rather than on the aesthetic values of their work. "The point," one publisher told us, "is to make money, not art."

Having a product image is to shape a piece of work so that it is most likely to be accepted by decision makers at the next link in the chain. The most common way of doing this is to produce works that are much like the products that have most recently passed through all the links in the decision chain to become commercially successful.

With such a product image everyone in the chain can make appropriate decisions without having to share a common world; there does not need to be an entrepreneur in charge; people don't need to agree on an audience image; and the recipe for making hit tunes can evolve rapidly without jelling into a rigid formula.

A product image, seems to guide the work of professional newspaper photographers, book publishers, and the British Broadcasting Corporation, as these symbol-producers have been described by Rosenblum (1973), Powell (1978) and Burns (1977), respectively. What is more, the idea of product image has long been used to explain why artists paint the way they do. In 1915, the art historian Wölfflin (1950) suggested that painters do not try to copy nature so much as they try to reproduce and build upon or distinguish their work from prior paintings. The utility of the product image concept will be further tested in analyzing how the creative efforts of country music songwriters are shaped by this constructed reality.

## COPING WITH CONSTRAINTS ON CREATIVITY

Tracing songs through the decision chain has shown just how slight the chances are that a songwriter's creative efforts will reach a wide audience. At each link in the chain, most of the surviving songs are filtered out or altered. Facing these odds, many, perhaps most, writers adopt strategies and elaborate explanations for their failures that protect their own definitions of self worth, but, as Peterson and Ryan (forthcoming) have shown, these strategies and explanations virtually guarantee that the writers will not succeed in the commercial country music market. There are two general sorts of coping strategies, however, through which writers have a measurable chance of expressing their creative talents. The first involves becoming a commercial professional.

## COMMERCIAL PROFESSIONAL

The term "professional" is widely used to describe those writers who develop an accurate product image of what will and will not be accepted by publishers and others down the decision chain (Gant, 1974; Siman, 1976; Kosser, 1976). Commercial professionals enhance the chances of success of their songs by developing friendly contacts and exchanging favors with decision makers as far down the decision chain as they can (Peterson and White, 1979; Peterson and Ryan, forthcoming). As noted above, the exchange of favors may necessitate giving up part of the author credit and royalties to artists, producers, and other key decision makers.

Much individual expression may be sacrificed, but publishers, producers, and others who regularly coach writers put this compromise in positive terms, saying that by frequent rejection and rewriting, the individual is "paying dues" in learning how to write a "good song," that is, one that fits the current product image held by the publisher.

The impact that such coaching has on writers is hinted at by the successful commercial professional, Billy Ed Wheeler. He said in a 1972 interview that he wrote two types of songs, "commercial songs" for the industry and "artistic songs" for himself. And yet he went on to note that his "best" songs were usually written for money. Writing for a market may be a spur to creativity; alternatively, his definition of creativity has become synonymous with "marketability." The published research on creativity does not suggest whether product image and such constraints inhibit or spur creativity (Martindale, 1975).

## SINGER/SONGWRITER

The second strategy for coping with the constraints on creativity is to circumvent the decision chain by presenting one's songs directly to the paying audience. Such singer/songwriters need have no product image. Instead they adopt the role of the self-expressive folk balladeer (Schmidt and Rooney, 1979; Klein, 1980).

While such folk singers may seem to have no place in contemporary commercial industry, from time to time they have played a vital role. An aesthetic revolution took place in popular music in the mid-1960s when such individualistic balladeers, trained in the live performance urban folk music circuit and the small clubs of England (Scaduto, 1971; Melly, 1971; Davis, 1975; Denisoff, 1975; Schmidt and Rooney, 1979) were merchandised to the mass market by the large music industry firms. The major record companies became the marketing agents for independent artistic production companies (Peterson and Berger, 1971). In this way the singer/songwriters circumvented much of the old vertically integrated decision chain for producing Tin

Pan Alley formula popular music which had operated in the 1940s much as country music operates at the time of this study (MacDonald, 1941).

Bob Dylan, the Beatles, and the Grateful Dead led the way toward the mass popularity of singers/songwriters. Whatever personal expression there was to begin with, however, did not always survive the integration of the singer/songwriter balladeer into the nexus of commerce (McCabe and Schonfeld, 1972; Davis, 1974; Stokes, 1976; Markovitz and Freund, forthcoming). The older Tin Pan Alley-oriented writers and publishers that could not adapt were frozen out of the pop music market (Denisoff, 1975). But the incorporation of the singer/songwriter system was highly profitable for all involved and fueled a sustained growth of the popular music industry. There may be parallel examples in other symbol producing systems of persons who are marketed to the public as authentic creative geniuses because they project their own personalities while circumventing the normal channels of production. The designation singer/songwriter obviously does not fit them, so following Becker (1978), the term "romantic genius" is used to refer to this larger class of creative persons.

Singer/songwriters are sometimes given the chance to create an album of their own country music songs. But two things happen that virtually guarantee the failure of these efforts. Sometimes their well-meaning producers, so concerned that individualistic songs will not succeed, arrange and overdub the music so extensively that it loses its distinctive edge and sounds much like any run-of-the-mill formula music. When singer/songwriters are given a free hand to produce their own work, they typically create records that do not fit neatly into the current product image. Being unusual, little record company money and effort are expended to promote and market these records. As a result, radio programmers are not likely to consider the works seriously for air play. When they do, they are likely to reject them because they do not fit neatly within their current product image.

Country music industry executives assert that their country music equivalents don't succeed because the genre of country music as appreciated by its audience is incompatible with the highly personalistic songs and mode of presentation of singer/songwriters. And yet, most of the early stars of the genre, including Jimmy Rodgers, the Carter Family, Woody Guthrie, and Hank Williams were singer/songwriters (Malone, 1969; Klein, 1980; Flippo, 1981).

It seems more likely that recent singer/songwriters have not had much chance to succeed because the influential decision makers at each stage of the decision chain have an interest in maintaining the present system with its complex division of labor and predictable product image song. Our recent study of novices trying to "break in" to the field of country music (Peterson and Ryan, forthcoming) supports this view. Many young people arrive with the examples of Bob Dylan, John Lennon, and Hank Williams in mind, hoping to succeed as singer/songwriters. A few become artists and are asked for the sake of their careers to sing the songs that their promoters consider the best available, usually the works of professional commercial songwriters. Some become instrumental musicians playing in bands for other artists, or in recording studios. Fully absorbed in the rigors of the road and maintaining a high degree of musicianship in a very competitive atmosphere, they do not often continue to write songs. The majority of the novice would-be singer/songwriters who do not drop out of the business become full-time professional commercial songwriters with their creativity harnessed to produce songs in the current product image for the established decision chain (Gant, 1974; Kosser, 1976; Peterson and Ryan, forthcoming).

If the revolutions in the popular music and film industries are any guide (Peterson and Berger, 1975; Denisoff, 1975), the chances for the creative singer/songwriter in country music are not likely to improve except as part of a major restructuring of the industry and the way its products are marketed. Such changes are not out of the question. The impetus for breaking the current decision chain which perpetuates the narrow product image of country music may come as a result of the various alternative video technologies that promise to bring a wide range of entertainment directly into the home.

## CONCLUSION

Clive Davis, a pragmatic executive who has headed both CBS Records Division and Arista Records, has asserted that "being in music is much like being in the shoe business." Both are fashion conscious consumer product industries in which problems of merchandising, promotion, inventory control, and successfully predicting or shaping consumer tastes are essential to financial success. But the analogy defocalizes the crucial problem that the music industry shares with all the collaboratively produced media arts, regularizing creative inputs without alienating or choking them off.

The production of culture perspective has helped to illuminate the problems of creativity in contemporary country music. It may prove useful in other domains of communication research as well. All of the topics discussed in this chapter—the decision chain, product image, commercial professionalism, and romantic genius—can be viewed as more devices developed to channel, integrate, manage, and use creativity without destroying it. Much is yet to be learned, however, concerning the best ways to structure systems of collaborative creativity in the media arts to foster—and control—creativity.

# REFERENCES

BALIO, T. (1976) United Artists. Madison: University of Wisconsin Press.

BARNOUW, E. (1970) The Image Empire. New York: Oxford University Press.

BASKERVILLE, D. (1979) Music Business Handbook. Los Angeles: Sherwood.

BECKER, G. (1978) The Mad Genius Controversy: A Study in the Sociology of Deviance. Beverly Hills: Sage.

BECKER, H. S. (1976) "Art worlds and social types," pp. 41-57 in R. A. Peterson (ed.) The Production of Culture. Beverly Hills: Sage.

———— (1981) Art Worlds. Berkeley: University of California Press.

BEHARRELL, P. (1976) Bad News. Boston: Routledge & Kegan Paul.

BENSMAN, J. and R. LILIENFELD (1973) Craft and Consciousness. New York: Wiley.

BRAESTRUP, P. (1978) Big Story: How the American Press and Television Reported and Interpreted the Crisis of Tet 1968 in Vietnam and Washington. Garden City: Doubleday.

BRIGHTON, A. and N. PEARSON (1978) "Art worlds: divergent views of professionalism among visual artists." Paper presented at the Conference on Culture of the British Sociological Association, April.

BROWN, R. T. (1968) "The creative process in the popular arts." International Social Science Journal 4: 613-624.

BUFWACK, M. A. and R. K. OERMANN (1980) Songs of Self-Assertion: Women in Country Music. Somerville, MA: New England Free Press.

BURNS, T. (1977) The BBC: Public Institution and Private World. London: Macmillan.

BUTSCH, R. (1981) "How does it happen? The production of culture." Paper presented at the 51st annual meeting of the Eastern Sociological Society, New York.

CANTOR, M. G. (1971) The Hollywood TV Producer: His Work and His Audience. New York: Basic Books.

———— (1980) Prime-Time Television: Content and Control. Beverly Hills: Sage.

COHEN, S. and J. YOUNG [eds.] (1981) The Manufacture of News: Social Problems, Deviance and the Mass Media. Rev. Ed. Beverly Hills, Sage.

CORBIN, E. J. (1980) Storm over Nashville: A Case Against Modern Country Music. Nashville: Ashlar Press.

COSER, L. (1965) Men of Ideas. New York: Free Press.

CSIDA, J. (1975) The Music/Record Career Handbook. New York: Billboard.

DAVIS, C. (1975) Clive: Inside the Record Business. New York: Morrow.

DENISOFF, R. S. (1975) Solid Gold: The Record Industry, Its Friends and Enemies. New York: Transaction Books.

DRANOV, P. (1980) Inside the Music Publishing Industry. White Plains, NY: Knowledge Industry Publications.

FAULKNER, R. R. (1971) Hollywood Studio Musicians. Chicago: Aldine.

FLIPPO, C. (1981) Your Cheatin' Heart: A Biography of Hank Williams. New York: Simon and Schuster.

FRIEDSON, E. (1980) Doctoring Together. Chicago: University of Chicago Press.

GANS, H. J. (1957) "The creator-audience relationship in the mass media: an analysis of movie making," pp. 315-324 in B. Rosenberg and D. M. White (eds.) Mass Culture. New York: Free Press.

———— (1979) Deciding What's News. New York: Pantheon.

GANT, A. M. (1974) Creating the Nashville Sound. Senior Scholar Thesis, Vanderbilt University.

GERROLD, D. (1973) The Trouble with Tribbles. New York: Ballantine.

GILLETT, C. (1972) The Sound of the City. New York: Outerbridge and Dienstfrey.

GITLIN, T. (1980) The Whole World is Watching: Mass Media in the Making and Unmaking of the New Left. Berkeley: University of California Press.

GREGORY, N. and J. GREGORY (1980) When Elvis Died. Washington, DC: Communication Press.

GRISWOLD, W. (1981) "American character and the American novel: an expansion of reflection theory in the sociology of literature." American Journal of Sociology 86: 740-765.

GUBACK, T. H. (1974) "Social context and creativity in mass communications." Journal of Esthetic Education 8: 65-83.

GUYON, J. (1981) "Record firms see profits by the score as city fans love country music more." Wall Street Journal, (March 3): 12.

HUGHES, E. C. (1971) The Sociological Eye. Chicago: Aldine.

KEALY, E. R. (1979) "From craft to art: the case of sound mixers and popular music." Work and Occupations 6: 3-29.

KIRBY, K. (1980) "Country lyrics reflect 1980's social permissiveness." Billboard (October 11): 3,32,65.

KLEIN, J. (1980) Woody Guthrie: A Life. New York: Knopf.

KOSSER, M. (1976) Bringing it to Nashville. Brentwood, TN: Cumberland Valley Books.

KUHN, T. S. (1970) The Structure of Scientific Revolutions. Chicago: University of Chicago Press.

KUROFF, B. N. (1980) Song Writer's Market. Cincinnati: Writers Digest Books.

LEE, C. (1980) Media Imperialism Reconsidered: The Homogenization of Television Culture. Beverly Hills: Sage.

LESTER, M. (1980) "Generating newsworthiness: the interpretive construction of public events." American Sociological Review 45: 984-994.

LYON, E. (1978) "States of theatrical rehearsal." Paper presented at the 73rd annual American Sociological Association meetings.

MacDONALD, D., Jr. (1941) "The popular music industry," pp. 65-109 in P. F. Lazarsfeld and F. N. Stanton (eds.) Radio Research 1941. New York: Duell, Sloan and Pearce.

MALONE, B. C. (1968) Country Music U. S. A. Austin: University of Texas Press.

MARKOVITZ, A. S. and M. FREUND (forthcoming) "So Amerikanish wie Drugen und Apfelkuchen: Andenkungen zum Jubilaum einer Rockband." Dollars Und Traume.

MARTINDALE, C. (1975) Romantic Progression: The Psychology of Literary History. Washington, DC: Hemisphere.

MAZO, J. H. (1974) Dance is a Contact Sport. New York: DeCapo.

McCABE, P. and R. D. SCHONFELD (1972) Apple to the Core: The Unmaking of the Beatles. New York: Pocket Book.

McNEEL, K. and M. LUTHER (1978) How to be a Successful Song Writer. New York: St. Martin's Press.

MELLY, G. (1971) Revolt into Style: The Pop Arts. Garden City, NY: Doubleday.

METZ, R. (1975) CBS: Reflections in a Bloodshot Eye. New York: Playboy Press.

MUKERJI, C. (1976) "Having the authority to know." Sociology of Work and Occupations 3:128-139.

PEARSALL, R. (1975) Edwardian Popular Music. Rutherford, NJ: Fairleigh Dickinson University.

PETERSON, R. A. (1975) "Single industry firm to conglomerate synergistics: alternative strategies for selling insurance and country music," pp. 341-375 in J. Blumstein and B. Walter (eds.), Growing Metropolis: Aspects of Development in Nashville. Nashville: Vanderbilt University Press.

————— [ed.] (1976) The Production of Culture. Beverly Hills: Sage.

_____ (1978) "The production of cultural change: the case of contemporary country music." Social Research 45: 292-314.

_____ (1979) "Has country lost its homespun charm?" Chronicle of Higher Education 29 (May): 22-24

_____ (1981) "Entrepreneurship in organization," in P. C. Nystron and W. H. Starbuck (eds.) Handbook of Organizational Design. New York: Oxford University Press.

_____ (1982) "Relative market shares of companies in the country music market, 1948 to the present." Nashville, TN. (unpublished)

PETERSON, R. A. and D. G. BERGER (1971) "Entrepreneurship in organizations: evidence from the popular music industry." Administrative Science Quarterly 16: 97-107.

_____ (1975) "Cycles in symbol production: the case of popular music." American Sociological Review 40:158-173.

PETERSON, R. A., and R. DAVIS, Jr. (1975) "The contemporary American radio audience." Journal of Popular Music and Society.

PETERSON, R. A., and P. DiMAGGIO (1973) "The early Opry: its hillbilly image in fact and fancy." Journal of Country Music 4: 39-51.

PETERSON, R. A., and J. RYAN (forthcoming). "Success, failure, and anomie in art and craft work: breaking in to commercial country music songwriting." Research in the Sociology of Work.

PETERSON, R. A. and H. G. WHITE (1979) "The simplex located in art worlds." Urban Life 7: 411-439.

POWELL, W. W. (1978) "Publishers' decision-making: what criteria do they use in deciding which books to publish?" Social Research 45: 227-252.

RITZER, G. (1977) Working: Conflict and Change. Englewood Cliffs, NJ: Prentice-Hall.

ROSENBLUM, B. (1973) "Photographers and their photographs: an empirical study in the sociology of aesthetics." Ph.D. dissertation, Northwestern University.

ROSENBLUM, R. and R. KAREN (1980) When the Shooting Stops . . . the Cutting Begins. New York: Penguin.

ROUTT, E., J. B. McGRATH, and F. A. WEISS (1978) The Radio Format Conundrum. New York: Hastings House.

RUMBLE, J. (1980) "Fred Rose and the development of publishing in Nashville." Ph.D. dissertation, Vanderbilt University.

RYAN, J. and K. BALES (1978) "Cultural change, expediency and the country music cross-over." Paper presented at the fifth annual meetings of the Popular Culture Association of the South, Nashville.

SCADUTO, A. (1971) Bob Dylan. New York: Grosset and Dunlap.

SCHMIDT, E. van, and J. ROONEY (1979) Baby, Let Me Follow You Down. New York: Doubleday.

SCHUDSON, M. (1978) Discovering the News. New York: Basic Books.

SEEGER, Jr., A. A. (1976) "Social control in the newsroom of the Berkeley Barb. Ph.D. dissertation, University of California, Davis.

SENNETT, R. (1977) The Fall of Public Man. New York: Random House.

SIMAN, S. F. (1976) Modeling the Success of Country Music Records. Senior Scholar Thesis, Vanderbilt University.

SMITH, T. S. (1974) "Aestheticism and structure: style and social network in the dandy life." American Sociological Review 39: 725-743.

STINCHCOMBE, A. (1959) "Bureaucratic and craft administration of production: a comparative study." Administrative Science Quarterly 4: 168-187.

STOKES, G. (1976) Star-Making Machinery: The Odyssey of an Album. New York: Random House.

TAYLOR, R. L. (1978) Art, an Enemy of the People. Sussex, England: Harvister.

THOMPSON, J. D. (1967) Organizations in Action: Social Science Bases of Administrative Theory. New York: McGraw-Hill.

TUCHMAN, G. (1978) Making News. New York: Free Press.

WILLIAMS, B. (1972) "Nashville writers sue record manufacturers." Billboard, (June 17): 3, 78.

WOLFE, C. K. (1975) The Grand Ole Opry: The Early Years, 1925-1935. London: Old Time Music.

WÖLFFLIN, H. (1950) Principles of Art History. New York: Dover. (Originally published in 1915).

WOOD, J. (1980) "Nashville publishers buck producers' song control." Billboard, (October 4): 1, 68, 94.

WOODWARD, J. (1965) Industrial Organization: Theory and Practice. New York: Oxford University Press.

ZOLA, E. (1968) The Masterpiece. Ann Arbor: University of Michigan Press. (Originally published in 1886.)

*Chapter 2*

# FROM CRAFT TO CORPORATION
## The Impact of Outside Ownership
## on Book Publishing

**Walter W. Powell**

BOOK PUBLISHING has grown enormously in the past two decades. Back in 1910, 13,470 titles were published. The annual output grew slowly to 15,012 in 1960. But in the next six years, the number of titles annually released doubled to 30,050. By 1974, more than 40,846 books were published and since then annual production has hovered near or above the 40,000 mark. Or take sales volume. In 1958 the value of industry sales receipts was approximately $1 billion. That figure exceeded $5 billion in 1977 and $6.6 billion in 1980.[1]

The rapid growth of book publishing has resulted from a number of societal forces: the expansion of higher education, the worldwide information explosion and the boom in the mass entertainment industry. At the same time, this growth has resulted in the entry into publishing of outside interests as the industry has become increasingly attractive to Wall Street. And this, in turn, has further fueled the industry's growth.

A number of major mergers occurred during the 1960s between publishing houses and electronics and/or computer corporations. Hoping to wed electronics and education, the electronics firm was to provide the hardware, capital, and management skills. The publisher, in return, was to supply the raw materials, marketing skills, and legitimacy. Among the corporate entrants were IBM, ITT, Litton Industries, RCA, CBS, Raytheon, Xerox, GE, and General Telephone. This activity was buoyed by the expectations of increasing school enrollments and a more widely educated and literate population with a great deal of leisure time on its hands. Trying to keep pace, a number of older, established houses, such as Houghton Mifflin, became public stock companies to raise capital for expansion or to avoid being broken up by estate-settlements. Some publishers amalgamated with other publishers; others, such as Harcourt Brace Jovanovich and Macmillan, embarked on expansion campaigns of their own, diversifying into other fields such as broadcasting, musical instruments, and entertainment.

The next wave of merger activity took place in the middle 1970s. In 1974 alone, publishing mergers took place at ten times the rate of mergers in mining and manufacturing industries. A distinguishing feature of publishing mergers in 1970s was that they took place almost solely within the media business. Most prominent were the mergers of paperback and hardcover houses, such as those between Doubleday (general publisher) and Dell (paperbacks), Viking (trade books) and Penguin (paperbacks). Also prominent were the mergers of media conglomerates with substantial publishing interests and previously independent publishing firms. For example, CBS, which already owned a paperback line and the hardcover house of Holt, Rinehart and Winston, purchased Saunders (a major medical publisher), Praeger (professional books), and Fawcett (paperbacks). Successful publishing houses, such as Harper and Row, bought up their less successful brethren (Thomas Y. Crowell and J. P. Lippincott). The Hearst newspaper empire, which owns Avon Books (paperbacks), acquired Arbor House (hardcover trade books) and then purchased William Morrow, a large trade publisher, for approximately $25 million from Scott, Foresman, an educational publisher. Time-Life, with major holdings in magazines and subscription books, bought Little, Brown and Book-of-the-Month Club.

Foreign publishers have opened American offices and started acquiring American firms. In addition to Penguin mentioned above, this trend includes the purchase of David McKay (college texts) by Longman (a British publishing firm), the purchase of majority stock in Bantam (the largest paperback house in the United States) by Bertelsmann Publishing Group (West Germany's largest magazine and book publisher), and the acquisition of E. P. Dutton (trade books) by Elsevier (a major Dutch-owned publishing firm). Canada's International Thomson purchased Wadsworth, a California based text publisher for $32 million in 1978.

The film industry has also gotten into the act. The Music Corporation of America (MCA) took over both Putnam (trade books), which had previously absorbed Berkeley (paperbacks), and Coward, McCann and Geoghegan (trade books). Filmways Pictures now owns Grosset and Dunlap and Warner Communications has founded Warner Books. Gulf and Western counts Paramount Pictures, Simon and Schuster, and its paperback subsidiary Pocket Books, as part of its leisure entertainment division.

The impact, if any, of these merger trends upon the structure of book publishing as an industry has not received much attention from social scientists. Nor has any attention been focused upon the manner in which the work of editors in trade publishing has been affected by changes in ownership.

This chapter attempts to fill these gaps. As other authors in this volume have suggested, alterations in the institutional and organizational contexts in which mass communicators work affect the nature and type of work they do. This chapter examines how shifts in ownership influence the marketing strategies employed by publishers, the internal organization of publishing firms, and, in some cases, the very way in which editors spend their time.

Over the past five years, Lewis Coser, Charles Kadushin, and myself have been involved in a study of the publishing industry as a major "gate-keeper of ideas" (Coser, 1975). Though the impact of mergers upon the industry has been only one of a number of topics we have researched, we have been in a unique position to observe this process first-hand. In the course of our research, we have interviewed more than one hundred editors in a wide variety of publishing houses and conducted participant observations in a dozen houses. The houses ranged in size from small independent firms with less than twenty employees to large conglomerates with more than one thousand employees. We have also interviewed many writers who published books with each of the houses where we did field work. In a less systematic manner, we interviewed literary agents, book reviewers, and booksellers (Coser, Kadushin, and Powell, 1981).

## CHARGES AND COUNTERCHARGES

The debate over the consequences of book publishing's continuing integration into the entertainment industry has been loud and contradictory. The Authors Guild has been the most outspoken, labeling the merger wave of the 1970s a "sinister process" that is diminishing competition. John Brooks (1978: 596), representing the Authors Guild, has argued:

> We have seen mergers in every imaginable permutation—hard-cover houses merging with each other; hard-cover houses merging with paperback houses; the combination thus formed being taken over, in turn, by huge entertainment complexes, involving radio-television networks and motion picture companies. And in some cases, perhaps most distressing of all, we have seen the business of choosing and purveying books, traditionally the province of more or less dedicated book men with one eye on profit and the other on literary and social values, falling under the control of businessmen with no prior interest in books—men, it has sometimes seemed to us, cursed like the Cyclops with having only a single eye, and that eye not trained on literary or social value but steadfastly on the bottom line of a company financial statement.

Winthrop Knowlton (1978: 567), former president of Harper and Row, has countered with statistics showing that his company's trade department had published approximately 400 books during the period 1977-1978. Of these, 132 were fiction, 21 were first novels, and 12 were volumes of poetry. Moreover, three-fourths of their trade books lost money. He stated that "this does not seem to me the kind of statistic that one ordinarily associates with undue economic concentration, the kind of concentration that makes it possible to manipulate the marketplace and consumers to one's own corporate ends."

Similarly, Townsend Hoopes (1978: 550), president of the Association of American Publishers, argues that "the most fundamental measure of the health and vigor [of book publishing] is the number of active firms in the industry." He maintains that the openness of the market is reflected by the steady establishment of new publishing houses.

Critics have focused on other "measures" however, and remain unconvinced. Senator Howard Metzenbaum of Ohio, speaking to the Senate Subcommittee on Anti-trust and Monopoly in March 1980, stated that, "a closer look at publishing leads me to believe that there is a cause for concern about the growth of concentration in the sectors of the business that have the most immediate impact on the consuming public." As reported in *Publishers Weekly* (March 9, 1980: 10, 12), he noted that the majority of book publishers appeal to specialized markets, but in two sectors he finds disturbing trends: "eight publishers have over 80% of the paperback market and the two largest general interest book clubs together have a market share of over 50%." And focusing more on taste than economics, the literary critic Alfred Kazin (1980) expressed dismay at the money and attention heaped on a few "big" trade books and concluded, "Like so much in American life, the book world is big, busy, and commercial, driven; not likely to be too aware of its compulsiveness, special interests, many blinders."

Making sense of the charges and countercharges is difficult. As Heather Kirkwood (1979), the lawyer who coordinated the Federal Trade Commission's media concentration project, remarked:

> I have been frequently startled by the amount and intensity of disagreement which revolves around the media. Yet I have found that little of this controversy involves disagreements on facts. Instead, people disagree on how the facts should be categorized, judged, analyzed or valued. Hardcover trade book publishing provides a good illustration of this type of controversy . . . frequently one side will point to a particular set of figures as proof positive that the industry is, indeed, concentrated. The next day, a different group will point to the exact same figures as proof positive that the industry is unconcentrated.

A dispassionate assessment of the effects of mergers must take into account both historical forces and the peculiar nature of book publishing itself. We must recognize that for over 100 years publishers have sought to market fewer books in larger quantities to achieve higher profits and at the same time virtually every house of any size was involved in mergers and acquisitions (Coser, Kadushin, and Powell, 1981). Moreover, in industries that depend on individual creative products which appear in sporadic bursts, that do not have sizeable sunk-costs in plant equipment or product development, and that face highly unpredictable markets, mergers and concentration trends are neither permanent nor irrevocable. Indeed, the anticipated "synergy" between publishing houses and electronics firms did not pay off quickly enough for some. Several mergers did not last. Enrollments declined in the schools and some corporate parents learned that many of publishing's arcane inefficiencies could not easily be rationalized. General Electric and Litton sold their publishing interests, Xerox sold its college division to John Wiley, and RCA sold the Random House complex, including Knopf, Pantheon, Vintage, and Ballantine, to Newhouse Newspapers.

While many critics look fondly at the past and consider present-day events disturbing, they forget that trade publishing in America has always been oriented toward the mass market. In the nineteenth century, elitist critics were embarrassed by the novel's intimate connection with the commercialization and democratization of culture in an emerging mass society. Only begrudgingly did they accord the novel the status of literature. In contrast to the present, serious American writers of the nineteenth century fared very poorly. They were, according to Perry Miller (1967: 255-256), "crushed before the juggernaut of the novel," by which he meant the popular novel of sentiment and adventure. "A damned mob of scribbling women," was Hawthorne's famous phrase for those who by 1850 had cornered the market in popular fiction (Douglas, 1977). His books were not selling and the sentimental writings of women novelists were selling "by the 100,000," he complained. "I should have no chance of success while the public taste is occupied with their trash—I should be ashamed of myself if I did succeed" (Smith, 1974). The nineteenth century market for books simply did not support serious writers.

Historically, book publishing has been a competitive industry primarily because of low capital entry costs. The easy availability of a range of services such as art design, copy editing and printing which can be contracted on an as-needed basis make it easier to establish new publishing houses than is possible in industries where economies of scale are so important. It is these same low entry costs which have made publishing so merger prone, because of the presence of numerous, often undercapitalized, small firms. Also, existing publishing houses with established backlists have always proved attractive to acquiring firms, especially in contrast to the risks and uncertainty of starting up a new house. An industry with numerous competing firms will naturally have a higher merger rate than an industry with few firms: there are simply more firms available for acquisition. It is the ease of entry and the competitiveness of the industry which has made it merger prone and with this in mind the recent merger trend seems somewhat less threatening. This does not mean, however, that the recent mergers along with the phenomenal growth have not changed the industry.

## EMERGENCE OF THE TWO-TIER INDUSTRY STRUCTURE

Sociologists and economists have been arguing for some time now that both labor and capital have become segmented in modern industrial societies. Dual labor market theorists have observed that there is a primary sector with greater job mobility, better working conditions and higher wages. The secondary sector is characterized by unstable employment and lower wages (Bluestone et al., 1973; Edwards et al., 1975; Gordon, 1972). These differences in the labor market are seen by some theorists as resulting from a fundamental split between industries which compromise the core of the muscle of the American economy and those which are more peripheral. Core, or first tier, industries are more likely to have an oligopolistic market structure. Firms within these first tier industries hold a large market share, are vertically integrated, and are large in size. The second tier, or peripheral, industries have a competitive market structure, are characterized by low entry costs, and firms within this second tier tend to be small (Averitt, 1968; Tolbert et al., 1980).

Tolbert et al. (1980) have developed an index of industrial differentiation that places industries on a continuum from periphery to core. Using this measure, the printing and publishing industries were classified as part of the core sector of the economy. Others may choose to regard publishing as peripheral in comparison with the steel or oil industries. I would argue that within the publishing industry there is a first tier which is more like core industries and a second tier which is similar to peripheral industries. First tier publishing firms deal in large investments and fast turnover and have a hectic promotion pace. Second tier firms are small and have specialized audiences.

### THE FIRST TIER

The recent merger waves have helped to create a number of large and powerful first tier firms which are well integrated into other communication and entertainment industries. For example, the Times-Mirror Company owns the Los Angeles *Times*, Long Island's *Newsday*, and the Dallas *Times*

*Herald* as well as several smaller papers and half of a major news service. It also owns eight magazines, seven television stations, two book clubs and at least seven publishing houses including the paperback giant, New American Library. Finally, it is currently the sixth largest cable television company. Similarly, Time Inc., in addition to its five magazines (*Time, Fortune, Sports Illustrated, People,* and *Money*) owns 17 weekly newspapers, five book publishing firms, the Book-of-the-Month Club, and a film company as well as interests in records and cable television. This integration of communication and entertainment industries has ushered in the era in which books along with film and television are seen as part of a total media package. Via talk shows, sexy advertisements and other media ballyhoo these firms effectively market their "blockbuster" bestsellers to mass audiences. The developers of these trendy products do indeed often pay more attention to advertising budgets than to book reviews. This is the era of the media "tie-in" (Powell, 1979). Much of trade publishing, that is, both hardcover and paperback books of broad appeal and sold in general bookstores, is now caught up in this emphasis on "big" books.

**THE SECOND TIER**

There is another sector of the publishing industry, however, where serious publishing continues to be carried on, albeit without much fanfare. This is the second tier composed of many small, often independent, firms which serve small and highly specialized audiences. Neither the successes nor the failures of these firms are very grand but thanks to them the publishing industry as a whole is the most differentiated and specialized media industry in terms of both products and the firms which produce them.

No one is quite sure how many small presses there are, but *Books in Print* lists some 12,000 publishers. A recent Congressional Research Service report states that the number of publishing establishments increased by 45.2 per cent to a total of 1,750 firms over the 1972-1977 period (Gilroy, 1980). And a February 23, 1981 New York *Times* story begins, "in an industry dominated by giants, small book publishers are having a bigger impact than ever." Many but not all small presses are tiny "mom-and-pop" independents located in publishing's hinterlands. Some small houses are subsidiaries of giant firms and some are located in Manhattan and compete directly with large houses. As the small press strategy of specialization succeeds, some big firms are even adopting it.

The result of this growth and specialization has been an expansion not only in the number of titles published but in the range of subjects covered. It is, in fact, highly inaccurate to speak of a single monolithic publishing industry. There are many different types of publishing—juvenile books, reference books, textbooks, subscription books, scientific monographs, and religious books, in addition to mass market paperbacks and hardcover trade books. The various industry sectors conceive of projects in different ways, use different marketing techniques, and rely on different distribution methods (Powell, 1978a).

### THE RESPONSE OF EDITORS

The shift from independent to corporate ownership is reflected in the perceptions and attitudes of editors concerning their firm. Every one of the 33 editors we interviewed who worked for a house which was part of a large corporation cited increased availability of capital as a major benefit of corporate ownership. The editors also cited the services and technical expertise as well as improved salaries as benefits. Though we pushed them on this point, none of the editors reported any attempts at censorship by the parent corporation and some even cited books they had published which were critical of their parent company. Eleven of the editors, in fact, specifically said there were no disadvantages at all to being "dependent."

Among the 22 editors who did mention disadvantages to dependent status, thirteen felt that their corporate overseers did not understand the essential nature of book publishing. Nine editors mentioned too much concern with the financial bottom line as a disadvantage of outside ownership.

The considerations of economics and independence were also central to the attitudes and perceptions of editors in independent houses. Twenty of the 22 editors we interviewed from independent houses mentioned lack of capital and financial insecurity as negative aspects of going it alone. On the other hand, the main advantage of independence as cited by 18 of the editors was fewer constraints upon their activities. Less pressure to be highly profitable was also cited as an important advantage.

## EMERGENCE OF NEW PUBLISHING STRATEGIES

Perhaps the most important question about the recent mergers concerns their impact on the books which are published. The Authors Guild admits that "it is not that fewer books are being published than formerly, or even, at least not provably, that books of exceptional merit are going unpublished." The Association of American Publishers argues that many mergers led to the survival of imprints that would have otherwise disappeared. They maintain that publishing could not have expanded as rapidly as it did over the past twenty years without the infusion of substantial new capital provided by mergers. Outside ownership has also brought new management and financial acumen to a business in which it had been reputedly lacking and, in many cases, has resulted for the first time in orderly budgeting, forecasting, planning, and marketing arrangements. These views combined with the editors' assertions that there is little or no corporate censorship suggest that the mergers have not drastically narrowed the selection of titles even among the large first tier trade publishers. Still, the mergers have had an influence on publishers' marketing strategies which, in turn, have had an effect on what is published (Powell, 1978b, 1979).

**BLOCKBUSTERS**

Almost all of the trade book editors we interviewed in large first tier firms said they are increasingly on the lookout for "big" books that will generate exceptionally high levels of sales. These "big"books are expensive, but the huge sums spent on them can be viewed as another part of the elaborate pre-release advertising and promotional campaign. One editor, whose house had paid over $2 million for a book summed it up, "We've been somewhat inactive and we needed to get back in the ball game. . . . You pay $2.x million and people pay attention. Look at all the free advertising we're getting." The blockbuster strategy is, then, to create the appearance of a successful product and it promises some hugely profitable successes. It also threatens some disastrously expensive failures, however. Some houses for which the threats of disaster have become reality are now beginning to question the strategy. Still, many houses pursue the strategy with enthusiasm by publishing and heavily promoting books by star authors and books with extensive tie-ins to other media.

The stakes involved in the quest for big books by established stars are now very high. Carl Sagan, for example, was offered $2 million by Simon and Schuster for hardcover and paperback rights to *Contact,* his first work of fiction. Simon and Schuster made the offer after seeing only a 115-page outline for the proposed book. Taylor Caldwell, the popular novelist, signed a two-book contract with G. P. Putnam's Sons for $3.9 million. Bantam Books paid $3.2 million for the paperback rights to Judith Krantz's *Princess Daisy.* Bantam also bought the paper rights for *The Right Stuff* by Tom Wolfe for $600,000 and the United Artists film company bought the movie rights for $500,000.

Although this reliance on well-known authors guarantees an interested audience, it also leads to a significant shift in negotiating status. Established stars command huge sums and have the bargaining power to demand up-front guarantees. Thus, they do not have to wait for royalties that may or may not be forthcoming. As the stakes involved have grown higher, authors have turned to agents and lawyers to represent them. They have been able to retain many of the subsidiary rights publishers have counted on. In the process, the blockbuster wars have escalated. A handful of stars, among them nonfiction writers like Tom Wolfe, Gay Talese, and ex-politicians, or best-selling novelists, now receive vast sums. Responding to a question concerning the size of advances to authors, one editor remarked:

> I've paid up to half a million, although I certainly have to get approval for something that big. But the amount has really gone up in recent years. I would have said $10,000 was the minimum several years ago, but now it's considerably higher. We have a highly effective publishing machine here, particularly on the promotional end, and it is not only hard to get them interested in a book that is earmarked as small, you have to wonder if it is even worth their time. We're finding that as competition gets more intense, you have to spend more money to make money.

A consequence of these "star wars" according to editors, is that there is less acquisition money available for other, less well known authors. This, combined with the gearing of the larger publishers' promotional machinery to marketing big books, has tended to squeeze out the middle sized books which are increasingly too small for the large first tier publishers and yet too large for the specialized second tier houses. Middle sized projects are deemed risky for without mass or specialized appeal they do not have a ready market. In the May 2, 1980 issue of *Publishers Weekly*, sixteen top executives in trade publishing were asked to comment on their current practices. A number of responses confirmed the decline of middle-level projects:

- "We're cutting middlebrow fiction—anything that is neither commerce nor culture."
- "We're not cutting back but we have an increasing reluctance to participate in auctions for intermediate books."
- "For anything below the blockbuster, the paperback reprint market is no longer the reliable source of income it once was."

Not only are middle sized projects being squeezed out but so too are middle sized publishers. Population ecology theorists have shown that firms compete most intensely with firms of similar size, thus the distribution of organizational size has important implications for competition. Hannan and Freeman (1977) suggest that competition between pairs of organizations within an activity will be a decreasing function of the distance separating them on the size gradient. For example, Hannan and Freeman note that small local banks compete most with other small banks, to a lesser extent with medium-scale regional banks, and hardly at all with international banks. When large-sized organizations emerge, they pose a competitive threat to medium-sized organizations but hardly any threat to small firms. The rise of large organizations may actually increase the survival prospects of small organizations. On the other hand, organizations in the middle of the size distribution may find themselves trapped. Whatever strategy they adopt to fight off the challenge of the larger firm makes them more vulnerable in competition with smaller organizations and vice versa.

Recent developments in book publishing illustrate very well the phenomenon that Hannan and Freeman describe. There has been simultaneous concentration among large firms and a proliferation of small, geographically dispersed independent companies. At the same time, middle sized firms, such as two of the most distinguished independent houses in the country, Charles Scribner's Sons and Atheneum Publishers, find themselves unable to compete with larger houses. Recently Scribner's and Atheneum merged in order to prevent possible takeover by a conglomerate and to capitalize on economies in shipping, warehousing and other areas.

## TIE-INS

With the emergence of strong ties between large publishing houses and film companies, editors and other publishing personnel spend a great deal of time arranging "tie-ins." In addition to the traditional pattern in which hardcover trade houses sell movie rights to already-successful books, a new pattern has emerged in which Hollywood studios engage in complicated ventures with both hard and softcover publishers to coordinate book publication with the release of a movie bearing the same title.

Tie-ins may take several forms. In one form, a book in either hard or softcover is issued six months or more before a film of the same title is to be released. The book's cover draws attention to the fact that it will soon appear as a motion picture and when the film is finally released, a newly packaged book appears on the racks as a mass market paperback. The film helps to promote the book and gives it a second life.

Of the movies produced each year about one-third are based on published books (Holt, 1979). Publishers have an advantage over film companies in initiating this form of the tie-in process because, according to one multimedia executive, book publishers "see more material in a week than a film producer does in a year." Further, beginning the process with a completed novel rather than merely an idea for a screenplay has an obvious advantage. Peter Gruber, producer of the film "The Deep," comments:

> Someone comes in and tells a 15-minute yarn, and you have to make the assessment of whether or not to gamble from $10,000 to $200,000 to develop the property for filming. But you read a novel and you can make that assessment based on a fully fleshed-out series of characterizations, a fully articulated plot and a clear indication of those incidents which make for exciting and successful films.

Not all tie-ins begin with a manuscript for a novel, however. Paperback publishers have increasingly taken to publishing novelizations or quickly-written, fleshed-out versions of successful screenplays such as "Star Wars" or "Close Encounters of the Third Kind." Still another form of tie-in is aptly described as "the spontaneous generation of literary property" (Whiteside, 1981). The aim here is fuse books and movies into a coordinated, packaged property. Such a package is composed of various elements. Whiteside (1981) captures the process well:

> A script is an 'element', so is a writer. So are a book, a producer, an actor or a troup of actors, a director. In contrast to simpler times, in which it was taken for granted that a published book originated with an author . . . the existence of even an unfinished manuscript may not be a necessary precondition for selling a book for a large sum of money to a publisher in these multi-media deals, since actual authorship often becomes an ancillary consideration. . . . [the package] does not have to take place in the mind of a writer; it can occur around a conference table in the office of a producer or an agent, who may then add to it 'elements' including the writer, who is 'acquired' sooner or later in the packaging process.

Richard Snyder, president of Simon and Schuster, did not exaggerate very much when he said, "In a certain sense, we are the software of the television and movie media" (Whiteside, 1981: 70). Certainly tie-ins are not the only thing published these days but as part of the "big book" syndrome they concentrate publishers' time, energy and money into a limited number of projects. And there may be other effects as well. One literary agent had this to say: "The indirect impact is much greater than the direct impact . . . it's very subtle, but I think it's there." He suggested, "material for books is being developed more and more along the lines of visual images, action structure, and externalized exchanges, rather than with internal character development. I think that TV has shaped readers',and publishers', appetite for books like that."

Along the same lines, Leslie Fiedler (1981: 143-144) argues that novels presently fall into the categories of "art or show biz"; not just after they are written and have been sorted out by self-conscious critics and/or the blind mechanism of the marketplace, but in their very conception. Writers tend to write as if for the academy or for Hollywood; "which is to say as if to be taught, analyzed, and explicated—or to be packaged, hyped and sold at the box office."

## SMALL PRESSES

We have found little evidence that serious or innovative books are not being published. It is important to note, however, that the two-tier structure has resulted in a major split in terms of the audiences publishers try to reach. The large trade houses are pursuing the mass market, while smaller trade houses, university presses, and scholarly houses publish for more specialized markets. Thus serious or original books are increasingly likely to be published by smaller houses, in smaller print runs, and at higher prices.

As many large trade houses have increased their expectations of the number of copies a book needs to sell in order to be deemed successful, they are less willing to take on titles with potential sales in the 5,000 to 25,000 copy range. In response, small, independent, "mom-and-pop" enterprises have sprung up, often outside of Manhattan where publishing has long been geographically concentrated. These houses survive on low overheads with small staffs. Some are only part-time operations. They have tended to favor the trade (large-size, quality design) paperback format. Although their output is but a fraction of the industry's total, several titles published by small houses have recently made the trade paperback bestseller lists.

Why have these small houses been successful? One independent publisher argues:

> Because our resources are limited, we have to specialize, to make our imprint stand for things that concern people these days—career-changing, parenting, health, solar housing, and the like. Few of our books are returned unsold by bookstores, most become steady backlist sellers. We've had to let very few of our books go out of print.

Smaller scholarly publishers are also exploiting the opportunity created by the large publishers' emphasis on big books by increasingly targeting their books of more than academic interest to larger audiences. The editor-in-chief of a small successful publisher of commercial scholarly books describes his firm's strategy:

> One of my duties is to pick several books a season from our list that I think have some trade potential and work on promoting them. We can't "make" bestsellers like trade publishers do, we don't have large advertising budgets. . . . In our business, and perhaps it is only in our branch of publishing that this is true, good books sell themselves because the book itself says something that is important. I try to help them along by bringing them to people's attention. . . . Our kind of publishing doesn't require a great deal of money. We rarely compete with other houses on the basis of money . . . our advances are quite small. We compete on the basis of services we offer authors. We like to think that we are continuing the traditions of editorial excellence.
>
> In the past it was uncommon for our hardcover books to sell more than 10,000 copies, except for the few textbooks we did. Now we are aiming for somewhat larger sales. We're advertising in places like the *New Republic* and the *New York Review*. But we aren't becoming trade publishers. Our books are still

budgeted to earn small profits on four-figure sales. If some of them do better, that's great. . . . It's a totally different business from trade publishing where books have to recoup their investments in six months . . . we do it on a two year basis . . . and if a book doesn't sell big, somebody loses his shirt. Trade publishers live off their front list sales. I couldn't sleep at night if faced with that . . . the majority of our sales are from our backlist, good books that sell year in, year out and that makes life a lot easier.

The Association of American Publishers points with considerable pleasure to the growth of small houses at the industry's bottom and even argues that their proliferation offsets recent concentration at the top. There is no question that the number of small entrants to the industry has been remarkable; but the idea that they mitigate the development of large vertically integrated publishing conglomerates is certainly debatable. Small houses encounter a number of problems, particularly in terms of distribution and access to bookstores. They have had to develop marketing techniques outside of normal sales and distribution channels. Herman Wouk (1978: 9), speaking for the Authors Guild, has pointed out that many small companies publish only a few titles per year and "lack the capital to produce, advertise, promote, and distribute their books effectively in the national trade book market."

## CHANGES IN THE WORK OF EDITORS

The acquisition of publishing houses by large corporations along with the new marketing strategies have changed the work of editors. Several of these changes became apparent in our interviews particularly with a number of editors-in-chief whose parent corporations are all on *Fortune* magazine's list of the 1,000 largest corporations. We also conducted observations in several houses to further study the pressures and demands placed upon these firms by their corporate owners.

### PRESSURE FOR MORE

The recent changes in large-scale trade publishing have created a high stakes game. Editors told us they felt that they must produce more "big books" to compete in the game. The editor-in-chief at one paperback house commented:

> With the large amounts of money we are spending on advertising, we have to have at least four really big books a year. . . . that means editors have to change their habits and spend more time working on deals.

The pressure on editors in the smaller corporate-owned houses was not for bigger books but for more books. The editor-in-chief of a prestigious small house under corporate ownership responded to our questions about pressure from above this way:

> The main pressures we feel are not pressures for greater profits. They don't even look at the figures on individual titles. What we feel are pressures for growth, to expand and do more books. . . . We cannot sustain growth really, they don't understand that. . . . They've bothered us partly by forcing more growth than we would normally have. They want us to do more books and we keep telling them there may not be any more books of real merit that we can do justice to.

As a result of pressure for more product, many editors in both large and small firms now find that they have less time to edit manuscripts. At the office they spend their time acquiring manuscripts and working on deals. At home in the evening, they go over manuscripts and suggest changes. Editors also attempt to cope with the pressure for more by signing books that do not require much work. A good example is novelization of a film script, or a packaged multimedia tie-in. Fiction churned out by independent book-factories is another example of nonbooks that are custom-tailored for mass audiences and require little editorial attention (Coser, Kadushin, and Powell, 1981).

**POWER WITHIN THE FIRM**

The recent changes in publishing have brought about shifts in the power of individuals and departments within the large trade houses. Hardcover houses as well as paperback firms have established sophisticated and expensive publicity departments. Personnel in these departments are now consulted before a book is purchased and, in some cases, they have a formal vote in the decision-making process. Similarly, subsidiary rights directors are increasingly the key actors in trade houses. These publishing houses are dependent for their very survival on subsidiary rights sales (that is, sales to book clubs, paperback houses, film companies, and television) and it is the subsidiary rights directors who now routinely auction off these rights for huge amounts of money. It is, then, hardly surprising that editors frequently clear projects with subsidiary rights directors before proceeding. Editors no longer can simply sign a book and then tell their house to sell it. Salancik and Pfeffer's (1974) research on decision-making within a large university has demonstrated that the power of a department is a function of the amount of resources that it contributes to the organization. So it is in publishing houses as well.

**LOSS OF CONTACT**

The biographies and autobiographies of nineteenth and early twentieth century editors and publishers show that many of them were closely associated with their authors. A recent study, for example, has shown the considerable amount of time that editors like Maxwell Perkins and Edward Aswell spent with authors such as Thomas Wolfe (Halberstadt, 1980). Aswell, in fact, produced three of Wolfe's posthumous novels from a million-word collection of finished and unfinished chapters. To be sure, contacts with authors and major intellectuals may loom larger in retrospective accounts than they were in reality, but even discounting for some exaggeration, such interactions seem to have been more frequent in the past than they are today.

As publishing houses are integrated into complex corporate structures, communication lines grow longer and the organizational hierarchy becomes steeper. Publishers work at a distance from writers, spending more time maintaining their organization than working on manuscripts. As one publishing director whose small house was acquired by a large diversified publishing corporation complained, "After we were bought, I never had time to see authors. I spent all my time in meetings with various corporate execs and 'selling' our imprint within the parent company."

Another senior trade editor voiced the same complaint: "I'm spending a lot more time planning the life of a book. Much less time is spent with authors and much more time with other departments—marketing and subsidiary rights especially."

Other factors in addition to merely lack of time have contributed to the loss of contact between editors and authors. According to one trade editor, "It is becoming harder and harder to keep bestselling authors without paying huge amounts of money." Further, "With multiple submissions, editor and author never get together to judge the chemistry between them, and we find ourselves up against 15 other houses, having to make fast decisions." Indeed, authors in quest of the highest price for their work are moving from house to house more frequently now, according to editors. Further, authors submit only very brief outlines for review and editors must buy quickly or lose the project to a competitor. Finally, most trade publishing contracts today are no longer negotiated with the author but rather with an agent or lawyer and this too reduces the contact between editor and author. All of these factors have disrupted the craft-like atmosphere of editing.

One editor-in-chief who recently left a small, high-quality house to head the trade department in a large house summed up the move from craft to corporation with the comment that in his new position he saw mostly lawyers and agents and was in danger of losing contact with creative writers and their manuscripts. He said that in his previous position he could assist in the creative development of his authors but now he was in danger of becoming simply a well-paid retailer of ideas and entertainment.

## CONCLUSION

The events of the last two decades have altered the structure of the publishing industry. There has been concentration among large vertically integrated publishing conglomerates. These are often the firms which produce the blockbuster bestsellers by established star authors. At the same time there has been a proliferation of small, geographically dispersed independent houses. These are the firms which are frequently responsible for "serious" books published in small press runs at high prices.

Some of the important differences between these large and small houses are neatly captured by Hirsch's (1978) distinction between producer-oriented and distributor-oriented media. Producer media generally serve a small audience. They rely on qualitative criteria and reward originality. These media are characterized by a close artist-audience relationship. The distributor media, on the other hand, cater to a mass audience and hence demand more formulaic writing and provide stylized genres. The main criteria for evaluation of success is quantitative. Distributor media are generally more centrally administered and oligopolistic. For example, off-off Broadway theaters serve small audiences and have a close artist-audience relationship. Indeed, the audience is often filled with people who are themselves involved with the theater. In contrast, Broadway productions cater to large audiences not intimately involved in the theater. The criteria for success in the off-off Broadway theaters are often no more than the approval of one's colleagues. Some noted performers even attempt to restrict entry to their pieces. In contrast, the main criteria for success on Broadway are quantitative. Without large audiences, Broadway plays close. Thus prospects for delivering original and complex ideas are clouded from the outset by the economic organization of distributor media.

Trade book houses have become the Broadway of publishing and this has had significant implications for the type of work that editors do. Editors spend more time negotiating deals and consulting with lawyers, corporate managers, and marketing and subsidiary rights directors. This not only signals a power shift within publishing houses, one in which editors are on the decline and others are in ascendance, but it has led to a change in the traditions of book publishing. Editors spend less time with authors and other editors and the old sense of a community of bookmen is fragmented.

There are, to be sure, large trade publishers who do not concentrate solely on the high-powered world of mass entertainment. One of the industry's current paradoxes is that distinguished old houses are hiring professional managers and highly commercial houses continue to publish a few books of real merit. For example, Simon and Schuster, owned by Gulf and Western and with quite a reputation for doing big, splashy, successful books, appears to be following a strategy of growth by becoming more diverse. Within the company, they have set up a number of smaller lines, among them Linden Press, Summit Books, Wyndham Books, Timescape Books, and Touchstone. Each is headed by an individual with a considerable reputation within the industry. This process of growth through the formation of small, personal imprints is an attempt to counterbalance many of the forces that are buffeting the industry. Other large, corporate-owned trade houses have also set up similar arrangements in order to retain top editors who have grown frustrated with corporate bureaucracy.

It should be emphasized that nowhere did we encounter any examples of corporate censorship. However, corporate pressures to increase growth, to go after high "ticket" books, to maintain a constant and steady flow of products do, in some ways, affect the type of books that are published. These pressures encourage editors to pursue authors with well-known track records whose work can be "exploited" in a variety of media formats. More time and energy are spent on "big" books. Serious, noncommercial books do not go unpublished; however, they are less visible since they are often done by smaller houses lacking distribution muscle.

Although there have been major changes in the work process and internal organization of trade publishing, they should not be overstated. Trade publishing is only one sector of the publishing industry and it has always operated under the twin pressures of the marketplace and the literary and intellectual currents of the times. The quest for profitability and the demands for high standards of excellence have rarely coincided. That this tension is exacerbated by outside ownership and multimedia conglomerates in which book publishing houses are expected to "feed" other media should not surprise us. It is important to recognize, however, that the vagaries of public taste are not always predictable and that creative individuals and the ownership of ideas, by their very nature, form an impermanent union.

## NOTE

1. These data are reported in the *1977 Census of Manufactures,* U.S. Dept. of Commerce, Bureau of the Census, U.S. Government Printing Office.

# REFERENCES

AVERITT, R. T. (1968) The Dual Economy. New York: Norton.

BLUESTONE, B., W. M. MURPHY, and M. STEVENSON (1973) Low Wages and the Working Poor. Ann Arbor: Institute of Labor and Industrial Relations, University of Michigan.

BROOKS, J. (1978) "Concentration and conglomeration in book publishing," pp. 549-648 in Proceedings of the Symposium on Media Concentration, Vol. II. Washington, DC: Bureau of Competition, Federal Trade Commission.

COSER, L. A. (1975) "Publishers as gatekeepers of ideas." The Annals 421 (September): 14-22.

—————— C. KADUSHIN, and W. POWELL (1981) Books: The Culture and Commerce of Publishing. New York: Basic Books.

DOUGLAS, A. (1977) The Feminization of American Culture. New York: Knopf.

EDWARDS, R. C., M. REICH, and D. GORDON [eds.] (1975) Labor Market Segmentation. Lexington, MA: D. C. Heath.

FIEDLER, L. A. (1981) "The death and rebirths of the novel." Salmagundi 15 (Fall 1980-Winter 1981): 143-152.

GILROY, A. A. (1980) "An Economic Analysis of U.S. Domestic Book Publishing: 1972-Present." Congressional Research Service Report No. 80-79E.

GORDON, D. M. (1972) Theories of Poverty and Underemployment. Lexington, MA: D. C. Heath.

HALBERSTADT, J. (1980) "The making of Thomas Wolfe's posthumous novels." The Yale Review 70 (October): 79-94.

HANNAN, M. and J. FREEMAN (1977) "The population ecology of organizations." American Journal of Sociology 82 (March): 929-963.

HIRSCH, P. M. (1978) "Production and distribution roles among cultural organizations: on the division of labor across intellectual disciplines." Social Research 45 (Summer): 315-330.

HOLT, P. (1979) "Turning best sellers into movies." Publishers Weekly (October 22).

HOOPES, T. (1978) "The book publishing industry," pp. 549-564 in Proceedings of the Symposium on Media Concentration, Vol. II. Washington, DC: Bureau of Competition, Federal Trade Commission.

KAZIN, A. (1980) "American writing now." The New Republic (October 18): 27-31.

KIRKWOOD, H. (1979) "Remarks." Presented at the Pubmart Workshop on Concentration of Ownership in Book Publishing, New York, April 11.

KNOWLTON, W. (1978) "Competition in book publishing," pp. 565-572 in Proceedings of the Symposium on Media Concentration, Vol. II. Washington, DC: Bureau of Competition, Federal Trade Commission.

MILLER, P. (1967) "The romance and the novel," in Nature's Nation. Cambridge, MA: Harvard University Press.

POWELL, W. (1978a) "Publishers decision-making: what criteria do they use in deciding which books to publish?" Social Research 45 (Summer): 227-252.

—————— (1978b) "Competition versus concentration in the book trade," pp. 573-582 in Proceedings of the Symposium on Media Concentration, Vol. II. Washington, DC: Bureau of Competition, Federal Trade Commission.

—————— (1979) "The blockbuster decade: the media as big business." Working Papers for a New Society (July/August): 26-36.

SALANCIK, G. and J. PFEFFER (1974) "The bases and use of power in organizational decision-making: the case of a university." Administrative Science Quarterly 19: 453-473.

SMITH, H. N. (1974) "The scribbling women and the cosmic success story." Critical Inquiry 1 (September): 47-70.

TOLBERT, C., P. M. HORAN, and E. M. BECK (1980) "The structure of economic segmentation: a dual economy approach." American Journal of Sociology 85 (March): 1095-1116.

WHITESIDE, T. (1981) The Blockbuster Complex. Middletown, CT: Wesleyan University Press.

WOUK, H. (1978) "Statement Before the Antitrust and Monopoly Subcommittee, U.S. Senate, May 12." New York: The Authors Guild.

# Chapter 3

# SCREEN ACTING AS WORK

## Anne K. Peters and Muriel G. Cantor

ACTORS—at least star actors—are influential in American society in two ways: as culture bearers and as celebrities. As culture bearers, they portray the images and myths found in modern literature. In a sense, actors are only a vehicle for the writer, director, and producer. Yet, actors can be creative because they must be convincing in the roles they play. No matter how brilliantly a script is written or how well the film is otherwise directed, if the actors are not convincing the impact is negligible. Thus, actors add to the symbolic messages by their own interpretations of the roles. Their personalities and acting skill, in the final anlysis, can determine the success or failure of a film.

As celebrities, star actors generate influence in their own person (Mills, 1956: 71-94). As their names become familiar and their lives are opened to public scrutiny, they become topics of conversation among a wide variety of people (Tuchman, 1974). According to some analysts, such celebrities provide one of the elements that integrate various classes and ethnic groups which might otherwise have little in common (see Hirsch, 1978). Actors of varied political persuasions have used their celebrity status as a means to propagandize for all types of causes, ranging from those considered liberal (such as civil rights and women's issues) to those considered conservative (such as anticommunist activities and states' rights). Some actors have also transformed their celebrity status into formal political power. The most obvious example is, of course, President Ronald Reagan.

Because producers think it is the star actor rather than the story which draws the audience, actors can be influential within the entertainment indus-

AUTHORS' NOTE: We spent six weeks in research at the main headquarters of the Screen Actors Guild in Los Angeles, and the Guild was helpful in providing most of the statistics used in this chapter. We are particularly grateful to the Controller, Pauline Golden, for her cooperation, and to Kat Brady, Assistant Executive Secretary of the New York branch, for her continuing support.

try as well. Star actors are often the most powerful people on the set, determining subject matter as well as interpretation of the script. Star actors also have the power to stop production for months, as they did during the summer and fall of 1980 when the Screen Actors Guild and the American Federation of Television and Radio Artists went on strike. Only because stars are willing to strike does the acting occupation as a whole have power (Ross, 1941). But stars with such power are, then, but one side of the coin. The other side is the vast majority of actors who have little social influence and absolutely no power at all within the industry.

The visibility of actors and the roles they play tell little about the occupation of screen acting. When actors are viewed as workers in society, somehow the mythology surrounding their occupation takes over. On the one hand, acting as an occupation conjures up visions of glamour and sexuality; on the other hand, actors are seen as struggling artists who pound the pavement looking for work—artists who would rather act than eat. While both images contain some truth, actors must also be viewed as part of the system in which they work. Organizations, customs, and behaviors have developed which routinize and structure both the paid work and the related unemployed time of actors. Screen actors, we would argue, provide an ideal example of how artistic endeavors have become part of the market economy and industrial complex of the twentieth century.

Some sociologists (Marshall, 1964: 163-164; Cullen, 1978: 6) have compared all artists to professional and white-collar workers who provide services rather than a material product. Supposedly, artists and professionals cannot labor in a detached, impersonal way, but rather perform in a uniquely personal context (Marshall, 1964: 164). For actors, each role is slightly different and, while not necessarily challenging, the work does vary from day to day. Still, there is little autonomy or creative freedom for most of those in the occupation. There is a large oversupply of actors to fill the available roles; most actors are lucky to work at all. When they do work, it is likely to be for a large, bureaucratically organized production company and most actors are unable to exercise much influence over the parts they play. Others create the parts, choose the individuals who play them and, most importantly, finance the entire production. Although it is quite true that actors rarely have the job security that those in other occupations have (or are perceived to have), the occupation of screen acting is still located in the same industrial and technological milieu which has developed for most of the workforce in the United States.

A vast majority of actors are, then, powerless. They depend for work on an industry which encourages an oversupply of artists in comparison to the demand for their services, an industry which offers them little autonomy or creative freedom when they do find work. Only a tiny minority of actors

enjoy wealth and power. It is the contradiction between the rich and powerful few and the poor and powerless many within one occupation that has
generated our interest in actors and acting.

## THEORETICAL PERSPECTIVE

Except for a handful of studies of media creators in Hollywood and
elsewhere (for example, Cantor, 1971, 1972; Faulkner, 1971; Moore, 1961;
Peters, 1971, 1974, 1977; Powdermaker, 1950; Turow, 1978), there has
been little written from a social science perspective about the work of the
people who create film and popular drama.[1] Of particular interest here is that
Lewis (1978), in a review of the literature on popular culture, did not report a
single study on actors. Most of the recent studies of how popular culture is
created are organizational studies which use a systems analysis approach
attributing little importance to artists themselves. Rather, they concentrate
on how parts of the larger system impinge upon or act as a gatekeeper for the
artists. While there are some studies of various performers which focus on
socialization processes and work tasks, few have approached the topic of
artists as workers in industrial societies or considered how the power of
artists relates to the industrial and economic conditions of work.[2]

We believe that actors provide the ideal example of how artists really will
fare in what Daniel Bell (1976: 39-40) and others call a "post-industrial"
society. Although we have many disagreements with Bell's analysis of social
relationships, it is difficult to question the important changes he emphasizes
in the occupational structure and the division of labor in the United States
which have occurred since the end of World War II. In particular, the growth
of telecommunications and knowledge-producing industries has changed
the nature of work (Bell, 1976; Montagna, 1977). Part of the change is
reflected in the growth of the white-collar labor force. Classified as white-
collar workers are those whose activities relate to the gathering and distribut-
ing of knowledge, information, and entertainment. Bell reinforces his contention that the United States is entering a "post-industrial" era by claiming
there is a decline in importance of economic elites and an increased influence of professions involved in the production and dissemination of knowledge. Modern society, according to Bell, is increasingly characterized by
and dependent upon the use of abstract theoretical knowledge. The mind
rather than the machine is becoming the tool of production.

Bell and some other postindustrial theorists believe that social relations in
the workplace are different for those who use their minds as tools than for
those who use machines. They believe that workers who have skill and
theoretical knowledge control their own work processes. Bell (1976: xviii)

claims that rewards in work are achieved on merit (skill and education) rather than from inheritance or property. Creative and professional workers, because they have theoretical knowledge, talent, and skill are upwardly mobile and powerful in the political sphere as well.[3]

The arguments for the emergence of a postindustrial society are based partially on labor force statistics. There is little doubt that both average salaries and employment are higher for those categorized as "professional, technical and kindred" workers by the U.S. Department of Commerce (1971, 1979) when compared to most others in the labor force (Montagna, 1977). Certain workers are likely to be among the most technically skilled as Bell contends.[4] However, when one studies each of the specific occupations within the larger category, another pattern emerges. Within each occupation, there are at least two kinds of workers: those with power, prestige, and control over the work process and those who are controlled and less autonomous. Large discrepancies in power, employment, and salaries exist within specific occupational categories. Certain members of an occupational group enjoy much power, prestige, and control while others with equal access to the same theoretical knowledge and training are less favored.[5]

Moreover, Bell's claims are also disputed by those who have studied workers such as journalists and television producers and by those who have studied the organization and economics of media industries (Brown, 1971; Cantor, 1971, 1972, 1980; Epstein, 1973; Gitlin, 1979; Johnstone et al., 1976; Melody, 1973; Tuchman, 1978). In actuality, those who do creative work for media organizations have little control over their employment or the content of their work. Power in the marketplace, inherited wealth, and property are as influential in the media world as they are in the worlds of commerce and manufacturing. Neither most people in media jobs nor most media jobs are at a controlling level. It is our contention that although the content of work is different for those employed in the media, such workers (especially actors) experience many of the same limitations as do pink- and blue-collar workers when it comes to mobility and control over the work process.

## METHOD

The material presented here is based on information from a number of sources. The primary source of information is fifty semistructured interviews with actors seriously pursuing careers in Hollywood and New York, the two major film production centers in the United States. Most of those interviewed were members of the Screen Actors Guild. (No one can act in television or movie production in the United States more than once without joining the Guild or its sister union, the American Federation of Television and Radio Artists.) Most actors who work regularly, and many who do not, belong to both unions and other acting unions as well.[6] Our sample is not representative of the 45,000 people who are presently members of the Screen Actors Guild, because as we have shown elsewhere (Cantor and Peters, 1980), many members of the Guild are not serious actors as we have defined them. Those we interviewed are serious in the sense that their primary occupation is "actor," that is they spend their time either working in films or trying to work in films. They were chosen for our study based on two criteria: they were presently working in a television or movie production or had worked in one in the last few years, and they considered acting their primary occupation. In addition to these fifty actors, many of whom were active in Guild affairs, six paid officials of the Guild were interviewed as were several aspiring actors who were not yet members of the Guild. The majority of interviews were conducted in Los Angeles and New York in 1976 and 1977.

In addition, we extensively reviewed trade publications directed to people working in the industry: *Daily Variety* (Western Edition), *Hollywood Reporter, Screen Actor* (the publication for members of the Screen Actors Guild), and *Broadcasting*. The Guild itself provided some records which were very useful. We observed the production of television series episodes and movies and attended acting classes both as observers and as students. Congressional hearings, FCC reports, and other documents were also used when appropriate.

## THE ORGANIZATIONAL CONTEXT OF ACTING

Filmmaking became an industry early in the twentieth century. By the time sound was introduced in the late 1920s, the industry had become one of the top fifty in the United States (Sklar, 1976: 250). Although films were made in Germany, England, France, Russia, and other places, Hollywood became the world center for the movie industry. During the 1930s and 1940s, as many as 500 films a year were made in the Los Angeles area (Sklar, 1976). The large studios such as Metro-Goldwyn-Mayer, Paramount, Universal, RKO, and Twentieth-Century-Fox were household words. Screen magazines told the stories of stars; fan clubs and beauty contests provided a means for vicarious identification with those actors who had star status. The movies of the 1930s and 1940s also provided definitions of proper manners, sexual mores, and success and failure for many Americans.

Even when the movie industry was at its height, the work opportunities and the power of actors were limited. At most, only several thousand actors have ever been able to earn their livelihood from screen acting. Further, the contract system used by the studios usually favored the production company rather than the actor. Before World War II, the studios were monolithic, paternalistic bureaucracies. Control and power were vested in the heads of the studios, and the cadre of actors under contract was small enough so that it was possible for a studio head to make most of the decisions about them (Sklar, 1976; Powdermaker, 1950). Although some actors were fortunate enough to have had the necessary apprenticeship that went along with being a contract player, most who aspired to become actors never made it and were dropped from the studio rolls. The contract system did, however, produce stars who are still among the best known and most revered people in American society (Dyer, 1979).[7]

After World War II, the film industry changed. The large studios stopped making so many films, and the number of contract players had dropped from 742 in 1946 to 229 by 1956 (Bernstein, 1957). The changes in the industry were due to lower movie attendance and lower profits for the studios. Television had become the national mass medium. When television was introduced, the movie industry fought its growth by refusing to sell old films to the television networks. By the late 1950s, however, the movie industry had capitulated to television and since then the demarcation between the two industries has become more blurred each year. There are few television shows or theatrical movies made in the United States which are not directly or indirectly connected with the major studios: Universal, Twentieth Century-Fox, Paramount, Columbia, MGM, Warner Brothers, and Walt Disney (FCC, 1980). The independent television producers such as Aaron Spelling and Norman Lear have no facilities to make shows but must rent space from one of the studios. Even when a film is not actually made in a Hollywood studio, a studio may finance the film, provide technical assistance, or distribute it. Moreover, almost every film made in the United States and many which are co-produced in Europe and elsewhere are eventually shown on American television.

Even with the coming of television, jobs remain scarce and actors remain powerless. The three major areas where screen actors work (television, movies and TV commercials) still provide only limited employment opportunities in comparison to the number who seek them.[8] Further, the contract system has disappeared and the star system has changed—though not to the benefit of the actors. Rather than having a cadre or company of players, producers go into the open market and select actors from the large available pool. Under this system, the actor who has had success in the past, measured by box-office receipts or ratings of television appearances, is in a good competitive position. However, under this system actors, even star actors, have become commodities which are procured as needed by producers from the large available supply. It is the fierce, open competition for limited work which structures actors' work lives, leaves them powerless in the workplace, and denies them a rational route to a career in acting.

The Screen Actors Guild does little to alter this situation. The ambition of all aspiring actors who arrive in Los Angeles is to join the Guild because without membership it is practically impossible to maintain a career in screen acting. The most common way to become a member is to work once for a producer who has signed a Guild contract. (All major producers have such contracts.) Although there are other routes to membership, such as joining a sister union, membership is not open to all who wish to join. We have met aspiring actors who were having trouble either getting hired for their first job or finding another way in, although it is our impression that most who wish to join find a way to do so. However, even for those who do become members, work may still not be available. The Guild has 45,000 members but only 3,400 of these earned over $10,000 from acting in 1974 (Cantor and Peters, 1980).

For an organization which began with seventeen actors and little money in the middle of the depression (1933), the Screen Actors Guild's growth and accomplishments are phenomenal[9] (Cantor and Peters, 1980; Ross, 1941; Tunstall and Walker, 1981). Yet its very size and growth raise a number of questions about the relationship of the movie and television industries to the workers who aspire to employment. The Screen Actors Guild is not exactly a union of workers, at least not of working screen actors. Only about 1 percent of its members are stars, and about 10 percent of the Hollywood members are working at one time. For the occasionally employed actor, the Guild can do little. It is not a hiring hall; it provides almost no training.[10] Membership primarily benefits actors who work with some regularity and who are somewhat established in the field. As a labor union, the Screen Actors Guild's primary function is to negotiate working conditions, residual payments, and minimum wage levels with its three major contractee groups (television producers, film producers, and TV commercial producers).

Because of the large number of members and the few jobs available, some have suggested that the Guild could be more effective if it limited membership to those who fit established criteria, rather than remaining an open union (Tunstall and Walker, 1981). Yet no one—neither Guild officials, producers, directors, nor actors themselves—seems to favor this change. For a combination of sentimental, ideological, and economic reasons, all of the people we have interviewed are adamantly opposed to defining who is and who is not an actor. They believe that *anyone* should have the opportunity to compete for a part in a production regardless of background or present status. Thus, the effective decision as to who qualifies as an actor is made by the casting director and others involved in the casting process.

## BEING A SERIOUS ACTOR

One outcome of having such a large supply of actors compared to demand is that most of the actual work actors do is preparatory to getting a paid job in a production. Almost all actors except perhaps the very big stars spend a great deal of time looking for work. According to one Screen Actors Guild member:

> We spend more time looking for work than any group in any other profession. Looking for work is really what we do for a living. Actually, it's not looking for work so much as looking for the opportunity to *apply* for work; i.e., looking for the opportunity to audition [Nassif, 1975: 22].

The majority of the activity in the work life of actors is necessary but technically unwaged. It includes studying acting, seeking agents, going to casting interviews, and other activities such as keeping the body in shape, socializing with other actors, and making contacts with people who might potentially further an actor's career. Analyzing these activities from the perspective of how actors attempt to control their work dramatizes how little autonomy actors have.

### STUDYING ACTING IN HOLLYWOOD

Most serious actors, as we have defined them, believe that acting is a thoroughly engrossing and enjoyable activity. Some call acting fun; some call it an emotional growth experience, especially when they have the chance to identify with a character in a script, and some call it a challenge. Not one actor we have interviewed would prefer another occupation. For those people who seriously pursue it, actually working in movies and television is involving and enjoyable in and of itself, regardless of the other benefits that might accrue from success in the field.

Ideally, acting totally involves the body and the intelligence of the actor who *becomes* the part being played. However, there are few opportunities for this kind of acting. Not only are jobs few and far between, but many television and movie scripts contain underdeveloped characters. Thus, even when actors find work, the work may not be satisfying. Serious actors must find ways of acting other than through employment. The most common and obvious way is to take acting classes or, in some cases, to give acting lessons.

All 28 actresses Peters (1971: 82) interviewed during her participant observation study had taken some classes in acting. The actors we interviewed also had studied acting either as drama students in college or through an acting school or both. Many continued to take lessons of some kind even after they had established themselves. A few have their own "schools" or give lessons to others. Throughout Los Angeles and New York there has developed a semiprofessional network of schools located in lofts, apartments, and theaters where both aspiring and established actors study the art of acting. Well-known teachers both in New York and Los Angeles may award "scholarships" to those they consider talented. Combined with the requirement of auditions to get into their classes, the reduction of fees assure the more well known teachers of having stimulating, talented students. Although all require auditions, those who teach to supplement their own incomes when not performing are less selective.

We found that the content of an acting class is similar no matter who the teacher but there are some distinct advantages to studying with a well-known teacher. One advantage is that people who cast shows tend to be more impressed by actors who can list a famous acting teacher on their resume. Another is that these teachers, who may often act professionally themselves (such as Sanford Meisner, Jeff Corey, Uta Hagen), are very apt to have contacts in show business and can help students in whom they are particularly interested to get jobs. Beyond these benefits, many take acting lessons simply to have an opportunity to act. It is very common for actors who have developed considerable skill in acting to continue to take lessons.

## AGENTS

An actor's agent is technically a person hired to arrange casting interviews and negotiate salary and other conditions for a percentage of the actor's earnings (usually a 10 percent commission). However, because of the oversupply of unemployed actors, the actors themselves must seek out and attract agents rather than vice versa. In Hollywood it is impossible to get into a casting interview without the sponsorship of an agent. It is absolutely crucial that much time and energy be spent in making the rounds of agents. This unpaid work is necessary to the work life of actors.

Agents want the clients they sign to have the potential for becoming very successful. Successful may mean either becoming a star or just a regularly working actor. An agent's judgment of success potential thus becomes an important element in determining whether a career as an actor is possible. Every actor in the context of the commercialized competitive world of show business must stand apart from every other actor in order to be noticed. Or in contrast, actors must be very much like a popular actor, that is, a "type."

More than competence, agents want actors with appeal who can be sold to casting directors and, in turn, the audience. It is this saleability which turns some actors into a commodity with considerable exchange value—very valuable to the agent and the producer as well. However, very few actors reach this status, and the ones who do never know how long their cherished position in the market will last.

## CASTING INTERVIEWS

Another significant part of the work life of actors is going to casting interviews, if the actor is fortunate enough to have an agent making interview appointments. Again, the work that goes into interviews is not waged.

There are different types of casting interviews, some more and some less demeaning to actors. Sometimes hundreds of actors are screened for a role in a show. This type of casting is dubbed a "cattle call" and seems to be universally hated, perhaps because it reminds everyone involved of how much competition there really is. After the cattle call is over, some of the more favored actors are requested to return within a few days for a second, more intense interview. These and other more concentrated interviews are considered more pleasant.

Unless very well known, actors have virtually no control over the roles they will be hired to play. It is casting directors who make most of the decisions about who is to be cast in a role. According to Turow (1978: 22), agents understand that time pressures often cause casting directors to rely on their "repertory companies" and to ignore those actors agents offer to them. Nevertheless, some talent agents said they do submit suggestions to friendly casting directors and producers who respect their judgment.

Turow argues it is the casting director in conjunction with the producers who establish the stereotypes and cliches so familiar to moviegoers and television viewers. He suggests that accidental decisions may become part of a caster's repertoire and spread throughout the industry, particularly if the choices are seen to fit emerging notions of credibility and can be used to forestall pressure group criticism (see Cantor, 1980, for a review of pressure group activities in the industry). A new cliche is established when a decision is made to break a mold, and then a new mold is established. In other words, casting directors (along with the producer or director) have an image in *their* heads that an actor must fit. Actors know they are not hired on talent but rather because of some other qualities which cannot necessarily be determined before the interview. According to one actress interviewed:

> You may be a good actress, but when you're starting out in the beginning and you're not well-known, then . . . if you don't look the part, they're not going to give you the part. Once you're an established star, perhaps like Julie Harris—

she's a good actress, and they take a gamble on her being a sex bomb in a picture and then Plain Jane in the next. But if she were just struggling, they'd put her into Plain Jane . . . no matter how good an actress she was [Peters, 1977].

## WORKING IN HOLLYWOOD

Once an actor does acquire an acting job, it usually lasts for so short a time that it is difficult to see it as an enduring feature of a work life. A job may last only a day or two. Further, the work itself in films and television amounts only to acting in disconnected scenes. It appears to be less satisfying than stage work, although some actors interviewed found it quite challenging. Another condition of screen and television acting is that there are long periods between takes, so even when a person has an acting job, there is much idle time. This time is probably best spent in making contacts with people on the set who might know of other jobs or who might put in a good word for the actor with a casting director.

Informal contacts with others in show business might also be made during the long periods of unemployment. There are places where actors hang out, and they are very apt to talk to each other about their work, lack of work, and the projects of which they have heard. Common interest and shared discrimination bind actors together to some extent, although the nature of the occupation forces them into individual competition with each other. There is a desire to socialize with and learn from other actors, but there is a defensiveness also, born out of the intensely competitive structure of acting.

The minimum wage for actors appears to be very high. For example, the least amount of money a member of Screen Actors Guild can earn for one day's work is nearly $300 and for one week's work is nearly $1,000. Coupled with unemployment benefits and residual payments, the money from only one job may enable an actor to live for several months. Thus, some of an actor's idle time is paid, but averaged over unemployed periods, the rate of pay is low.

Because acting jobs are sporadic, again except for a small cadre of actors, unemployment compensation often does not cover the time between jobs. To exist under such circumstances, most members of the Screen Actors Guild work at other occupations when not acting for money, which is most of the time. The majority take minimal work while the better known are able to invest in businesses and capitalize on their names. In Los Angeles various stars have become car dealers, realtors, restaurateurs, and politicians.

For the struggling actor, outside employment is a serious problem connected to the organization of work in the entertainment business. One must be ready to accept a part if offered. It is clearly impossible to become too involved in outside employment if an actor is seriously committed to acting as a career. The physical attractiveness of actresses often qualifies them for such jobs as receptionist or model. Some become high priced prostitutes, but most take the low-level, unskilled jobs that have been called "pink collar" occupations: waitress, temporary secretary, or salesclerk. The male actor also faces similar problems in deciding how to earn money during times of unemployment as an actor. Throughout Los Angeles, bartenders, waiters, construction workers, gas station attendants, and even plumbers and electricians will claim to be actors. Although these workers may not be committed to their "temporary" employment, having to work takes time from pursuing a career in acting. When one must go to work daily, regardless of how uninvolving the work is, little time is available to take acting lessons, to make the rounds of agents, and, if lucky, to go to casting interviews.

## STARDOM

Although most actors are unemployed or underemployed, certain individuals work regularly, are very well paid for their work, and enjoy celebrity status. A few of these can be considered stars. They are very much in demand in the industry. Their names are household words. They command enormous salaries. And they have power and influence in the workplace and often in the larger society as well (Mills, 1956).

In terms of income, it is clear from the reports of the Screen Actors Guild that there is a real gap in earnings between those who have achieved some success and all others. In 1974, for example, 0.6 percent of all Screen Actors Guild members earned over $100,000 while 75 percent earned less than $3,500 from acting (Cantor and Peters, 1980).

In terms of control in the workplace, star status can be translated into the power to choose one's own scripts and then to determine the interpretation of those scripts as well as other aspects of the production. Star actors may, in fact, become more powerful than the director or producer in controlling work on the set. Some actors are also able to translate their star status and wealth into behind-the-scenes control by becoming directors or producers themselves. Robert Redford, Katharine Hepburn, Burt Reynolds, and Jerry Lewis are examples of stars who direct and/or produce films.

Stars command wealth and power because they are a very valuable commodity—but they are still a commodity. In a sense, stars are the real product of the entertainment industry. They are what the industry sells to the public. The process by which stars are produced by the industry, however, is unclear. There is no credentialing process and no established career ladder. Still, unknown players do sometimes rise to stardom and it is this feature of the occupation which, we believe, helps account for the tenacity we have observed among the aspiring actors whom we interviewed.

# CONCLUSION

Throughout this article we have stressed how little control most actors have over both their working conditions and over the process of creating film and television. The dependency of actors upon agents and casting directors for work is only part of the story. The major problem of finding work which is creative and provides a living wage arises from the organization of the industry combined with the acceptance of the ideology of stardom by the actors themselves. There are no longer any apprenticeships in the industry and no formal qualifications to enter the occupation imposed either by producers or by the Screen Actors Guild. Anyone can claim to be an actor and attempt to get work. This organization, combined with the lure of stardom, maintains the huge oversupply of actors and, in turn, the scarcity of jobs and lack of control for most actors.

If this system does not function to the advantage of actors, it does function very much to the advantage of production companies. If the pool of actors were smaller, their cost to the production company would probably be higher. Moreover, if actors were organized on criteria related to talent and training, they would be more likely to have some input into the kinds of dramatic productions produced. The system also functions to the advantage of the unions by providing a large pool of dues-paying members. The benefits to the production companies and unions are, then, financial. The benefits to the actors are the promise of fame and wealth for a few.

There is little question that the "post-industrial society" described by Bell does not include actors. For them, power in the workplace is not based on skill or knowledge, nor has a meritocracy developed. The individual merit so highly valued by Bell is not the criterion for success as a screen actor. Rather, the criterion is nebulous and, in fact, is considered undefinable even by the agents, casting directors, and producers who apply it. Still, there is always the possibility for a person to begin with virtually no capital or credentials and to become eminently successful. It is this feature of the occupation which probably explains the remarkable persistence of many aspiring actors in the face of deprivation and compromise. It is also this feature of the occupation which makes most actors powerless to control their own work lives. This, we would argue, is the contradiction which confronts the artist in contemporary society.

# NOTES

1. We are, of course, excluding the large number of memoirs and biographies of stars, profiles of actors and directors, and film criticism available in the literature.

2. Paul Hirsch (1969, 1972) makes only passing reference to artists in his analyses of how cultural industries operate. He says, "the status of artists resembled more closely the salaried employee's than the freelance professional's" (1972: 641), and in another publication says, "the artist provides the creative input. He [sic] is in constant demand because of the rapid turnover of product. The novelist, the politician, the playwright, and the clothing designer, all exemplify the artist." (1969: 59) Hirsch's evidence that novelists and playwrights are in "constant" demand is weak. Certainly, the ordinary screen actor is rarely in demand. Because a film can be seen over and over again, the demand for the artists, including script writers and other performers as well as actors, is never high. Rather, the supply of actors far exceeds the demand (Cantor and Peters, 1980; Ennis and Bonin, 1977).

3. Kevin Phillips (1975) has suggested that journalists exercise great political power in the United States. He believes they are a force for liberal social change. Bell (1976: 342-376) is less clear than Phillips on political power of "new professional groups," but he does state that they may become a coherent class in society, wielding more power than those who own or control property.

4. Bell (1976: 134) uses, as part of his argument to show the emergence of a post-industrial society, the growth in the proportion of white collar workers in the labor force (17.6 percent in 1900 compared to 42.0 percent in 1960). The U.S. Department of Commerce (1979: 415) reported that such workers were 50 percent of the labor force in 1978. These figures are not being disputed. However, included in the category are clerical workers who cannot be considered part of the new professional class. Moreover, the professional and technical workers in the larger category are only 10.8 percent of all workers. In all, 195 occupations are included under the category "professional, technical, and kindred workers." (U.S. Department of Commerce, 1971: 1-22). Among the 195 occupations are a variety of workers such as physicians, rodeo riders, and seeing eye dog trainers. Actors are included in that category as well.

5. The literature (mostly case studies) is too vast to be cited here. For example, many studies which compare women and men in the same occupation show that women who are equally qualified as men workers do not have equal prestige or power (Kanter, 1977; Epstein, 1974).

6. Rules about joining the Screen Actors Guild are somewhat complex. A person may and usually does join the Guild when hired for a first role. However, because of the way the union interprets the Taft-Hartley Act, a person is not required to join until the second role is secured. This is beneficial to those "real people" who are used in commercial advertisements. Another way to join the union is by becoming a member of a sister union. The Screen Actors Guild is one of several unions known as the Four As, Associated Actors and Artistes of America. The major affiliates of the Four As are Screen Actors Guild, Actors Equity Association, and the American Federation of Television and Radio Artists. Lesser known affiliates include the American Guild of Musical Artists, Screen Extras Guild, Hebrew Actors Union, Italian Actors Union, and Puerto Rican Association of Actors and Show Technicians. At one time almost anyone could join the American Federation of Television and Radio Artists and then transfer to the Screen Actors Guild. Several years ago this route into membership was made more difficult.

7. Richard Dyer in his book, *Stars,* written in 1978, uses as examples of stars mostly actors from the Hollywood films of the 1930s, 1940s, and 1950s. An analysis of his index, for example, shows that he does not consider television actors to be stars.

8. With the advent of cable television and the increased popularity of made-for-television movies in the last five years film production in the United States has increased somewhat. In 1980-1981, for example, ABC contracted for 20 films from various production companies in Hollywood.

9. Because so many films are made on location, the number of branches of the Guild has increased as well as the membership. In 1948 there were three branches, New York, Detroit,

and Los Angeles. In 1975, there were 11 offices and as of October 1980 the number has grown to 24 including New York and Los Angeles. The 45,000 members, however, are concentrated in New York (approximately 16,000, including extras) and Los Angeles (20,000, not including extras). This information was provided by the Washington, D.C. branch of the Guild.

10. The Screen Actors Guild, in conjunction with the American Film Institute, established a conservatory in 1975 to provide some training for a few actors who had little experience in front of a camera. Actors receive fellowships to attend.

# REFERENCES

BELL, D. (1976) The Coming of Post Industrial Society: A Venture in Social Forecasting. New York: Basic Books.

BERNSTEIN, I. (1957) "Hollywood at the Crossroads: An Economic Study of the Motion Picture Industry." Prepared for the Hollywood AFL Film Council.

BROWN, L. (1971) Televi$ion: The Business Behind the Box. New York: Harcourt Brace Jovanovich.

CANTOR, M. G. (1980) Prime-Time Television: Content and Control. Beverly Hills: Sage.

——— (1972) "The role of the producer in choosing children's television content," in G. A. Comstock and E. A. Rubinstein (eds.) Television and Social Behavior. Vol. I. Content and Control. Washington, DC: Government Printing Office.

——— (1971) The Hollywood TV Producer: His Work and His Audience. New York: Basic Books.

——— and A. K. PETERS (1980) "The employment and unemployment of actors in the United States," in W. S. Hendon, J. L. Shanahan, and A. J. MacDonald (eds.) Economic Policy for the Arts. Cambridge, MA: Abt Books.

CULLEN, J. B. (1978) The Structure of Professionalism: A Quantitative Examination. New York: Petrocelli Books.

DYER, R. (1979) Stars. London: British Film Institute.

ENNIS, P. and J. BONIN (1977) "Understanding the Employment of Actors." Washington, DC: National Endowment for the Arts.

EPSTEIN, C. F. (1974) "Ambiguity as social control: consequences for the integration of women in professional elites," in P. L. Stewart and M. G. Cantor (eds.) Varieties of Work Experience. Cambridge, MA: Schenkman.

EPSTEIN, E. J. (1973) News from Nowhere: Television and the News. New York: Random House.

FAULKNER, R. R. (1971) Hollywood Studio Musicians: Their Work and Careers in the Recording Industry. Chicago: Aldine.

Federal Communications Commission (1980) An Analysis of Television Program Production, Acquisition and Distribution. Federal Communications Commission Network Inquiry Special Staff, June.

GITLIN, T. (1979) "Prime-time ideology: the hegemonic process in television entertainment." Social Problems 26 (February): 251-266.

HIRSCH, P. (1978) "Television as a national medium: its cultural and political role in American society," in D. Street (ed.) Handbook of Urban Life. San Francisco: Jossey-Bass.

——— (1972) "Processing fads and fashions: an organization-set analysis of culture industry systems." American Journal of Sociology 77 (January): 639-659.

_____ (1969) The Structure of the Music Industry. Ann Arbor, MI: Survey Research Center.

JOHNSTONE, J. W. C., E. J. SLAWSKI, and W. W. BOWMAN (1976) The Newspeople: A Sociological Portrait of American Journalists and Their Work. Urbana: University of Illinois Press.

KANTER, R. (1977) Men and Women of the Corporation. New York: Basic Books.

LEWIS, G. H. (1978) "The sociology of popular culture." Current Sociology 26 (Winter): 3.

MARSHALL, T. H. (1964) Class, Citizenship, and Social Development. Garden City, NY: Doubleday.

MELODY, W. (1973) Children's Television: The Economics of Exploitation. New Haven, CT: Yale University Press.

MILLS, C. W. (1956) The Power Elite. New York: Oxford University Press.

MOORE, J. (1961) "Occupational anomie and irresponsibility." Social Problems 8: 293-299.

MONTAGNA, P. (1977) Occupations and Society: Toward a Sociology of the Labor Market. New York: John Wiley.

NASSIF, F. (1975) "Aren't auditions fun?" Screen Actor 17 (Winter): 22-24.

PETERS, A. (1971) "Acting and aspiring-actresses in Hollywood: a sociological analysis." Ph.D. dissertation, University of California, Los Angeles.

_____ (1974) "Aspiring Hollywood actresses: a sociological perspective," in P. L. Stewart and M. G. Cantor (eds.) Varieties of Work Experience. Cambridge, MA: Schenkman.

_____ (1977) "The work life of actresses." Presented at the annual meeting of the American Sociological Association, Chicago.

PHILLIPS, K. P. (1975) Mediacracy: American Parties and Politics in the Communication Age. Garden City, NY: Doubleday.

POWDERMAKER, H. (1950) Hollywood: The Dream Factory. Boston, MA: Little, Brown.

ROSS, M. (1941) Stars and Strikes: Unionization of Hollywood. New York: Columbia University Press.

SKLAR, R. (1976) Movie-Made American: A Cultural History of American Movies. New York: Random House.

TUCHMAN, G. (1978) Making News. New York: Free Press.

_____ (1974) "Assembling a network talk-show," in G. Tuchman (ed.) The TV Establishment. Englewood Cliffs, NJ: Prentice-Hall.

TUNSTALL, J. and D. WALKER (1981) Media Made in California. New York: Oxford University Press.

TUROW, J. (1978) "Casting for TV parts: the anatomy of social typing." Journal of Communication 28 (Autumn): 19-24.

U.S. Department of Commerce (1979) Statistical Abstracts of the United States (100th edition). Washington, DC: Government Printing Office.

_____ (1971) Classified Index of Industries and Occupations: 1970 Census of Population. Washington, DC: Government Printing Office.

*Chapter 4*

# THE PRODUCER AS ARTIST
## Commercial Television

**Horace M. Newcomb and Robert S. Alley**

WE BEGIN WITH a commonplace. "Television is a producer's medium." Not only within the industry, but in analytical and descriptive literature about it, the producer's control is cited as a dominant factor in a highly collaborative enterprise. In spite of this recognition, however, most discussions of the producer's role focus not on freedom and creativity, but on restriction and limitation, on the nature of "systems" which restrain individuals and prevent them from achieving potential goals. Some of this analysis is based on naive misreadings of the industry or on unreflective theories of popular culture (Ravage, 1978; Stein, 1979). Far more sophisticated readings, however, such as Gitlin (1979) and Cantor (1971, 1980) move in a similar direction, assuming that limitations thwart creativity rather than that producers, clearly aware of the limitations, work within, around, and through them to achieve creative goals.

At a deeper level, all these previous forms of analysis fall short because they are rooted in an inadequate model of television and its role in American culture. All of them assume what Carey (1975) refers to as a "transportation" model of communication. In this model "the archetypal case of communication . . . is persuasion, attitude change, behavior modification, socialization through the transmission of information, influence, or conditioning." Whether it is the producers unconsciously "falling into line" and attempting to sell their product to network or audience, thus reproducing their social class or the dominant culture, or whether it is the network molding the work into what it has decided is "workable," persuasion is the goal and transportation is the model.

AUTHORS' NOTE: The authors are completing a study of the creative role of the producer in commercial television to be published by Oxford University Press. They would like to thank the John and Mary R. Markle Foundation for support during the preparation of this chapter.

We suggest instead that television is better defined with what Carey terms a "ritual" model of communication, and modify his general insights with an analysis of ritual provided by anthropologist Victor Turner. Turner has suggested (1977) that the function of ritual is filled, in postindustrial societies, by the arts. That function is not merely to conserve or express the dominant cultural system, but to serve as a form of meta-commentary *on* the culture. Values and attitudes, beliefs and codes of meaning, metaphors and their applications, are dismembered, rearranged, reformed, and analyzed. New models can be suggested and old ones repaired. In this view the creation of cultural meaning and of societies built on applications of those meanings is a process of constant negotiation. Popular entertainment is, in our view, central to that process. And a primary means of understanding the role of the producer is to examine individual contributions to this ongoing process.

Television, then, for us, is not an easily read, simplistic, homogeneous mass of meaning. We find in it significant differences in content, form, and meaning. We also see that producers, working within the same patterns of organizational restraint, develop varied work patterns, intentions, and styles. They use these individual patterns and styles to express individual values, beliefs, attitudes, theories, evaluations, or world views. We are suggesting that it is relatively easy, at this point in the history of television, to identify those producers who have personalized their work. We refer to them as self-conscious artistic producers.

We have never intended to argue that this concept could define the larger professional or sociological category of producers. Nor have we any intention of suggesting that the concept provides a general theory of television. What we do want to suggest is that the concept offers a powerful critical tool that can be applied to specific questions about both the content of television and the production process. What we provide here is a beginning step that may enable a more thorough, more sophisticated comparative analysis of the work of individuals in the television production community, of the work that they create, and perhaps of the nature of creativity itself.

To a point our approach to these matters is a simple one. Through critical analysis of television programs it was relatively simple for us to select a group of subjects. Everyone included in the study has clearly established an identifiable personal style, has used television presentations to offer consistent patterns of meaning, and has made a significant impact on the history of television programming.[1] We then arranged with the producers to conduct extensive, informal, conversational interviews. Although the actual content varied from situation to situation, we explored several basic areas of concern.

The first deals with the producer's control. Under this heading came personal descriptions and evaluations of the industry, career narratives, comments on relations with network offices, public interest groups, and so on. The second topic focused on the uses of television as a means of personal expression. Here we explored statements of basic personal values, political perspective, and world view. We examined individual aesthetic theories and looked closely at the medium, discussing examples of programs, series, and episodes. A third area overlaps and contributes to these two large topics, and concerns the producers' use of control for the creative purposes. This area concentrates on interaction with other members of the production process: writers, actors, directors, editors.

Gathering material in these areas, and in dozens of smaller areas that bear on them, was not difficult. Its final application is far more complicated. Many orders of information emerge from such interview material, and through it all there is the persistent possibility of succumbing to the intentional fallacy or of placing emphasis on post hoc creations of meaning.

Our approach to these problems is twofold. On one hand we count the interview material as merely another text. Like others it is an interpretation of experience rather than a recounting of fact. Like other texts it must be interpreted and not merely accepted and applied. One of our primary aims has been to make this material available to other scholars who may disagree with our interpretation and application.

Simultaneously, we argue that we do offer a "controlled" reading of the interview material. We "read" the interviews "through" the actual programs made by the producers as often as we read the programs through the producers' descriptions or their stated intentions. Often we disagree with a producer's evaluations, and this disagreement was accepted as part of our study.

Inevitably, as we move from reportage to interpretation of the programs, and finally to an interpretation of a producer's body of work, we move away from the obvious and into analysis. The final portions of this chapter demonstrate this process, demonstrate the move into interpretation. It is a move made possible, we argue, by the new body of information we provide. But we recognize the possibility that other scholars will disagree with our interpretations, just as we have disagreed at times with the producers.

What follows here is a condensed case study focused on our work with Quinn Martin. The actual selections of material we present here provide a smattering of the total material gathered. It indicates the kind of material solicited and how we have chosen to apply it. We also offer, by way of conclusion, some very brief indications of how Martin's work forms part of the total text of television by demonstrating how the work of other producers might be used to properly contextualize Martin's.

## CONTROL

The idea of control is central to the concept of the self-conscious artistic producer. To a degree the terms are synonomous. There are few producers who seem to have recognized this so early as did Martin, or who realized, as he did, that the producer would be the only professional in television who could actually sieze and use that control. This recognition rose from history and biography, from an observation of his own environment. He grew up in Los Angeles and "patterned, without even thinking about it," on the great movie producers: "Mayer, Cohen, Warner, Zukor." The patterning, the recognition, the image creation may have been almost unconscious in the beginning. Now, however, it is clear that Martin can carefully recount the process by which he gained control and made this image into a reality. Among the more interesting comparative questions rising from this study is that focusing on the variations and patterns in achieving access to control. In Martin's case the process was closely tied to the rise of the ABC television network.

> I've always had more control than most because I carried a lot of control before I carried a lot of money. I always had an instinct to form my own company. I saw that the biggest problem is control. So when I had ABC trying to make a deal with me to make shows exclusively for them, I had a lot of power. *The Untouchables* was number one. I just reached for total creative control and I had it.

> I don't mean to sound like a braggart when I say control. You've got to relate it to the period and, as I say, the whole reason I formed my own company was to get away from all the bureaucracy. I was given total control by a network which was looking desperately to get on the boards and I really pulled it off. I was the only one who did. I had four shows in the top ten for ABC at the time when it was really tough because we used to start off with fifty stations short the first of every year and have to prove ourselves. Be tougher than anybody. I earned my spurs in a very tough market.

As a result of these events Martin did gain important concessions. He was able to convince the network, for example, that he should not have to submit completed scripts for all his episodes. Instead he submitted "notions" or story ideas. With those he and his staff would block out an entire season for each series, assign writers, and maintain a consistent point of view for each production. Individually, Martin approved each story idea, each script, each match between idea and writer. He was willing to show the network the working idea, even to have it approve the basic outline. From that point on, however, the actual production conformed to the company idea. Additionally, Martin was given authority to select actors and directors without network approval.

## THE COMPANY

When all this merged into an ongoing operation, it developed into what might be called a company style. Authority was delegated by Martin, but only *after* the basic agreements regarding style, content, point of view, and attitude were firmly in place. Subordinates could be defined as having substantial freedom, but only within rather tightly constrained boundaries.

> I've set up a system where, honestly, once a script is done and everything's been talked out you can put it into the system and it will get made. It will look as if I did everything because I've got a head casting guy, a head editorial guy, a head production guy. I mean we all worked together to a point where the company is the producer. I'm the executive and the producer is really the story editor. There's nothing wrong with that. I think it's good. I think it's the only way you can have mass produced quality. My producers have always like it.

> We're going into a phase now where we're changing it. We're making them the executive producer. However, during the twenty year phase of [the previous model] they did not have to bother with the wardrobe, locations, all the stuff that makes guys groan about twenty-four hour days. Because I split the responsibility. I was the producer and the producer was a high-class story editor making a lot of money and getting credit as a producer.

Clearly, what Martin has done transcends the idea of the producer as little more than a remote supervisor. It goes beyond the idea of the producer as mere entrepreneur, concerned solely, or even primarily, with the final entry in the financial report of his various enterprises. Martin's true prize-winning creation, in spite of Emmys won by his shows, is his company, as thoroughly designed, as skillfully polished as any fictional construct. It is a company tuned to the process of creating mass entertainment that meets Martin's standards of quality.

Within it there are functions and roles to be filled and played by those carefully cast in the parts. Often there appears to be a training period, as if the individual were an understudy, an apprentice, intent on polishing a craft. This period may be followed by elevation to a post of greater responsibility, sometimes to a post only partially related to the previous status. Writers, for example, may become line producers where they, like the executive, can perform many functions. Significantly, Martin looks for skill and craft rather than for conventionally defined creativity. He sometimes takes script clerks, or assistant directors, and transforms them into directors. In this manner he assures his own control and eliminates battles with "creative" directors who might wish to change the concept of an episode or of a series.

> Again, we lay out the style of the show, whether it's low angle, or it's moody, and these people get the coverage. We cast it. We do the script. They come in and they shoot the show and we get the pace, the angles, whatever, and we put it together. And we come back at the end. They get their credit if they want it and have gone off doing something else.

While this might sound like a brutal sort of restriction, the removal of creative potential from those roles with which it is traditionally associated (directors), it expresses, in our view, precisely the sort of redefinition necessary. In examining the function of the producer we discover many patterns of this use of creative control. In Martin's case, because he is superbly versed in the technical aspects of filmmaking, the function of the director is minimized.

Another example of the appropriation of creativity is expressed in his description of dealings with actors. Here we have something a bit more conventional, a recognition that the actor may require special handling, that this function is not so easily learned or appropriated by those in the producer's seat. Still, there is good indication here of where the producer must reassert the hard-won control that is necessary in exercising creative vision.

> With Karl Malden, with Bob Stack, anybody, I would sit down for hours before I ever started a series and find out everything about that guy. Just as you're doing, we'd get a tape going and I know what he eats for breakfast, his hobbies, whatever. I tried to get that man's emotional attitudes involved in the character because I feel that the character in a show should only be about fifteen percent of the person. If you're playing a college professor I've got to play it as you because you're going to play it better. Especially in television you're not trying to be creating something different every two minutes.
>
> So we would do that. We'd give them scripts ahead of time. An actor comes in and wants to talk about his role, I gave my permission, carte blanche, if there's anything within reason, rewrite it for them if it makes them more comfortable. But we get on the set and you shoot the script. That's the rule. We give you all the leeway ahead of time, but once we're in agreement you don't start playing games because we don't make shows like that.
>
> I'm a big believer in organization. I think you get as loose as you have to before you start. But once you get in there the only way you can manufacture quality, I think, is to have control. It's a word I use a lot. I believe in control.

Obviously, in this particular example, control is defined in terms of sequence, and in terms of reason. It is Martin who determines what is "within reason" in the rewrites, in the efforts to make the actors comfortable. It is, nevertheless, a major concession in a tightly defined, time-bound enterprise. The tradeoff is made in terms of creative return. To the degree that the quality of the production will be enhanced, to the degree that ultimate control is not sacrificed, the gifts are made. Perhaps Martin's own description offers the best definitions of creativity. Here he expresses it in terms of a ratio between creativity and craft. It is a viewpoint expressed in other ways by other producers, but it is closer to the definition being developed in this study than to given, accepted, romantic definitions of creativity.

> I teach at UCLA sometimes, an extension course on advanced television. And most of the people do look upon the whole thing as magic. I think it's about seventy-five percent craft and twenty-five percent creativity. The people that don't learn their craft don't make it, or if they do make it they'll blow up along the way. Because in the middle of the night, if you're blocked or something, you can go back to square one if you know your craft. But you can't just expect it all to come by inspiration. I have found, in my lifetime, a couple of people who were marvelously talented guys who didn't know their craft. They had this attitude that if they dug into the craft they would lose their creativity. And I say nonsense. It's just the other way. . . . You have to know the rules before you break the rules. I'm a big believer in being steeped in education, the right way to do things. And then you can use your individuality.

**THE TECHNIQUE**

In order to examine Martin's own use of that creative individuality, we move to a much more specific level of analysis. We deal with his own descriptions of his technique in making television shows. The descriptions are those of the craftsman who never moves far from considerations of content and meaning, from ideas about the nature and role of television in society. While the choices often reflect economic or technical change, they are made with a clear view of final results. If something is changed it must fit within a larger pattern. If public response, positive or negative, results in a shift of tone or style, the shift is not judged in terms of expediency, but in terms of its relation to other aspects of the program and to other programs.

In this systematic view of television and television programs, only the self-conscious creative producer can control the various pressure points. For Martin the control begins when the *producer* has articulated a precise style for each show, a style that will establish a particular set of meanings, a range within which writers and directors and actors may work without tampering with the central concept.

> I always try to put a stamp on every show so that you viscerally know what show it is just by seeing it and feeling it. *The Fugitive,* if you will, is more

"John Ford" in that it's the great country, wide and open, and a little more straight forward, eye level camera and forty millimeter.

"The Streets of San Francisco" was getting inside the city with a twenty-five millimeter desk level camera, being a little more emotionally distorted, being inside the melodrama. In every show I would try to pick a camera style and a photographic style and have it be something that is recognizable.

I really believe people. I get letters saying, "I know your shows and I know this and I know that." So there is a definite feeling for them.

This brief comment offers an excellent example of the interaction of producer, program and audience. First there is the producer's desire for immediate audience recognition. Martin wants his shows to be known for the obvious reasons; financial success, mass market, and so on. He is rewarded with the letters indicating that he has achieved a recognition that matches his highly stylized designs. The audience is not merely viewing television. It is watching a QM production.

Interestingly, however, his conception of the visual mark of the specific programs is far more detailed, more precise than that required by mere "recognition." The visual style is selected and executed with an eye to content. These shows reflect different attitudes toward adventure, different types of American experiences of melodrama, intrigue, action, and mystery.

Any quick judgment that these theories, choices, and personal expressions are the ultimate factors in making design decisions about programs would run the risk of error. They are simply some of the very significant elements in a complex mix. The personal preferences are modified by shrewd analyses of the market and of the audience responses Martin receives. Even more important is the fact that like all successful producers, he must operate with an overall view of the role of television in American society. This does not mean that he must conform to some theoretical political notion about the function of television in maintaining the status quo. It does mean that Martin, because of his continued success, is able to articulate an overview of the history of American audiences, of technical innovations, and of programming in the last twenty years. His insider's analysis is a close parallel to those offered by more scientific researchers. It is not expressed in the abstract terms of the sociologist or historian, but in the concrete terms of one who must sell products shaped in forms acceptable to a spectrum of markets.

Here, for example, he notes a response to a perceived change in audiences, and elaborates on the manner in which he sought to modify his shows according to that response.

Fifteen years ago, which was *The Fugitive,* we used to shoot ten pages less because we finished out scenes. We had entrances then. There was a need for people to have more time to absorb. With the advent of commercials speeding up and society speeding up, I shoot anywhere from ten, eleven, twelve, thirteen, fourteen more pages to get the fifty minutes today than we did then. So right there you're going to have a different style.

We used dissolves then. We use straight cuts now. We come right in in the middle of scenes. You can't let people get bored today. They will just walk away from you. They're just going to keep shopping, so there is definitely a visual change I'm sure you see.

We used to say it and say it again and say it one more time, if it was an important story point, because people did not get it. Because it was on a smaller tube and . . . it was a newer medium. My epilogue used to really reinforce a point. I get—say—eight hundred, nine hundred letters a month, that's been fairly standard. On a successful film through the years I get a certain amount of mail. Well, I read it. Or I have people read it and then I look at the different parts of it. You should keep aware of what people's reactions are. When people said, "I don't have to be told twice," we stopped telling them twice. Part of that you get from the feeling and part you get in input.

I would say the major change has been the speed with which we tell a story— which also makes it more costly. If I now have forty percent more setups to tell that story than I used to, because we're not having the long walks, the exit, etc. every time you move a camera, it's more money.

That final comment may come as a surprise to television critics who reduce everything to financial considerations or to sociologists who wish to find the sources of television in the constraint mechanisms surrounding the industry. What such a comment truly indicates is that in many cases artistic choices, identified in a reading of the audience and the culture, control the economic choices. Doubtless, attempts are still made to reduce the necessary number of setups, but the fact that they are viewed as necessary on certain grounds, that they determine the nature of the show itself, is crucial.

The point is that neither choice is separable or identifiable as primary. While the economic decisions, pure and simple, will determine what happens in the realm of content and technique in some cases, the opposite is equally often the case. The self-conscious artistic producer must recognize the fact that the economically motivated decision will affect his artistic choices. Indeed, that is how the self-conscious producers determine what to fight for. Pressure, in the form of audience response, Nielsen ratings, or network clout may affect either sort of decision.

Our own view is that there are no strict lines, finally, that separate the artistic from the financial from the technical from the social. Economic choices are symbolic choices. Symbolic choices must be expressed technically. Audience response and network pressure are indications of distinctions among values, perceptions, and aesthetic preferences. Those critics who overlook the systematic nature of popular art, and those producers who cannot or do not cope with the interactions at all these levels are unlikely to succeed, certainly to the degree that Martin has.

Control, gained and established, is used to mold techniques into identifiable products. It is also used to translate personal, individual ideas into television content. What follows now is a brief description of Martin's expression of his own ideas about content, ideas derived not from theories of television, but from personal values and attitudes. Mixed with the description is commentary on the ways in which those ideas are translated into his work. This hardly means that every show must, or can, be read as a one-to-one reflection of what he believes about any given topic. As our own later analysis shows, there are other considerably more complex readings that must be offered for some of those shows. These comments do indicate, however, that for certain individuals, television can be used as a medium of personal expression—in spite of enormous pressures and contrary to popular opinion and certain esoteric theories.

## CONTENT

Like other self-conscious artistic producers, Martin has fashioned a style and a form that serve to best advantage his own merger of artist, businessman, and citizen. The patterns of those forms are broad ones because that is the best way, in his view, to capture the concerns of a mass audience. Reading that audience, understanding its concerns and values while still expressing a strong personal commentary, is the core of the art of the television producer.

> You can't work in a vacuum. I think initially you have to believe in [what you do]. Then I truly believe that I related to a general audience. I think if you do things that are emotionally solid that it doesn't matter whether the guy is undereducated or in a lower socioeconomic area. I think you can hit a very broad spectrum of audience because you're hitting people where they live. If things are emotionally correct, then they hit everybody.

> So I always try to make sure that the characters are motivated properly, that people understand, that they get a feeling of what's going on. I've always been rather proud that my shows really hit a very broad section. I get the college kids and I get the truck drivers. I've always gotten a very broad section of the audience.

> [What is an example of a show that is emotionally *incorrect?*]

I think that many shows today—rather than be specific—are superficial in that they're based on plot and not character. Go, go, go. No point of view. No depth. I think more television is that way than less.

I'd rather give you a show that I think is the epitome of what I'm talking about positively. That's *Lou Grant,* a show I fought for with M-T-M. The network really tried to turn it into a glorified cop show and pressured and pressured and pressured. I supported those people by mail and everything else because I thought they were really doing something good, and it finally emerged.

You know, I turned down *Batman* and I turned down *Wonder Woman,* things that just weren't to my taste. I wouldn't want to do them. I couldn't care less about how successful I would have been. It's just that I think that people see your name and it ought to stand for something and that's what a guy has in his life.

My point of view has always been to do the truth about things, but to have an idealized version. If I do *Streets of San Francisco,* which is about people under stress in a big city told through the eyes of two cops, I want those cops to be idealized. I'll do a story about a bad cop, but the system will get rid of him.

I don't like to make people paranoid about the system. I like to be positive about the system and give some hope and some optimism. Maybe that sounds like a corny attitude, but that's always been my point of view.

[Today] we are less heroic. I've always had a point of view of telling an idealized version of life in that if it's a cop show, the police department is going to be a decent police department. . . . I believe that we have too much of a power [in television] on our hands and if we're going to make everybody feel uncomfortable all the time that we're doing a negative thing. Well, then you say, what right do I have to take this attitude?

It's my belief. I think in general things are better. I'm a glass-is-half-full guy rather than half-empty. I believe in the positive attitude. I've always wanted to tell a more idealized version of things in an honest manner.

But today I wouldn't be as heroic as I was fifteen years ago because people, young people especially, think you've got to be more laid back. You've got to be cooler. You still have a hero and you still win and so on, but you don't make as much out of it. I'd say, just in general, we're talking about the same kind of thing, but we're telling you faster and we're telling it in a more sophisticated manner.

I used to be ultra-liberal. Right now I'm a little left of center. I think part of that comes with age, part of it comes with success, part of it comes from getting smarter. I think every high I.Q. college kid, I don't mean becomes a communist, but begins looking for a utopian world. So you get into an ultra-liberal attitude and the welfare state and you have to help everybody. But as I've gotten to be a business man that's changed. This doesn't mean I'm voting my pocketbook or anything else. I still feel that the haves have to help the have nots.

But on the other hand I understand about gross national product and about business and about a lot of things so that I don't have simplistic answers like I used to. And while I might be very liberal in one attitude I'm very hard nosed about not believing in detente and not trusting Russia, and so on. Where I used to think, at a very young age, that there were simple answers under simple labels for everything, I think I've matured and my work reflects that.

Again, whether I was liberal, conservative, moderate, whatever—you can have an overall point of view, but you shouldn't use your vehicles to try to do a polemic. I've had some big fights with people down in the creative department. One writer, he's an ultra left-wing rich kid, is always trying to put a very close to communist point of view in shows. I'd just say, "Now stop already." He'd load it up figuring that if I changed part of it he'd still have part of it left.

I don't think that's what our business is. I do think that you have to have some point of view. But we shouldn't really be trying to be very strongly political in shows. We're an entertainment medium. Underneath, though, I tried in every episode of the fifteen hundred to have a theme that you are making a statement about something. But it doesn't have to be heavy. I do think you can have a little substance in what you are doing.

We'd start out saying, "Let's do an episode about old people, geriatrics, and how they're treated and what's the right way and the wrong way." Then, out of that you say, "How do you do that story in *Barnaby Jones*?" and you do a crime that occurs because of the treatment of old people.

So that we tried all the way to have a little more underneath shows than the average person and then put melodrama on top. I think I've gotten more sophisticated. I think I used to be a little more obvious about it than we are now.

In the general overview of television, Martin's dramas have often been dismissed as prime examples of slick, violent, formula shows. The total body of work also bears the brunt of two forms of criticism. First is the attack on that violence. Second is the more subtle suggestion that the shows are examples of television's social and political repression, its defense of the status quo, its ability to thwart radical or even moderate forms of social change.

Martin has never shied away from recognizing and discussing these issues. As we have seen, he openly discusses his idealization of authority structures and individual figures such as police officers or federal agents.

When fully presented, as it is in our interviews, his position is more adequately argued than it often has been in brief quotations. It is also more thoroughly placed with regard to other elements in the shows, in the formulas with which he works, and in the context of the medium. These comments go beyond the simplistic and offer material for a new perspective on Martin's work. It is an analysis that leaves behind easy cultural and literary analysis that lumps him with similar producers, because it is able to identify and apply the distinguishing characteristics of his series.

**STRUCTURE**

A television show for Martin is structured in three layers, each with special significance. Every element is assigned to one layer, its placement indicating a priority, a sign of its meaning and value. In the process of sorting out the elements we begin to understand the reasons for various judgments, decisions, and choices made by this producer.

The constituents, or layers, of television drama are, in Martin's terms, Melodrama, Emotion, and Theme. Melodrama should be equated with plot or action. Emotion is a shorthand term that includes motivation, characterization, and the universal dimensions of human response. Theme indicates specific social or political significance or small moral "lessons" that can be drawn from the dramatic events. These aspects of television drama are ordered in the sequence given here. Melodrama is the surface, Theme the substructure. The central quality of any QM production, the quality Martin uses to evaluate shows by other producers and the element that he works most for in his own shows, is Emotion. The relationship among these factors is crucial, so much so that one of the producer's primary responsibilities is to work with them, manipulate them, until the successful mix is achieved.

Shows that focus on melodrama, on plot, are those that offer the sizzle without the steak. They are the "go, go, go" shows. Although Martin recognizes that such shows can be very successful, and even cites examples from works produced by friends and acquaintances, they are, for him, best defined as "bubble-gum" television. They represent much that is wrong with the content of the medium. The clear impression is that this layer of TV is the most formulaic, the most easily accomplished and copied. Although it is an essential element it is as likely to lead to trouble as to success. Martin often demonstrates this troublesome aspect of melodrama, and the problems of maintaining balance, when he discusses network interference in program design. In one example network program executives, eager to grasp every rating point, keyed on high audience response to a villain in one of Martin's pilots. Insisting that the villain be kept in the series as a side-kick to the central character, they were dismayed at the show's failure. To Martin, the explanation was simple. The network choice ignored the dramatic function of the character, and with a thoughtless and uninformed decision, the balance of the show was wrecked.

On the other end of the spectrum of internal elements is Theme. This is the realm of journalistic currency, of hot news topics molded into the formula of a series. This factor, too, is secondary. One "teaches a little" in all shows. One has a theme that is "making a statement about something." Still, "it doesn't have to be heavy." It is possible to have "a little substance in what you are doing." These apparently condescending descriptions should not be taken to indicate that the issues are not significant ones for Martin. They do indicate, however, that he avoids turning the shows into explicit, immediate statements about current social problems. Above all, at this level, one is to avoid the "polemic." When this element overwhelms the others the production becomes a tract instead of real drama, real entertainment.

## "VIOLENCE"

Given these distinctions it is easier to see why the idea of "violence" has never been a vital issue for Martin except as it affects the design and programming of shows he has constructed. As part of any action-adventure, police, or law enforcement series, violence, in his view, is technique. It is clearly relegated to the realm of the melodrama, the action, the formula, the go, go, go. It is used there to attract and hold audiences upon entry from other shows, through commercials, and above the distractions that surround them in the home. Given the fact that it is part of every show of this type, in Martin's view part of every one-hour format, it should hardly be taken with undue seriousness or isolated from its context. In response to pressure, of course, one can merely change the nature of the representation of violence. These technical changes can be quickly and easily accomplished because the violence is not directly related to the essential content of anything that Martin is trying to present to his viewers.

If, on the other hand, violence is to be treated in and of itself as a subject, it should not be treated as a "theme," as a social statement. That would require a precise sort of political position statement and Martin would then enter the ball game of opposing views surrounding the "topic" of television violence. Even more to the point, the thematic or polemical response to violence would not be the truest, most significant response that could be offered. That best response comes in the realm of emotion, where truth, for Martin, always resides.

It is in the properly motivated human response of strong characters that one must deal with such issues. Thus we have episodes in which police officers anguish over the violence they encounter and in which they must indulge. Most likely such characters respond to these situations ambiguously, for there are few easy answers in these fictional worlds. In spite of the charges that Martin's characters are one-dimensional, that all of them represent the same point of view, that is not often the case. Although stories are resolved in terms of repeated reaffirmations of roles and values, the characters are most often people capable of being profoundly troubled by the worlds in which they live. If, finally, they must act in ways that are predictable, ways that can be classified socially or politically, they must do so as a decision central to the drama, and not merely as a matter of formula. To do otherwise would actually undercut the power of the values and reduce them to mere thematics, to polemics. In Martin's view such a choice is a sure step toward losing the audience.

## EMOTION

Emotion, then, in Martin's view, is the layer in any television show which must govern the ratio of melodrama and theme. It is emotion, the universality of human response, that is crucial in building a successful show. Located here is the honesty that cuts across socioeconomic lines and builds the mass, general audience.

Still, this is not an honesty patterned on reality as we experience it. Even emotion as a dramatic element, is governed by Martin's concern for Idealization. A translation of this term makes apparent his intention to present things "as they should be" rather than as they are. Such a view is part of a strong tradition, one always open to the artist. The swerve toward "realism," so prevalent in the history of modern fiction, and the "realistic" nature of visual media, tend to distort the historical importance of the tradition of idealism. But such a perspective is strong within the popular arts. Martin's work is obviously tied directly to heroic American types, to the heroes of popular westerns and to the protagonists of detective fiction. And as astounding as may first appear, there are equally direct links to the strong central figures created by Hemingway or Stephen Crane, to a wide range of "respected" American artists in fiction and film. They, too, idealized characters who face danger, who are able to participate in violent acts without flinching. Theirs are, in important ways, characters defined by Martin as "bigger than life." Yet they are ordinary, flawed, romantic, pressured individuals as his are.

All these creators draw on a similar vein in American cultural thought. Their characters ultimately affirm some of the values of "the system," and say that whatever needs doing can be done by individuals if not by society. Always, explicit political or social notions are subordinated to specific human response. Always the brave, compassionate hero stands central, and in his actions we affirm our universal ties.

In Martin's fictional worlds, then, two ratios are at work. As creative controller he must establish the relationship among his three layers within each show and he must regulate all of them toward a presentation of his own idealizations. Each show becomes a variation of this ideal world as expressed in the frame of action-adventure. The details of each world highlight the distinctions among his programs.

## THE IDEAL WORLD

The world as it *should be,* is presented as a world in order. When order is disturbed, those in positions of traditional authority are called upon to set it right. The characters, police officers and detectives for the most part, are in fact, symbolic representations of "the system," by which Martin means the American system of society, government, and justice. Threats to the system come in the form of individuals, but they, too, are representative. They may stand for those who do not abide by the system, those who choose to place themselves above authority. Or they may simply be indicative of larger forces, "the forces of the big city," for example. In a show such as *The Streets of San Francisco,* it is the city itself which is the villain, which is out of order, and thus causes confusion, pressure, distortion, violence, and crime. In these situations humans must test themselves, their systems of order, and the compassion that must reside in that order.

The system can demand respect, but it must be tempered with human warmth, compassion, with human expectations and failures. The people who represent the system are most honest when their own weaknesses show. There is, obviously, in *The Untouchables,* and *The F.B.I.,* a weighting in favor of strong authority. Rarely do the central figures of these shows display weakness or vulnerability. The human factors are most obvious in *The Fugitive* and *The Streets of San Francisco,* where questions of human frailty repeatedly emerge.

But the system itself has weaknesses, as demonstrated both in *The Fugitive* and its weaker imitation, *The Invaders.* In such cases ordinary citizens find themselves called upon, in almost Hitchcockian fashion, to try to correct the distortion. Interestingly, the disorder in these shows results in large part from a refusal on the part of the official authority to accept compassion as part of its role. Over and over Lt. Garrard comes up against Richard Kimball's humanity only to reject it in favor of an abstract, *disordering,* reliance on the law.

It is, again, a matter of ratio, of balance, of controlling point of view. Martin's decisions in shaping these shows offer some of the clearest examples of the making of television art. His discussions of *The F.B.I.* and *The Fugitive* illuminate his theories of television and his own sense of the idealized nature of his "worlds."

In very early episodes of *The F.B.I.*, for example, Inspector Erskine is remarkably open and vulnerable. In one episode from the first season he is clearly relieved when a sympathetic bank robber outruns him and escapes into Mexico. Like Erskine, the man is a Korean War veteran. Like Erskine he has lost a deeply loved wife and has only a single child remaining as his family. His life, however, unlike Erskine's has not gone according to plan, has not moved toward success and self-definition. Erskine says to his assistant that he can envision himself in the man's position. He even questions his job, a job that forces him into strong, potentially violent confrontation with such a man. In spite of these doubts he arranges for the man to learn that his son is still in this country, knowing that the loving father will return for him. When he does so he is captured. Justice prevails, but it is justice confused, cognizant of the weaknesses in "the system."

Such a perspective is quite in keeping with many of Martin's other shows, but in this case it was not judged a success. He describes those early days of the show by pointing out that Erskine was portrayed as very like a typical member of the audience in "human" terms, a portrayal apparently unacceptable to some members of the audience.

> I really thought a general consensus from my mail in reaction to that was that the people got uptight that the FBI guy had the same kind of problems they can have. The show didn't start off that succcessful and I took that out because the people wanted to relate to the FBI as a super-protector and to get their emotion from the guest star. I switched to that direction and it was immediately successful. So that didn't come from the FBI; that came from the people.
>
> The FBI liaison said, "Is it good to have the FBI guy question his job?"
>
> And I said, "It's good."
>
> And then he said, "Fine."
>
> They did not bother me about story content. They bothered the hell out of me in terms of procedure.

The most interesting result of this change, of course, is that there was created an emotional tie to the guest star, most often a star portraying a criminal or a member of the criminal's family. Such a structure would seem to be dangerous, given Martin's views. But he clearly trusted the outcome of his stories to stand as affirmations of appropriate American attitudes.

By contrast, *The Fugitive* seemed to be pointed in another direction, one that more obviously seems to cut across the aim of idealizing the system. Here, drastic mistakes are made, and an innocent man is threatened. When questioned, however, Martin's answer again demonstrates the values that determine the structure of his fictional worlds.

If a man has done everything ethical [he] has a right to protect himself. That was my justification, because I thought long and hard about whether I was really doing something wrong in making a show that says a man is living outside the law. We made it very clear. He had all the appeals. He had tried to do everything and now he escapes. He's trying. You know, he didn't go out and play around. He's not a jet-setter. He worked beneath his station. He did a lot of things to try to find out who killed his wife. And he did.

The idealization then, includes both justice and mercy, strong authority and temperate compassion. Ultimately, it comes down on the side of "the system" because Martin believes that an appropriate range of varied responses can actually be found there. The system works, though not always in harmony.

This is precisely the point at which a large question emerges. As we have indicated, Martin poses the question for us.

"What right do I have to take this attitude?"

It's my belief. I think in general things are better. I'm a glass-is-half-full guy rather than half-empty. I believe in the positive attitude. I've always wanted to tell a more idealized version of things in an honest manner.

It is precisely at this level, we suggest, that the large political statements are made. Martin cites the smaller "theme," the "message," underlying his shows as the locus of political content. But it is in this other choice, this choice of world view, that the more potent, because more pervasive, political content resides. There is no polemic here. There is the far more powerful undercurrent, the substructure of assumptions which orders and governs the mix of other factors.

Again, this view, like the aesthetic one, mines a strong American tradition and one could ask the same questions of Hemingway or Crane that one asks of Martin. They are moral and political questions. Harshly put, they go like this. How far can the idealization go and remain honest? For whom are things really better? Is this particular idealization the only one, the best one, the appropriate one? Is it too related to visions that involved us in moments of failure, moments like Watergate, that have lead to the negativism that Martin deplores? Do too many of us accept too easily the idealized versions of authority? These are the questions often cited in political analysis of television, analysis from the right and the left. Martin's productions are marked as evidence of the medium's strong support for the conservative right. By attending to Martin's own views, to the deeper level of an undercurrent of basic assumptions, the harshest judgment becomes too simple.

The easier political indictment of television and specific television content is moderated by a closer look at both the medium and those who create

for it. The intermix of elements within shows clearly makes multiple interpretation possible for viewers. In Martin's case, in spite of the definable
political assumptions, emotion is always central. We are asked to involve
ourselves in the lives of characters from many sides of the political spectrum, and this cushions the idealizations whether the cushion is intended or
not. Even when characters with opposing views are presented negatively,
when those views are oversimplified or ridiculed, the element of fictional
choice is present. On a more elementary level, we often experience an
understanding of the criminal, and sympathize even more directly with those
who, as family and friends, are touched by criminal actions. We feel something of lived experience in the best shows, something of victimization,
frustration, even anger at "the system."

It is possible to make qualitative distinctions among Martin's shows on
such a basis. The sense of humanity is strongest in *The Fugitive* where the
system itself is questioned. This show, for us, remains Martin's central
achievement. The same sort of sympathy is powerfully present in *The
Streets of San Francisco,* a show originally planned as a story of newspaper
reporters rather than of detectives. *The F.B.I.,* by contrast, is weakened in
its insistence on the role of authority at the cost of compassion. In still other
series, *Cannon* or *Barnaby Jones,* there is simply too little room for emotion
to develop and we are left with a residue of melodrama and a touch of theme.

## CONCLUSION

These distinctions within Martin's work demonstrate, for us, the strength
of television's internal variety. Neither the clearest intention nor the most
extensive control can assure homogeneity. It is this pattern of variety within
similarity that is more apparent when we examine the work of other producers with individual styles, definitions, descriptions, and intentions.

For us, this indicates a fundamental question regarding the nature of the
television text, a question that should demand that many sorts of analysis be
reexamined. Convinced as we are that there must be an internal variety in
every producer's work, we are even more adamant that the individual visions
of individual producers resonate with one another in a complex dialogue.
Thus, the work of a producer like David Victor can be placed alongside
Martin's to demonstrate a range of perspectives on American society and
culture. In works such as *Dr. Kildare, Marcus Welby, M.D.,* and *Owen
Marshall, Counsellor-at-Law,* Victor suggests that significant parts of the
American "system" fail at the level of individual service. His characters,
also idealizations, represent the dreams by which we measure our failures,
the hopes that indicate our flaws. Similarly, the work of John Mantley in

*Gunsmoke* or of Earl Hamner in *The Waltons* suggests that neither our social institutions nor our emotionally defined families are to be seen as perfect. In these shows individuals are always learning, always being forced to admit their inadequacy.

All of these producers, all of the others that we examine in the full study, are bound by one another. The serious worlds of melodrama are questioned by the inherent irreverence of comedic structures, and vice versa. The story forms with which all these producers work bear cultural meaning developed in literature, vaudeville, radio, and film. These meanings, too, act as boundaries.

What we are suggesting is that creativity is never a process of total freedom. Even the most innovative artist, the most removed from broad communication, cannot afford the slide into total solipsism, into private, esoteric codes of meaning. In this regard television is no different from other media. What we have tried to establish in addition to this given set of generalities, is that certain individuals choose the constraints of television as the boundaries in which they work to create special forms and meanings. Not all of them succeed. Not all persons in their roles even try. What should emerge from a more complex study of the producer's role, however, is that for those who do choose and who do try, television, "the producer's medium," is as open as other media to creative manipulation, to the making of art.

# NOTE

1. Included in the full study are the following producers, identified here with a few representative works: Quinn Martin *(The Fugitive, The F.B.I., The Streets of San Francisco)*, John Mantley *(Gunsmoke, Buck Rogers in the 25th Century)*, David Victor *(Dr. Kildare, Marcus Welby, M.D., Owen Marshall: Counsellor-at-Law)*, Earl Hamner *(The Waltons)*, Richard Levinson and William Link *(Columbo, That Certain Summer, The Execution of Private Slovik)*, Garry Marshall *(Happy Days, Laverne and Shirley)*, Norman Lear *(All in the Family, Maude)*, and James Brooks, Alan Burns, and Grant Tinker of the Mary Tyler Moore Company *(The Mary Tyler Moore Show, The Bob Newhart Show)*.

Obviously, even within the terms of our own definition, we have not exhausted the ranks of self-conscious creative producers. We were unable, for example, to persuade Jack Webb to participate in the study, despite the good offices of other participating producers. This is a lamentable loss. We were unable to see Aaron Spelling, even though we were less sure about an application of our definition in his case. Larry Gelbart is perhaps an example of a problematic aspect of our definition. As an original creator of *M\*A\*S\*H*, and even more, as the creator of *United States*, he is a prime example of the sort of individual we wish to study. Yet Gelbart left *M\*A\*S\*H* claiming that television restricted his creativity too severely (a view that we do not totally share). And *United States*, one of the most powerful instances of the work of a self-conscious creative producer, was removed from the air and defined as a failure after only a few episodes. Gelbart's own work therefore has had little impact on the medium except as example or by way of contrast. While he might cite the same evidence as an example of the restrictions within the medium, we argue only for a range of definition regarding the problematic term "creativity." The case will be explored more fully in our complete study.

# REFERENCES

CANTOR, M. G. (1980) Prime-Time Television: Content and Control. Beverly Hills: Sage.
_____ (1971) The Hollywood TV Producer: His Work and His Audience. New York: Basic Books.
CAREY, J. (1975) "A cultural approach to communications." Communications 2: 1-22.
GITLIN, T. (1979) "Prime-time ideology: the hegemonic process in television entertainment." Social Problems 26 (February): 251-266.
RAVAGE, J. (1978) Television: The Director's Viewpoint. Boulder: Westview Press.
STEIN, B. (1979) The View From Sunset Boulevard: America as Brought to You by the People Who Make Television. New York: Basic Books.
TURNER, V. (1977) "Process, system, and symbol: a new anthropological synthesis." Daedalus (Summer): 61-80.

# Chapter 5

# THE ORGANIZATIONAL CONTEXT OF CREATIVITY
## A Case Study from Public Television

### James S. Ettema

THE PRODUCTION OF messages by the mass media has typically been examined through one of three conceptual lenses. One lens is focused on the attributes and activities of individual media personnel. This lens reveals the form, content, and meaning of messages to be the fruits of individual labor. Another lens is focused on the production routines of media organizations. It reveals the form, content, and meaning of messages to be the result of constraints imposed by these routines. The third lens is focused on conflict within and among media organizations. And it reveals the messages to be compromises negotiated in the course of organizational politics.

These three lenses offer views of the mass media which, to some extent, overlap, yet no one lens provides a complete image. In the study which follows, all three lenses are used to examine the development of a children's series for airing on the Public Broadcasting Service. When the development process is viewed through the lens focused on individual labor, the series is seen to be the creative achievement of one person—the executive producer. However, when the process is viewed through all three lenses the series is seen to be the result of a complex organizational process in which the creative activity of the executive producer was activated and energized by problems or puzzles arising from the production routines and conflicts within the organization in which he labored. Used together the three lenses can, then, offer a multidimensional view of how messages are produced.

## LITERATURE OVERVIEW: THE VIEW THROUGH EACH LENS

Mass media scholars have peered through the lens focused on the attributes and activities of individuals for several decades now, and their observa-

AUTHOR'S NOTE: Thanks are due to Jerome Johnston for his unfailing support in this project. This research was supported by the National Institute for Education, contract 4000-76-0096.

tions provide a richly detailed view of the life and work of individual com-municators. Cantor (1971), for example, found three distinct value systems among Hollywood television producers. Some producers valued their work as an opportunity for self-expression; others as an opportunity to learn the craft of filmmaking and still others as an opportunity to earn a good living. Similarly, Johnstone, Slawski, and Bowman (1976) found two value sys-tems among journalists. Some endorsed a neutral and detached stance to-ward the events they reported while others endorsed a participatory stance toward them.

The work habits and processes of individuals in particular have come under close scrutiny. Research on the exercise of news judgment, for exam-ple, ranges from White's (1950) pioneering observation of a single gate-keeper to Dimmick's (1974) multidimensional scaling of story selection criteria. Recently, corresponding studies of decision-making in entertain-ment organizations have begun to appear (such as Virts, 1980) though much of what we know about program selection and other such decision-making is based on the anecdotes of columnists (Brown, 1971) and the reminiscences of industry insiders (Miller and Rhodes, 1964: 3).

Looking beyond how individuals choose messages, researchers have begun to observe how individuals generate them in the first place. The impact of journalists' (Flegel and Chaffee, 1971) and television writers' (Greenberg, 1969; Stein, 1979) attitudes upon the messages they produce have been analyzed with varying degrees of sophistication. Similarly, the perceptions of the audience held by media personnel have been examined (Martin, O'Keefe, and Nayman, 1972; Cantor, 1971) though their impact on the content of messages is more often assumed than analyzed. Pool and Shulman's (1959) classic research on audience-related fantasies is a rare study which actually specifies a psychological mechanism by which the perceived audience can influence media content. Despite these tentative probes and despite the substantial literature on the psychology of creativity, the processes by which individuals generate mass media messages remain, for the most part, still locked in their black box.

Whatever is yet to be learned about individual creativity and other individual processes, it is clear that they occur in a context of both produc-tion routines and organizational conflict which shape those processes. Hirsch's (1977) reanalysis of White's (1950) gatekeeper study, for example, suggests that influences on media messages which have often been traced to the work of individuals may more accurately be traced to production rou-tines. The reanalysis revealed that the amount of news in various categories (such as national political) used by "Mr. Gates" was proportional to the amount of news in each of the categories transmitted by the wire services. Thus Mr. Gates' behavior, which appeared rather idiosyncratic when viewed by White through the lens focused on individual labor, appeared to be powerfully influenced by the techniques of news processing when viewed by Hirsch through the lens focused on production routines.

Many scholars who view the mass media through this lens focused on production routines begin with an interest in organizational theory. For example, Hirsch (1972), building upon the work of Thompson (1967), has analyzed the strategies employed by the book publishing, recording, and motion picture "industry systems" to cope with their highly uncertain business environments. These strategies include the development of both organizational structures (that is, the deployment of "contact men" at organizational boundaries) and processes (that is, over production and differential promotion of products). Other scholars who use this lens have begun with an interest in the sociology of knowledge. Tuchman (1978, 1977) has studied the methods by which news organizations routinize the processing of daily "occurrences" into news "events." These methods include the establishment of a reliable and productive, though biased, "news-net" and the use of standard operating procedures for production of objective reports. In the same vein, Elliot's (1970) case study of documentary production by the BBC reveals how reliance on a variety of production routines results in merely a repackaging of the conventional wisdom on the subject.

The processes which serve to routinize the tasks of media organizations do so in part by increasing organizational control over the workers. For example, Tuchman (1978) reveals how the organizational vocabulary of news work (such as, "hard news," "soft news") reflects the tasks of news gathering and thus provides a system for perceiving the world which is conducive to performing the tasks required of newspeople by their organizations. Organizational vocabularies and standard operating procedures as well as socialization of new recruits are all discussed by March and Simon (1958) as mechanisms by which organizations control workers (and thus routinize production) through establishment of the premises by which the workers make job-related decisions.

These control mechanisms serve to reduce conflict within organizations (see Breed, 1958; Sigelman, 1973) but when the media are examined through the appropriate lens, conflict can indeed be found (see Argyris, 1974; Cantor, 1971; Hahn, 1972; Tunstall, 1971). Showing more than mere squabbles among media personnel, this lens reveals a complex process of conflict development and management. Dimmick (1979), for example, suggests that media organizations can be viewed as political coalitions and Cantor (1979) argues that popular drama is the outcome of a "negotiated struggle."

The political scientist Graham Allison (1971) has outlined a simple but useful model of organizational politics. The model, which was originally devised to explore the "bargaining games" within governmental bureaucracies, includes four key concepts. One is "players-in-position." The players in the game of organizational politics are those individuals whose roles place them in a position to play (that is, to participate in the decision-making of the organization). In media organizations, players of interest include, of course, reporters and editors, writers and producers, publishers and network executives.

The second concept is the "stakes and stands" of these players. Each player's views on the issues at hand are shaped by individual values, attitudes and goals, but these, in turn, are influenced by the particular view of the issues afforded by the player's position within the organization. Organizational theorists have long realized that position in an organization is related to the development of a specific and predictable "orientation" toward organizational issues (Lawrence and Lorsch, 1967). All of this is captured in the aphorism: "where you stand depends on where you sit" (Allison, 1971: 176).

It is differences among the "stands" or "orientations" of the players-in-position which give rise to organizational conflict. For example, the conflict which Tunstall (1971) found in his study of English newspapers was between editors who were oriented toward the readers and revenue goals and reporters who were oriented toward their sources. The conflict which Cantor (1971) found in her study of television producers included that between producers and network executives over the content of scripts. This conflict was particularly intense for those producers oriented toward self-expression in their work. In media organizations, where you stand does, then, depend on where you sit—though perhaps not entirely.

The third concept in the Allison model is power. When power is shared, at least to some extent, by the players, then negotiation and compromise become necessary to get things done. Power rests both on formal structural bases (that is, position in the hierarchy) and informal bases such as expertise or control of information (see Hickson et al., 1971, for a review.) Analysis of the power of media personnel within their organizations has been limited, for the most part, to that of publishers and other executives to influence the messages produced by their organizations (Bowers, 1967; Donohew, 1967). There has been little explicit analysis of the ways in lower ranking personnel such as reporters accrue and exercise power.

The fourth concept is "action channels." These are the regularized means for taking action on an issue which serve to structure and regulate the bargaining games. In media organizations, action channels which provide the forum for negotiation of media content include contacts between writers and producers concerning scripts, assignments by editors to reporters and conferences among the editors themselves. Sigal (1973), for example, found that the editorial conferences at the New York *Times* were the forum for some hard bargaining among the national, foreign, and metropolitan desks on the content of the front page. Compromise was facilitated, however, by the standing agreement that, on the average, the front page would be evenly split among the three desks.

In overview, the explanatory powers of Allison's four concepts (1971: 173) are utilized by "displaying the game—the action channel, the positions, the players, their preferences and the pulling and hauling—that yielded as a resultant, the action in questions." Substituting only "the form, content and meaning of the messages" for "the action in question," Allison provides the third of the three lenses necessary for a complete, multidimensional image of the production of media messages.

## A CASE STUDY: THE MULTIDIMENSIONAL IMAGE

In the following study all three of the conceptual lenses are used to observe a critical point in the creation of a children's television series: the design of three experimental pilot shows. The development of these pilots and, later, the entire series was based on three fundamental ideas which have come to be called the Children's Television Workshop (CTW) model of educational television, thanks to CTW's successful application to them.[1] First, the pilots and series were planned around a well defined educational goal: countering sex-role stereotypes and expanding career awareness among 9-to-12 year-olds. Second, the shows were designed to be entertaining as well as educational because they were intended to reach not only captive audiences in the classroom but also volunteer viewers at home. And third, the shows were developed by an organization which brought together top television professionals, educators, and researchers.

The organization which developed these shows was actually a temporary consortium of organizations. A nationally known public television production house was responsible for the production of the shows themselves and an executive producer was hired to head the project. An educational publisher was responsible for the development of supporting printed materials, including a teacher's guide to the shows. The activities of these consortium components were guided, in part, by a statement of educational objectives prepared by a curriculum planning team drawn from a large educational agency and by the research of a formative evaluation team drawn from a university school of communication. Each of these separate consortium components was represented on a central planning and policy-making body called the core committee and the entire project was funded by an agency of the federal government.

Admittedly, this was an uncommon media organization but it is of particular interest for several reasons. The consortium, in bringing together television professionals, educators and formative researchers, was similar to several other organizations (such as Children's Television Workshop, Agency for Instructional Television) which are major sources of quality educational and instructional television for children.[2] The consortium offered an opportunity to analyze how television is produced in this uncommon but significant organizational setting. Further, the consortium is of interest because it readily revealed individual and organizational processes which are present but may remain hidden in other media organizations. The consortium, like other television production organizations, conceived, wrote, and produced television shows, but unlike other organizations, the consortium had to share information among components, open discussion of problems and solutions to various experts and justify decisions to a funder. The operation of this particular media organization was, then, particularly open to scrutiny by a participant observer.[3] Finally, the consortium is of interest because its work was a significant creative achievement. The series which it produced embodied complex pro-social messages in shows which were artistically successful. The series accomplished many of its educational objectives while winning numerous awards including an Emmy.[4] Together these characteristics recommend this organization as a worthwhile study of creativity within a complex organizational context.

**THE CASE STUDY**

As the project got under way the core committee decided to produce three different pilots, test them for entertainment value and educational effectiveness, and then select one as the prototype for the entire series. While each pilot was to be different from the others, certain constraints applied to the design of all three pilots. The budget, of course, imposed constraints on all of the pilots but so too did the consortium's plan to produce a series which could be broadcast both into classrooms as instructional programming and into homes as entertaining yet educational programming. The first and most general constraint imposed by the plan was that the shows had to "carry the educational cargo," in the words of the executive producer, but do so in an entertaining way. The series could not depend on a captive audience when broadcast into homes and would have to win an audience against competition which did not have the burden of educational cargo. A synthesis of entertainment and education was essential in all three pilots. A second, more specific constraint arising from the plan was the requirement that each pilot be produced in a half-hour version for prime-time broadcast into homes and that each of these half-hour shows be structured so as to allow editing into two stand-alone quarter-hour shows for daytime broadcast into classrooms. This requirement grew out of the experiences of the educators in the project with the demands of classroom teachers regarding the length of instructional programs.

The executive producer, as the ranking television professional on the project, was ultimately responsible for designing program formats which met these requirements, but as a seven-year veteran of the Children's Television Workshop, he was very receptive to the ideas of educators and to the use of educational objectives in planning television content. The curriculum planning team was, however, behind schedule in their work and the executive producer was forced by his own schedule to begin work with very little information on the objectives to be addressed in the shows. With no information to lead him elsewhere, the executive producer fell back on his experience with CTW and proposed a format very much like that of *Sesame Street*. This show was to be composed largely of short animated and filmed segments (approximately 17 per half-hour) which the executive producer called the "sizzle factor." Each segment was to deal with one or more educational objectives and all of the segments were to be loosely tied together by "wrap-around" material taped in the studio.

The three influences shaping this format—the executive producer's past experience, the divisibility requirement, and the budget—became apparent in the presentation of the proposed format by the executive producer to the core committee. The executive producer argued that this format would both entertain and educate its audience as evidenced by the success of *Sesame Street* in both areas, though his argument overlooked the facts of *Sesame Street*'s younger target audience and emphasis on cognitive rather than affective goals. The executive producer also argued that this format would be the most successful in meeting the condition that each half-hour be divisible into quarter-hour shows because the use of short segments would offer natural division points within the half-hour. Two other arguments in support of this format were based on budget considerations. One was that the short segments could be used several times during the life of the series thus amortizing the cost of expensive animation and live-action film over several shows in the series. This the executive producer called the "repeat factor." The other argument was that the use of short segments would allow those segments which testing showed to be low in either educational or entertainment value to be eliminated without losing the entire show.

The executive producer envisioned two somewhat different variations of the short segment format for the first two pilots to be produced. The first pilot would be a cross between *Sesame Street* and an adult variety show. A company of four young actors and actresses along with a guest star would perform several musical numbers and comic sketches. This studio material would open and close each quarter-hour and introduce a number of short animated and live-action films. The second pilot by comparison would be more story-like. The adventures of four youngsters would be portrayed in a number of short segments all taped on location. Although music and comedy would remain important elements, the slightly longer and more realistic segments would give the second pilot more continuity and coherence. The executive producer credited the more story-like quality of the second pilot to the formative researchers whose interviews with 9-to-12 year-olds and analysis of Nielsen ratings data had shown that children of this age were more attracted to shows with narrative formats (such as sit-com, action/adventure) than to those with short segment formats. In both pilots a "bridge segment" would be placed in the middle of each half-hour show. This segment could be removed to divide the show into quarter-hours.

With the formats for the first two pilots in place, the executive producer began to generate premises or story ideas for the short segments. These premises were created to address one or more of the project's educational objectives but, of course, to do so in a highly entertaining way. An important source of ideas for the premises, according to the executive producer, was the notes he had taken during the curriculum planning activities. The curriculum plan which had finally emerged from these activities contained a formal statement of educational objectives and a lengthy review of scholarly literature. The executive producer's notes, on the other hand, were a jumble of images, ideas, and interpretations which could help him—but only him—translate the stuffy curriculum plan into lively television. For example, one objective concerned the limitations which sex-role stereotypes place upon the opportunities of both sexes. When confronted with the task of generating a premise to capture this idea the executive producer recalled a comment by an educator that the abstraction of stereotyping ought to be made real and concrete to children as "a beast with claws." This inspired a premise for a segment in which the word "stereotype" metamorphoses via animation into a three-head monster. This "stereotyping beastie" turns out to be more silly than fearsome and its attempts to make children conform to sex-role stereotypes are comically unsuccessful.

As the executive producer refined the short segment format and generated premises, discontent with the whole approach was growing among the educators within the consortium. In a number of core committee meetings one of the curriculum planners, acknowledging her desire for a series which would be, above all, educationally effective when used in the classroom, reviewed several educational problems with the short segment format. One of her arguments was that short segments did not allow for the in-depth treatment of characters, problems, and solutions which was appropriate to both the interests of 9-to-12 year-olds and to the affective content of the series. Another of her arguments reflected her concern for accommodating the demands of the educational system. A show with a good deal of music and comedy would be perceived by teachers as waste of precious classroom time, she argued, because teachers tend to think of entertainment and education as antithetical. She concluded that in light of renewed emphasis on basic skills, a program which appeared to entertain rather than educate would have little chance for teacher acceptance. The curriculum planner was joined in a similar argument by the person responsible for developing the teachers' guide. Together they maintained that a large number of short segments in a show, particularly if each segment dealt with a different educational objective, made the organization of a coherent lesson around each show very difficult. While they did not argue that the short segment approach should be abandoned the curriculum planner, the teachers' guide developer, and others pressed the executive producer for a format in which one or two topics could be explored in some depth.

The executive producer, acknowledging his own desire for a show which could attract an at-home audience, admitted to creative problems in designing a show with a narrative format which could also be divided into two separate and complete shows. At one point he suggested that a narrative show be produced only in a half-hour version but the curriculum planner and the other educators all reaffirmed their interest in the school use of the series and argued that a half-hour show, in their experience, would have difficulty in gaining teacher acceptance. This argument rested on the notion that because the time required for airing a half-hour show plus the time for preparation and followup activities would total at least 45 minutes, teachers would feel that using the show required too large a block of time from any given school day. The educators also argued that the daytime instructional schedules of public television stations were structured around quarter-hour shows and that a half-hour show would have difficulty finding a spot on the schedule of many stations.

At a later point the executive producer suggested to the core committee that the third pilot be dropped and the money earmarked for it be used to revise and improve the first two pilots after some preliminary testing. The curriculum planner, however, remained firm in her conviction that a more in-depth approach should be tried. She suggested that the problem be viewed not as dividing a single show in half but rather as joining two shows together. Her example was a show which would examine an instance of sex-role stereotyping from a child's point of view in the first quarter-hour and from a parent's point of view in the second quarter-hour. Ultimately, the executive producer acknowledged the tenacity of the curriculum planner on this issue and agreed to attempt to develop a show which would meet her demands.

The executive producer's solution to the problem of dividing a single narrative into separate shows was to design a two-part soap opera. In the first quarter-hour the protagonist would confront a crisis which would climax just as the episode ends. In the second quarter-hour the protagonist would over-come and learn from the experience and go on to achieve a significant goal. The cliffhanger device allowed the half-hour show to be divided but in a way likely to stimulate rather than dull the interest of the audience. This solution to the problem did not, however, meet the condition originally imposed by the educators that each quarter-hour be able to stand alone as a complete show. And, if chosen as the prototype for the series, this format would have required the executive producer to alter the write-test-assemble production routine planned around the short-segment format. Still, everyone agreed that this solution was an acceptable compromise.

With this dramatic structure in place, the executive producer faced the task of generating a premise. To begin, he selected several educational objectives which he felt had not been adequately addressed in the other pilots. Reasonable risk-taking, for example, had been portrayed in one pilot as a girl asking a boy to dance—a trivial interpretation of a behavior closely related to career success. The idea had to be taken more seriously and, further, a distinction between reasonable and unreasonable risk-taking had to be drawn.

The structure imposed by the cliffhanger device and the requirements of the risk-taking message finally all came together in a premise based on the "sorcerer's apprentice" theme. Chris, a girl keenly interested in auto me-chanics, seeks a summer job in a service station, risking disapproval of her friends and the insults of the station's crusty owner. Chris wins the job and works hard but one day when she is left in charge of the station she takes an unreasonable risk by attempting an auto repair for which she is untrained. The first quarter-hour ends with Chris standing amidst the parts of a car which she has needlessly disassembled. In the second quarter-hour Chris gets up her courage to return to work and the station's mechanic begins to instruct her. Later, when there is another emergency, Chris is able to save the day in classic television fashion.

Chris' story became the third of the three pilots.

## ANALYSIS

Viewed through the lens focused on individual labor, the three pilots are undeniably the creative achievement of a single individual—the executive producer. He chose the short segment format for the first and second pilots and devised the "bridge segment" to adapt the format to the constraints of the project. He also devised the cliffhanger dramatic structure to adapt the narrative format to these constraints. And he managed to combine educa-tional messages with television entertainment in his premises.

At least some of these ideas can be readily traced to particular attributes of the executive producer. For example, his past experience with the Children's Television Workshop and his rather undifferentiated view of children-as-audience caused him to rather mechanically adapt the *Sesame Street* short segment format for the first pilot. Also, his ability to make remote associations—a classic definition of creativity—is clearly displayed in his generation of the stereotype beastie and sorcerer's apprentice premises.

The pilots, each a slick Hollywood product, were clearly the work of a top television professional, but the executive producer was not the only professional to have an impact upon them. Indeed, the most significant feature of this organization was its harnessing of a variety of professional expertise to achieve its goals. The greater continuity of the second pilot and the narrative format of the third are traceable to the educators' more sophisticated perceptions of children-as-audience and to the data-based "perceptions" of the formative researchers. A primary reason for including the researchers in the organization in the first place was, of course, to increase the veridicality of the consortium's perceptions of its audience. If the executive producer, as revealed through the lens focused on individual labor, is the creator of the pilots, then the educators and evaluators are revealed as his faithful advisors.

The other conceptual lenses add much to this image, however, by revealing the organizational context which structured, regulated, and motivated the activities of the creator and his advisors. When the executive producer began work on pilot design he was searching for a format which could lend itself to a workable and economical production routine. The *Sesame Street* format could have allowed the production of the series to follow a routine in which segments were written for a particular educational objective, evaluated for comprehensibility and entertainment value, and those which passed the test assembled into a complete show. This assembly-line process would have reconciled the television routines of scripting and production with the use of objectives, formative evaluation data, and the restrictions of budget.

Educators—classroom teachers, educational broadcasters, and lesson planners—had routines of their own which the educational advisors wanted the pilot design to accommodate. The condition that each of the half-hour shows be divisible into two quarter-hours was prompted by the scheduling requirements of both teachers and educational broadcasters. The narrative format itself was prompted by the lesson planning needs of teachers and the educational publisher.

The routines of television production and of education were, then, not easily reconciled and this helped to set the stage for an exercise in organizational politics. As the consortium's attention turned to the third pilot, the executive producer and his educational advisors were players-in-position with quite different stakes and stands on the issue of pilot design. The executive producer was oriented toward the demands of television production and also toward the entertainment value of the shows. He was satisfied with the short segment format which promised both to accommodate production routines and to provide a slick and entertaining series within the divisibility constraint. The educators, on the other hand, were oriented toward the demands of the educational system and also toward the educational effectiveness of the shows. They wanted to try the narrative format which promised to communicate more meaningfully to children than an assemblage of short segments and to more readily accommodate the routines of lesson planning. The clash of professional orientations thus arose not only from differences in general professional values—entertainment versus educational effectiveness—but also from differences in the specific organizational demands—television production routines versus lesson planning routines. Where the various professionals stood on the issue of pilot design did indeed depend upon where they sat within the consortium.

The power of the players in the ensuing bargain game was clearly uneven. The executive producer, by right of formal position and television expertise, was clearly in charge. The educators were not powerless, however. The executive producer respected the expertise of his advisors, particularly in anticipating what other educators would find useful, and this gave the advisors influence. A particular action channel—the meetings of the core committee which brought together representatives from each of the consortium components—provided the opportunity to exercise this influence. The committee meetings provided the players with a forum for presentation of their stands on the issue, negotiation and, finally, compromise. Compromise on the design of the third pilot was reached when the executive producer reluctantly agreed that the narrative format should be tried. The third pilot is, then, the embodiment of a compromise worked out in the course of organizational politics.

## CONCLUSION: THE ORGANIZATIONAL CONTEXT OF CREATIVITY

If it is clear that the executive producer was the creator of the pilots, it is also clear that his creative endeavors cannot be understood apart from the perceptions and values of his co-workers, the demands of production routines, and the machinations of organizational politics. Further, it is clear that these processes cannot be understood apart from each other. Professional values as well as the production routines which had to be accommodated shaped the orientations of the various experts in the project. Differences among these orientations, in turn, gave rise to intraorganizational conflict. And all of these processes, in turn, interlocked into an organizational context which certainly constrainted but also guided and energized the creative activity of the executive producer. Professional perceptions and values, the demands of production routines, and the compromises of organizational politics were all pieces of puzzles which are the executive producer was called upon to solve.

The three pilots are, thus, each a solution to a puzzle formulated within the organization. The first pilot was a solution to the puzzle of designing a television show which was educational and yet highly entertaining as desired by the executive producer, amenable to the routines of television production as demanded by the budget and divisible into two separate parts as required by the routines of teachers. The second pilot was a solution to a puzzle which included all of these elements as well as the audience demand for continuity-of-storyline as perceived by the formative researchers. The puzzle of the third pilot added to all of these elements the agreement between the executive producer and the educators to use a narrative format.

The lens focused on the individual sees the executive producer as the solver of these puzzles and thus credits him with creating the pilots. The lenses focused on organizational routines and organizational conflict, however, see the context in which the puzzles were formulated. Scholars of creativity are coming to realize that puzzle formulation as well as puzzle solution is part of the creative process (Getzels and Csikszentmihalyi, 1975) and it was only with the assembly of the various experts and their interaction within the context of the consortium that the complete creative process of puzzle formulation and solution could operate as it did. In this sense, the shows are the creative achievement of the organization itself.

**POSTSCRIPT**

The three pilots each solved a puzzle but together they created another: which of the three to select as the prototype for the series. The educators had always favored the dramatic third pilot and they were joined by the executive producer when his own judgment told him that dramas were best able to sustain a whole series of shows without becoming repetitive and trite. Finally, the researchers concurred when they found a sample of children overwhelmingly preferred the third pilot to the others. Thus, the constraints of the educational system as defined by the educators, the requirements of quality television as envisioned by the executive producer, and the preferences of the audience as perceived by the researchers all converged on a solution.

The dramatic format chosen by the consortium and the complex pro-social messages specified in the curriculum plan, in turn, became the pieces of a puzzle which script writers were called upon to solve when scripting an episode of the series. Some of the writers complained about the constraints imposed by the format and messages but others took a different view of their creative task.

"I happen to believe that setting limits increases creativity," one of the writers said. "I think if you take a creative person and give him nothing to fight against, nothing to bump up against, he can't flex his muscles. He's flabby. I think that restrictions are very good creatively."

Another of the writers strongly agreed. "Writing for the series," she said, "is like solving a puzzle."

## NOTES

1. See Lesser (1974) and Mielke and Swinehart (1976) for a discussion of the ideas from which *Sesame Street* and subsequent CTW productions were developed.

2. Land (1972) provides an overview of the operation of CTW. Middleton (1979) and Sloan (1980) provide extensive reviews of two projects undertaken by the Agency for Instructional Television.

3. To conduct this study the author became a fulltime observer within the consortium for a period which included the development of the pilot shows. The author attended meetings, observed the work of individuals, collected documents and conducted both formal and informal interviews. The concepts outined in the literature review structured the study, first, by sensitizing the author to significant issues and events and later by organizing the reporting of those issues and events.

4. See Johnston, Ettema, and Davidson (1980) for an evaluation of the educational effectiveness of the series.

## REFERENCES

ALLISON, G.T. (1971) Essence of Decision. Boston: Little, Brown.

ARGYRIS, C. (1974) Behind the Front Page, Organizational Self-Renewal in a Metropolitan Newspaper. San Francisco: Jossey-Bass.

BOWERS, D.R. (1967) "A report on activity by publishers in directing newsroom decisions." Journalism Quarterly 44: 43-52.

BREED, W. (1958) "Mass communication and social integration." Social Forces 37: 109-116.

BROWN, L. (1971) Televi$ion: The Business Behind the Box. New York: Harcourt Brace Jovanovich.

CANTOR, M.G. (1979) "The politics of popular drama." Communication Research 6: 387-406.

———— (1971) The Hollywood Television Producer. New York: Basic Books.

DIMMICK, J. W. (1979) "The gatekeepers: Media organizations as political coalitions." Communication Research 6: 203-222.

———— (1974) "The gatekeeper: An uncertainty theory." Journalism Monographs, No. 37.

DONOHEW, L. (1967) "Newspaper gatekeepers and forces in the news channels." Public Opinion Quarterly 31: 61-68.

ELLIOT, P. (1970) "Selection and communication in a television production—a case study." In Tunstall, J. (ed.) Media Sociology: A Reader. London: Constable.

FLEGEL, R. C. and S. H. CHAFFEE (1971) "Influences of editors, readers and personal opinions on reporters." Journalism Quarterly 48: 645-651.

GETZELS, J. W. and M. CSIKSZENTMIHALYI (1975) "From problem solving to problem finding." In I. A. Taylor and J. W. Getzels (eds.) Perspectives in Creativity. Chicago: Aldine.

GREENBERG, B. (1969) "The content and context of violence in the mass media," in D. L. Lange, R. K. Baker, and S. J. Ball (eds.) A Report to the National Commission on the Causes of Violence and the Media. Washington, DC: Government Printing Office.

HAHN, T. (1972) "Structural control of the press: an exploration in organizational analysis." Ph.D. dissertation, University of Minnesota.

HICKSON, D. J., C. R. HININGS, C. A. LEE, and R. E. SCHENCK (1971) "A strategic contingencies' theory of intra-organizational power." Administrative Science Quarterly 16: 216-229.

HIRSCH, P. M. (1977) "Occupational, organizational and institutional models in mass media research: toward an integrated framework," in P. M. Hirsch, P. V. Miller, and F. G. Kline (eds.) Strategies for Communication Research. Beverly Hills: Sage.

———— (1972) "Processing fads and fashions: an organization-set analysis of cultural industry systems." American Journal of Sociology 77: 639-659.

JOHNSTON, J., J. S. ETTEMA, and T. N. DAVIDSON (1980) An Evaluation of Freestyle. A Television Series to Reduce Sex-Role Stereotypes. Ann Arbor, MI: Institute for Social Research.

JOHNSTONE, J. W. C., E. J. SLAWSKI, and W. W. BOWMAN (1976) The News People. Urbana: University of Illinois Press.

LAND, H. W. (1972) The Children's Television Workshop. How and Why It Works. Jericho, NY: Nassau Board of Cooperative Educational Services.

LAWRENCE, P. R. and J. W. LORSCH (1967) Organization and Environment. Boston: Harvard Business School.

LESSER, G. S. (1974) Children and Television. Lessons from Sesame Street. New York: Vintage Books.

MARCH, J. G. and H. A. SIMON (1958) Organizations. New York: John Wiley.

MARTIN, R. K., G. J. O'KEEFE and O. B. NAYMAN (1972) "Opinion agreement and accuracy between editors and their readers." Journalism Quarterly 49: 460-468.

MIDDLETON, J. (1979) Cooperative School Television and Educational Change. Bloomington, IN: Agency for Instructional Television.

MIELKE, K. W. and J. W. SWINEHART (1976) Evaluation of the Feeling Good Television Series. New York: Children's Television Workshop.

MILLER, M. and E. RHODES (1964) Only You, Dick Daring! New York: William Sloane.

POOL, I. and I. SHULMAN (1959) "Newsmen's fantasies, audiences and newswriting." Public Opinion Quarterly 23: 145-158.

RICH, L. M. (1973) "Sheriff Who?" in J. D. STEVENS and W. E. PORTER (eds.) The Rest of the Elephant. Englewood Cliffs, NJ: Prentice-Hall.

SIGAL, L. (1973) Reporters and Officials. Lexington, MA: D. C. Heath.

SIGELMAN, L. (1973) "Reporting the news: an organizational analysis." American Journal of Sociology 79: 132-151.

SLOAN, K. R. (1980) Thinking Through Television. Bloomington, IN: Agency for Instructional Television.

STEIN, B. (1979) The View from Sunset Boulevard: America as Brought to You by the People Who Make Television. New York: Basic Books.

THOMPSON, J. D. (1967) Organizations in Action. New York: McGraw-Hill.

TUCHMAN, G. (1978) Making News. New York: The Free Press.

_____ (1977) "The exception proves the rule: the study of routine news practices," in P. M. Hirsch, et al. (eds.) Strategies for Communication Research. Beverly Hills: Sage.

TUNSTALL, J. (1971) Journalists at Work. London: Constable.

VIRTS, P. (1980) "Theory building in media decision making." Presented to the Speech Communication Association annual meeting, New York.

WHITE, D. M. (1950) "The gatekeeper: a case study in the selection of news." Journalism Quarterly 27: 383-390.

# Chapter 6

# UNCONVENTIONAL PROGRAMS ON COMMERCIAL TELEVISION
## An Organizational Perspective

### Joseph Turow

THAT AMERICAN commercial network television is unadventuresome and derivative of its previous fare has become a truism among critics, practitioners, and academics (see, for example, Barnouw, 1975; Brown, 1971; Shanks, 1976). Possibly as a consequence of this viewpoint, research and writing on the production of television content have tended to focus òn the constraints which result in predictably patterned content (Baldwin and Lewis, 1972; Cantor, 1972; Melody, 1973; Tuchman, 1974; Turow, 1978). Left virtually unopened has been an entire research area relating to the possibilities of programming change within the commercial television system. The purpose of this chapter is not to challenge the notion that much of American commercial television is patterned and derivative. Rather, it is to explore the organizational and interorganizational conditions which foster those rare instances when unconventional programs are conceived, produced, scheduled and aired.

The analysis of unconventional programming must begin by considering the term "unconventional" as it relates to a term frequently used in writing about new products: "innovation." A definition of innovation common among sociologists of organizations is "the implementation of a new product, idea, or service" (Evan, 1976: 112). Because "new" has many meanings, writings on innovation often suggest the value of differentiating, per-

AUTHOR'S NOTE: Many thanks go to Patrice Buzzanell of Purdue University for her hard-working help during the preliminary stages of this project. Thanks are also due to Paul Rosenthal, Mardi Gregory, and other members of the Communication Studies Program at UCLA for their friendliness and support during the interviewing stage. A major portion of this investigation was funded by the Purdue Research Foundation.

haps along a continuum, between the development of new products that are recognized within the firm and the industry as essentially derivative of those currently available ("conventional innovations") and products recognized within the firm and industry as departing strongly from accepted approaches ("unconventional innovations"). From this standpoint, unconventional television programs are programs perceived within the TV industry as departing strongly from the norm when they appear.

A large body of literature has grown around the study of innovation in non-symbol producing organizations (see, for example, Burns and Stalker, 1961; Johnson, 1970; Khandwalla, 1977; National Industrial Conference Board, 1967; March and Simon, 1958; Marquis, 1976; Panel on Invention and Innovation, 1967; Rogers and Rogers, 1976; Rothberg, 1976; Schon, 1966; Steele, 1975; Wainright and Gerlach, 1968; Young, 1970). Though only a small number of articles even mention the concept of *mass media* innovation (see Crane, 1976; Hirsch, 1972, 1976; Peterson, 1976; Peterson and Berger, 1975), the two bodies of literature, taken together, do provide a useful framework for developing hypotheses about the conditions that foster unconventional television programs. Both note that innovations are risky and that a firm is not likely to develop new "symbolic" or "material" products when it is experiencing rather stable organizational and environmental conditions that encourage the status quo—for example, when it can keep out competition, when it has few competitors, or when it fears that market (that is, distributor or consumer) dissatisfaction might ensue if accepted approaches are abrogated (Hirsch, 1972; 741-742; Young, 1970: 53; Rogers and Rogers, 1976: 70-71). On the other hand, the writings stress that a firm is much more likely to produce innovative products when it or its environment experiences tension-inducing changes (see, for example, Panel on Invention and Innovation, 1967: 3, 48).

These bodies of literature also agree that changes among ultimate consumers (the "audience") are not the primary sparks to innovation within a firm. While consumers ultimately play an important part in accepting or rejecting innovations, the most important factors in a firm's environment which induce tensions toward innovation include aggressive competitors that ignite a fear of falling behind, changing technology which points a firm's current products or production techniques toward obsolescence, changing demands by distributors, and changing government policy (Rogers and Rogers, 1976; 156-163; Rothberg, 1976; DiMaggio and Hirsch, 1976). Developments *within* a firm which the writings cite as encouraging innovation include a desire by the company's executives to eliminate excess capacity (Rothberg, 1976) and the desire by an individual newly appointed to an important position to accumulate or exhibit power by taking risks and succeeding (Kanter, 1977).

Of course, a production firm is ordinarily dependent upon outlets for the presentation of its innovations to consumers. Outlet receptivity to innovation would likely be of special concern to production firms in the television industry, where three commercial networks purchase the great percentage of programs production firms create (Cantor, 1980). Therefore, it is important to point out that although the factors just mentioned suggest reasons for the generation of program innovation within TV production firms, they need only be rephrased slightly to predict situations under which the television networks would search for, and accept, innovations from those producers. That is, it is likely that tension-inducing changes that affect networks, production firms, or the relationships between the two, will have crucial consequences for the inception, development, and release of innovations.

When product innovation is crucial to a firm's survival, the firm often implements mechanisms to promote innovation. Often, special departments are formed to facilitate this task. In the television industry, where fierce competition for ratings encourages at least two "seasons" a year with new fare, the three commercial networks have program development departments to help production firms design new shows. Marquis (1976) states that such institutional responses to routine demands for innovation result generally in a certain level of innovation that is conventional for *that* firm in *that* industry. Unconventional innovations by the firm are produced in response to what, for that firm, is an extraordinary (that is, unpredicted and nonroutine) problem.

Other factors related to innovation are the size of the firm and the degree to which the firm is in the mainstream of its industry. Marquis implies, and Johnson (1970: 42) explicitly states, that large organizations tend to take a lot longer to consider and implement unconventional suggestions than they do to consider and implement mundane ones. Rogers and Rogers (1976: 144) argue that one important reason for this difference is an inflexibility and a hesitancy to take risks that often develops among the executives who control the routine communication channels by which organizational policy is made. They suggest that unusual ideas which find acceptance often have been moved through the organization by atypical agents, connections, and procedures. In the same vein, Marquis, in agreement with Perrow (1980) and Downs (1967), points out that relatively unestablished organizations have been more likely to come up with unconventional innovations than have large firms in the mainstream of their industries. The reason, Marquis (1976: 15) suggests, is that "technical people within [the mainstream of] industry are apt to be preoccupied by short-term concerns . . . cost cutting, quality control, expanding the product line, and the like." The staff of unestablished firms, with no large product lines to protect and expand, is more likely to concentrate on unusual problems and daring possibilities.

Applying these ideas from the literature on innovation to the television industry leads to six hypotheses about the genesis of unconventional programs:

(1) Unconventional shows tend to be produced by companies, and sold to networks, lagging in the ratings or experiencing extraordinary changes in their competitive environment.

(2) Unlike the conventional shows, the greatest percentage of unconventional shows tend to be developed by firms not comfortably engaged in the ongoing production of other programs.

(3) Since it is unestablished firms and firms in competitive trouble which are the most willing to risk innovation, it is likely to be the *coming together* of an unestablished production firm with a network experiencing extraordinary problems or changes that most favors the development and airing of unconventional shows.

(4) In large organizations (like the networks), unconventional shows tend to be championed by executives newly placed in their positions, or by executives wanting to risk their current positions to move to more powerful ones as a direct result of their involvement in the programs.

(5) Unconventional programs, more often than conventional shows, are conceptualized outside the normal channels of typical production firm/network program development.

(6) Unconventional programs, because they are perceived as risky from the start, take a much longer time than do conventional shows to move from the concept-generating stage to the production and airing stage.

The purpose of this investigation was to determine if these hypotheses are supportable and to explore other organizational and interorganizational factors relevant to the development of unconventional shows.


## THE METHOD

The core of the research was a comparative analysis of the genesis of three series generally accepted as conventional within the television industry when they appeared, and three generally described as unconventional. The six programs were chosen after an analysis of the past fifteen years of television reviews and articles in the trade journal *Variety* to determine the shows people in the TV industry described as unconventional or very innovative. Of 26 series and specials that fell into the "unconventional" category, three series—*Rowan & Martin's Laugh In, All in the Family,* and *United States* —were selected for study. Each of these was then paired with a conventional series that appeared around the same time, on the same network—*Kraft Music Hall, Arnie,* and *Facts of Life,* respectively. The pairing of these shows highlights the point that a network can accept both conventional and unconventional programs for airing in the same season.

The genesis of each show was traced carefully, through a review of articles in the popular and trade press and, more importantly, through interviews with people involved in the show's creation and airing. The executive producer of every show, as listed in its *Variety* review, was contacted and interviewed, using an open-ended question format with specific probes. The goal of the interview was to understand the sequence of events that led to the first airing of the program, and to specify that sequence as far as possible in terms of the people involved, the decisions made, the reasons for those decisions, and the time between them. In the process, names of key production, network, and (in the case of *Kraft Music Hall*) advertising personnel involved in the show's development were elicited. Many were contacted and questioned. In all, 32 people in Los Angeles and New York were interviewed.[1] Several were involved in more than one program. The interviews typically lasted about 20 minutes, though some were longer and a few were shorter. They were transcribed and compared—for each show, then across different shows—to determine if the hypotheses were supported.[2]

## THE COMPARATIVE CASE STUDY

The case study did uphold the hypotheses, though not without qualification. The findings are best conveyed and explained by describing the organizational processes in context—that is, by comparing and contrasting the geneses of the conventional and unconventional shows.

### THE CONVENTIONAL SERIES

Distilling the essential details about *Kraft Music Hall, Arnie* and *Facts of Life* that bear upon the hypotheses of this study highlights the three different kinds of organizations that have traditionally brought viable program ideas to the commercial networks—advertising agencies, established production firms, and the networks themselves. For various reasons (see Turow, 1980), the ad agency route is now very rarely used to generate network series programs. However, in the fall of 1967, when *Kraft Music Hall* made its debut, it was traveled somewhat more often.

Actually, while the specific format of Kraft Food's program was new in 1967, the title was not. In the 1930s and 1940s, a series called *Kraft Music Hall* with Bing Crosby was one of the most popular variety shows on radio. When Kraft moved to NBC television, it departed from the "Music Hall" title until the 1958-59 season, when *Milton Berle Starring in the Kraft Music Hall* appeared. Although a *Kraft Music Hall* with Perry Como aired regularly, then irregularly, in the early 1960s, and although a *Summer Kraft*

*Music Hall* with other hosts could be seen as mid-decade approached, the firm began to lend its name more often to television drama. *Kraft Suspense Theater* aired from October 1963 through the summer of 1965, and for the 1966-1967 season the company decided to sponsor an episodic drama of NBC called *Road West*. Ratings were poor. By the middle of the year, it was clear to many in the TV industry that Kraft would be interested in sponsoring a new program. Consequently, various television industry executives passed through Kraft's advertising agency, J. Walter Thompson (JWT) in New York, trying to pitch their ideas to Bill Highland, head of the television department.

One of these people was Lester Gotlieb, a notable New York figure in the then-powerful G. A. C. talent agency, which represented Perry Como, among other stars. Gotlieb suggested to Highland that Kraft bring back the "Music Hall" title in a prestigious weekly series which G. A. C. would populate with top talent. The prime week-to-week movers of the show would be Gary Smith and Dwight Hemion, two of G. A. C.'s clients, who were winning increasing acclaim together through the decade. Hemion and Smith had begun working together in the very early 1960s (as a producer and a set designer, respectively) on Kraft's Perry Como *Music Hall*. They had continued their professional comradeship through the *Andy Williams Summer Show* and had formed a production firm that concentrated on variety specials. Initially, the two had balked at Gotlieb's suggestion that they get involved in a series again. They feared building a program around one host's personality for several weeks would limit their creative freedom. They became interested when the agent explained the series would not have a regular host; in a sense, it would be like creating a "special" every week. Actually, all three realized that J. Walter Thompson executives would accept such a program only if they could get commitments from at least three famous hosts who would return several times a year. Initial probes to interest Bill Highland evoked Frank Sinatra (a G. A. C. client), among other names, but eventually the first year's list of "core" hosts lowered its sights to less stellar personalities—Bobby Darin, Alan King and Eddie Arnold. As long as ten to twelve shows used one of them, the other shows could have other hosts.

Gotlieb, his boss Sam Cohn, Smith and Hemion also presented their ideas to Kraft executives in the Chicago home office. Both the Kraft people and the agency executives liked the idea and the format. The firm prided itself on the "Music Hall" name and wanted it in front of the public on a regular basis. Smith and Hemion had a "track record" of polished programming. Moreover, the *Colgate Comedy Hour,* an early network TV show, had been successful using a similar format, and ABC's more recent *Hollywood Palace* had succeeded using various hosts. Kraft executives were assured the hosts and themes of the show would fit the contemporary, though at the same time rather conservative, family-oriented image the firm tried to exude. Comedian Alan King's sometimes biting humor did make the executives a bit nervous, but they realized that his urban style was needed as a counterbalance to Arnold's rural demeanor. They were also willing to pay a little more than was typical for variety programming to associate with a quality show. The earliest installments of *Kraft Music Hall* would be blockbusters, to draw attention to the series. The first program would star the popular Herb Alpert and his Tijuana Brass, and Louis Armstrong; a Rock Hudson salute to Broadway musicals would follow a week later. The Kraft executives agreed to the series, about five months after Gotlieb had first proposed it.

J. Walter Thompson executives proposed the show to NBC, the network Kraft had been associated with since radio days. The network, struggling behind CBS in the ratings, had been trying to interest Kraft in sponsoring a variety or anthology show. Program executives, led by Mort Werner, a former agent, felt those formats were the vehicles whereby they would overtake CBS. Werner and his staff accepted Kraft's alternative to the NBC suggestions, and they also accepted the JWT executive's insistence that the *Music Hall* be aired on Kraft's traditional Wednesday, 9 p. m. slot. (The slot allowed Kraft to advertise its products the night before the traditional American Thursday and Friday shopping days.) Since JWT controlled the show and G. A. C. packaged it, the network had very little to do with the program once it was scheduled. Given this go-ahead, Smith and Hemion hired writers, a choreographer (the prominent Peter Gennaro), and other staff members. The first program was ready to air within two months.

**Arnie**

*Kraft Music Hall* was typical of variety shows of the time in not having to test a "pilot" program. Situation comedies and other episodic series *were* expected to pass network audience tests, however. *Arnie* was no exception. The idea for the program began with a phone conversation between David Swift, a successful television and film writer/producer/director, and actor Telly Savalas, who had just finished a comic role in a film by Swift. Savalas indicated he wanted to star in a television show, and Swift responded somewhat later with a lightly funny storyline about a Greek American blue-collar worker (Savalas is proudly Greek-American) who is elevated to a white-collar job and finds himself making many adjustments as a result. Not wanting the exhausting burden of guiding a television series, Swift brought the idea in late spring 1969 to his friend Grant Tinker, who had recently moved from a position as West Coast production head of NBC to a position of production chief at 20th Century Fox Television. Liking the idea, Tinker and his boss,

William Self, took it through the normal development channels at CBS—to Frank Barton, a West Coast development executive, and Perry Lafferty, head of the network's West Coast development area. Both knew Swift's reputation for successful Disney films, TV shows, and particularly the TV comedy classic, *Mr. Peepers*. They liked the idea for *Arnie* and, in summer, 1969, ordered a script. Swift wrote it, along with additional storyline possibilities for the series. The CBS West Coast executives felt the pilot script was fine, but it was up to Michael Dann, the network's programming chief based in New York, to give the final approval to produce a pilot. Dann was a bit concerned the public might not accept a program about a blue-collar worker. Grant Tinker remembers convincing him to OK the pilot while visiting him at the Beverly Hills Hotel.

Around that time, Telly Savalas' agent met with Tinker and told him the actor was no longer interested in doing the show. Putting their heads together, the Fox people and CBS casting personnel came with Herschel Bernardi as a replacement; the actor had recently done *Zorba the Greek* on Broadway. Other casting was done in preparation for the pilot, which was to be directed by Swift. As Perry Lafferty recalls it, he and his staff had encouraged Swift to take advantage of the mechanical, predictable nature of audience testing:

> We had every kind of satisfaction for the audience. A man got promoted to a different level. His job improved. He got things for his wife, was kind to her and the family. So everything was wonderful. The program tested through the roof. We defeated the machine. . . . We designed it to test well, and it tested great![3]

Pleased with *Arnie's* audience response scores, Mike Dann scheduled it for Saturday evening, 9-9:30, between the long-running *My Three Sons* and the new *Mary Tyler Moore Show*. The pilot, taped in fall 1969, was ready to be shown to prospective advertisers on CBS' then-traditional new season announcement day, Washington's Birthday.

### Facts of Life

The six months it took from idea presentation to the completion and acceptance of the *Arnie* pilot about matched the time it took to develop and complete the first *Kraft Music Hall* installment. In the case of *Facts of Life,* the time was a bit shorter—fewer than three months. The impetus for the show—and for its quick development—was NBC's very low position in the ratings race during fall 1978 and spring 1979. Fred Silverman had recently taken over the presidency of the network, and he and his staff were looking for program ideas to shore up the network's sagging schedule.

One of the few shows debuting on NBC in the fall of 1978 which was evidencing even a glimmer of "hit" status was *Different Strokes,* a situation comedy about a rich white widower, his daughter (Kimberly), his two adopted black sons, and their white maid (Mrs. Garrett). The comic center of the show was the young Gary Coleman, but Silverman felt Charlotte Raye, who played the maid, had enough personality to carry a show on her own. In spring, 1979, he told a member of his West Coast development staff, Stuart Sheslow, to develop a spinoff from *Different Strokes* in which Charlotte Raye would have "something" to do with girls.[4]

Shortly thereafter, Sheslow suggested the idea of a *Different Strokes* spinoff to Al Burton, head of development for T. A. T., the very successful firm which produced the series. Sheslow's view of the new series, which he would call "Garrett's Girls," was to have the maid become a custodian of some rather tough students in a girls school; the show would be a kind of female *Welcome Back, Kotter,* the ABC hit of a few seasons back. For his part, Burton, reflecting on his own experience with teenagers as a father of girls and as a former coordinator of teenage beauty pageants, believed that a show with Mrs. Garrett and girls could have the potential of exploring some important issues of growing up—a kind of teenage *Passages.* His notion was that Mrs. Garrett would take a position at Kimberly's private girls school and become an anchor around which the problems of the girls could be played out. He saw a private school as more consonant with the kind of programs his firm developed. T. A. T. had a "quality" image of itself and tried to generate shows that resonated with the experiences of their creators. Even so, the company's principals, Norman Lear and Alan Horn, were skeptical that the program would be nothing more than "jiggles," Burton recalls, referring to the increased sexual suggestiveness then sweeping television. He assured them it would really be a teenage *Passages* (recalling the popular book by Gail Sheehy), and they acquiesced. They rejected the title "Garrett's Girls" as sexist, however; the tentative title became "Growing Up."

The "pilot" was to be Episode 22 of *Different Strokes;* the network was in a hurry to get the spinoff on the air. Two writers were hired to write the script which, because of the need for speed, was completed on the Monday before a mandatory Friday taping in May. T. A. T. executives were astonished at the crudeness of the script, which was to introduce Mrs. Garrett to the school. Rather than carry forth Burton's *Passages* idea, the writers seemed to have gone for low comedy in the vein of the successful film, *Animal House.* There was not enough time to completely reconceptualize the script, but two writers from *Different Strokes* were brought in to give it some "coherence" and "polish" (to quote Burton). Still, Horn informed Silverman that T. A. T. was taping the show under protest. That the episode was televised was due in large measure to Silverman's persuasive abilities. NBC, testing it on the night it aired, told T. A. T. that audience response was quite favorable.

Soon after the May airing, NBC executives informed Alan Horn and Al Burton that the network wanted to order 4 more episodes and run them as a "short flight" series. The network people realized the flaws of the *Different Strokes* episode but felt it had potential. Moreover, NBC had to fill the half-hour after *Different Strokes* on four Friday nights beginning late August. The series that had held that slot since mid-season, *Hello, Larry,* had produced only 13 episodes and, having rerun all 13 once, NBC programmers were wary of repeating some again. They felt a short flight series of "Growing Up" (soon to be renamed *Facts of Life*) would have a good chance in that time slot.

Horn and Burton, concerned about the bad experience with Episode 22 and the short lead time NBC was giving them, said they would consent to producing the episodes only if NBC first ordered four scripts. Only if both T. A. T. and the network were happy with the scripts would they then commit to the short flight series. Sheslow and the other development people agreed, and Glen Padnick, a T. A. T. executive, came up with a storyline he felt would establish the *Passages* theme of the program: One of the teens in Mrs. Garrett's dormitory is afraid she (the teen) is a lesbian. Sheslow liked the storyline, and two writers from the successful T. A. T. show *One Day at a Time,* Julie and Dianne Kirgo, were brought in to write the script. The lesbian theme tangled with the NBC censors, however, and in the end the script was diluted to portray a girl who is ridiculed because she is a tomboy. The Kirgo sisters angrily removed their names from the credits, replacing them with "Brad Rider," purposely a man's name, to emphasize their exasperation with "a bunch of old men" writing about girls' problems. Though a bit disheartened, Burton contended that the *Passages* flavor of the episode remained. As he said, "the pace of television production is such that we didn't have the time to be disappointed."

**THE UNCONVENTIONAL SERIES**

As a hypothesis presented earlier in this chapter predicted, the "conventional" pace of development was not followed with respect to the unconventional programs. *Rowan and Martin's Laugh In, All in the Family* and *United States* all took quite a bit longer than six months from the initial proposal to a network until the program's completion for airing. Moreover, in each case network executives had grave reservations about televising the show, even after it was scheduled. One crucial reason the series ultimately did air related to the initiative of particular network officials who, for both occupational and organizational reasons, decided to encourage the unorthodox.

### Rowan and Martin's Laugh In

In the case of *Rowan and Martin's Laugh In,* the primary network official to fit this role was Ed Friendly, NBC's Vice President in Charge of Special Projects during the mid-1960s. In the years prior to *Laugh In's* September 1967 debut, Friendly had often voiced to his colleagues the conviction that the network should experiment with "all comedy" formats. Since the mid-1950s, television humor that was not "situation comedy" had essentially meant monologues or skits on "variety shows" that also included songs and dance. Ernie Kovacks' ingenious "blackout" humor, short-lived on CBS during the early 1950s, had pointed in a different direction, but none had followed. Friendly, searching for all-comic possibilities, helped supervise NBC's rather ill-fated version of *That Was the Week That Was (TW3),* the biting British news satire program. After that experience, he decided that what television really needed was a television version of *Hellzapoppin,* the more frantically paced (and much less news-conscious) stage smash of the 1940s.

Creative interest in taking a risk on an unusual comedy idea came to Friendly from two sources—producer George Schlatter and the comedy team of Rowan and Martin. In the mid-1960s, Schlatter was developing a modest reputation for his work on television variety shows. His dream, however, was to bring outrageous, quick-paced humor to the medium on a sustained basis. He recalls going to all the networks for about three years in the early and middle part of the decade "trying to sell the idea . . . of bright and fast comedy" that would use a free-wheeling, multimedia format, no host, and a group of unknown comedians (Barthel, 1968: 154). Friendly recruited him to do a variety special with some of the ingredients he favored. Called *NBC Follies* and hosted by Steve Lawrence, the program had outrageous bits, such as Lucille Ball riding a pink elephant. However, no network seemed interested in giving Schlatter full reign with his all-comedy notions. He himself said that "this was just a nutty, weird idea, just a vehicle, and every network and ad agency in the business turned it down. We tried several titles: 'Wacky World of Now,' 'Stand Up and Turn Left,' and 'Just for Laughs' " (Barthel, 1968: 154). In the meantime, he took a job of producing *The Steve Lawrence Show* for CBS's 1966-1967 season. The show was cancelled after just a few months.

Dan Rowan and Dick Martin converged upon the scene from another direction. A struggling comedy duo for several years, they had shown strong potential for regular prime-time television in the eyes of NBC's brass when they replaced Dean Martin during the summer of 1966 and garnered good ratings. Network executives tried to interest them in starring in a variety program—either a special or a series—but the two insisted they wanted to make their major move into television in an unusual, all-comedy, vehicle. It is a matter of argument whether Ed Friendly, believing Rowan and Martin sensitive to the all-comedy notions he and Schlatter had been contemplating, introduced the producer and stars, or whether the comedy duo, searching for a producer to help execute their all-comedy theme, ultimately chose Schlatter. At any rate, Friendly became a champion of their show at the network. The initial program deal, arranged by him, was for one special. However, it was clear to all that, if successful, *Rowan and Martin's Laugh In* might go on to become a series. In fact, Friendly, who wanted to leave the network for the potentially more lucrative independent production business, seems to have been convinced of the show's prognosis. After buying the special for NBC, he resigned from the network to become Schlatter's business partner. NBC program chief Mort Werner gave his blessing to that unorthodox move, and Friendly retained much influence at the network. In a sense, the *Laugh In* company had a network executive in its midst and on its side, tilting the program toward a series commitment.

The program which Schlatter, Rowan, Martin, head writer Paul Keyes, and their staff put together was a collage of elements from vaudeville, burlesque, film, and television. Much of the comedy was obviously and admittedly derivative. What was new for television here were the manic style and the pace, quickened considerably over typical TV comedy through sharp electronic editing, which pruned jokes to their punch lines. Participants recall that the *Laugh In* special was actually not as fast-paced as the later series. All the same, NBC's program executives, while themselves finding the program funny, believed the general public would find it too quick-moving to be understandable. Also, they said the pace made some jokes seem "bluer" than they really were. Moreover, when the special was audience-tested, it received poor marks. Nevertheless, NBC had found a sponsor, Timex. Because the watch manufacturer had financed previous NBC specials, the network offered it the "Laugh In" special at a significant discount, in a time slot adjacent to the fall 1967 Miss America Pageant. The hope was that it would attract young viewers.

The program got mediocre ratings—about 26 percent of the audience. Nevertheless, the *Laugh In* principals tried to persuade the NBC Program Committee (headed by Mort Werner) to allow the show to air as a series. The special had drawn excitedly favorable comments from TV critics, a fact they were sure would impress the network executives. Yet the program people were not easily convinced. Aside from previously raised objections, they felt a quick-paced program like *Laugh In*, which relied on many rapid-fire jokes, could not maintain its energy for an hour each week. They suggested the show be shortened to a half-hour if it aired. Friendly and Schlatter demurred, contending that an hour-long weekly *Laugh In* was possible.

In the end, Werner agreed and entered the show into the NBC lineup as a mid-season replacement. Werner had begun to worry seriously that traditional variety programs and stars—the Jackie Gleasons, Perry Comos, and *Kraft Music Halls* —were losing their hold on the audience. Overall, NBC was running consistently behind CBS in the popularity of its prime-time programs. Since Werner, a former talent agent, was intent on cultivating variety-like shows to catch CBS in the ratings, he felt that perhaps an unconventional specimen like *Laugh In* should be given a chance. Moreover, the show, bereft of stars, was relatively inexpensive. Still, his scheduling of *Laugh In* seems to betray his ambivalence about the series. The program replaced the network's fast-fading *Man From U.N.C.L.E.* against two CBS Monday night powerhouses—*Gunsmoke* (then the number 2 rated show) and *Lucy* (then number 1). As a *Saturday Evening Post* article (Dietz, 1968: 35) later noted, "insertion into *U.N.C.L.E.'s* time slot was not exactly a vote of confidence." *Laugh In* writer Dighby Wolfe suggests that such scheduling reflected the network's exasperation at CBS's control over the Monday night time slot. *Laugh In* was considered expendable, and perhaps something as outrageous and different might indeed compete well with *Gunsmoke* and *Lucy*.

### All in the Family

The strong ambivalence which accompanied NBC programmers' acceptance and scheduling of *Rowan and Martin's Laugh In* as a series was also seen in CBS programmers' acceptance and scheduling of *All in the Family,* the situation comedy which the network began to air in January 1971. At first glance CBS was, as Richard Adler (1979: xvii) has observed, "the network least likely to broadcast a program like *All in the Family,* startling as it was in its direct confrontation with bigotry and its use of racial and ethnic slurs never before heard on television. The network had perennially led NBC and ABC in the ratings by striving for audience loyalty through a stable of proven stars in proven program vehicles. In 1970, however, CBS sought a program that departed from its traditional style, for two related reasons. One was the presence of a new network president, Robert Wood, who, despite a very limited experience in programming (he had been station manager at KTLA), was ambitious to show his leadership in the most visible of network areas— the selection and scheduling of prime-time series. The second reason was Wood's belief that while CBS was first in the overall ratings, it was falling behind NBC and ABC in reaching a population segment that was becoming increasingly important to advertisers: young (18-49-year-old), urban adults. In a speech to his West Coast development staff, Wood let it be known that he was willing to take a chance on something different, something with "ruby dust" that would begin to redefine the network's image and audience.

It happened that around that time Norman Lear and Bud Yorkin already *had* something that people in the industry deemed different from anything on American TV—a show they called *All in the Family.* Lear and Yorkin had worked successfully (as a writer and producer, respectively) in television during the 1950s, and in 1959 they had joined forces. Their firm's initial TV venture, a dramatic series called *Band of Gold,* was a failure, but they proved moderately successful through the decade with theatrical films *(Come Blow Your Horn, Divorce, American Style, The Night They Raided Minsky's).* In 1968, shortly after completing *Minsky's,* Lear came across an article in *Variety* about *Till Death do Us Part,* a hit British comedy series about a bigot constantly at odds with his family, especially his son-in-law. Intrigued by the idea, and energized with an identification of the bigot with his father, Lear acquired the American rights to develop a series based on the show. With his agent from Creative Management Associates (C.M.A.), he proposed the idea to development executives at ABC. The network's president, Marty Starger, liked Lear's "treatment" (his general idea for the show and his notes describing the characters), and he gave it the go-ahead for a pilot. It was shot in January 1979. When ABC executives saw the pilot, however, they became concerned the program was too controversial to air. Eventually, they rejected a second pilot as well. Neither version had done well in audience tests, and the executives decided the overall concept was just too risky for commercial television.

After the ABC rejection, Lear and Yorkin went back to making movies. Lear, who was finishing direction of his first movie, *Cold Turkey,* was offered a three-picture deal with United Artists. A film version of *All in the Family* was under serious consideration as one of those films. In February 1970, Bud Yorkin was visiting his agent, Sam Cohn, at C.M.A. in New York. After Yorkin mentioned to Cohn that he and Lear would consider working in television again if *All in the Family* were picked up, Cohn called Michael Dann, the program chief at CBS, and persuaded him to see the second of the pilots ABC had rejected. It so happened that before Robert Wood's appointment as network president, CBS program executives had rejected a property based loosely on *Till Death Do Us Part* called "Man in the Middle." Still, Dann screened the program, liked it, and recommended it enthusiastically to Wood. After conferring with an uncertain CBS Chairman William Paley and a nervous CBS chief censor William Tankersly, Wood decided to buy the show. Perry Lafferty, then head of CBS programming on the West Coast, was sure that Wood's novice status at the network helm encouraged his risk taking. Wood, looking back, agrees and adds that his early years as network president "were the freshest." Afterwards, "you learn the rules too well and don't think in new directions."

After Wood bought *All in the Family,* however, his executives questioned the advisability of airing the pilot as it stood; they specifically urged less objectionable language. Lear, buttressed by the three-picture deal awaiting him at United Artists, held firm. He had no desire to return to television if it were not on his terms. Debate within CBS about the show stretched through the early summer. Audience tests paralleled those at ABC and upheld those at CBS who wanted to change the pilot. Finally, Wood decided that, despite its negative test results and its controversial material, the pilot should air without major script changes. *All in the Family* fit his youth-oriented, urban image for the network; he hoped the controversy over the show would generate viewership. It was mid-summer 1970 when he gave Lear the go-ahead to produce 13 episodes. Somewhat later, Wood decided to begin airing the show in January.

Lear reshot the pilot in order to accommodate a recasting of the bigot's daughter and son-in-law, but he would brook very few attempts by the local CBS censor or the programming department's liaison person to change words or ideas. Quickly, word spread that *All in the Family* was Wood's concern, and crucial problems of phrasing became a matter of discussion between the network president and chief censor Tankersly. Wood stood by Lear in maintaining the language and plot of the pilot. However, that the CBS president was less than fully secure in his conviction that the show would succeed is evidenced by his decision to slot it on Tuesday at 9:30 p.m. in place of the failed *To Rome With Love*. Thus doing, he scheduled the show against two very strong movie series—the ABC *Movie of the Week* and the NBC *Tuesday Night Movie*—and after CBS's own *Hee Haw,* a rustic version of *Laugh In* that, as a lead-in, cultivated the very audience that *All in the Family* was presumably purchased to counter. Lear and Yorkin argued against this "death slot" to no avail. But even more troubling to them was a decision by Wood and several other CBS executives that it would be more prudent to begin the series with what was to have been the second episode. The executives deemed that one to be less shocking (and to have fewer racial epithets) than the first. After conferring with Yorkin and Rich, Lear refused, and he threatened to disband the *All in the Family* company if the network aired the second episode in place of the pilot. He prevailed.

Comparing the genesis of *All in the Family* with the genesis of *Arnie* illustrates the claim by CBS personnel that *All in the Family's* journey through network development was quite different from that used on more typical shows. The initial involvement of corporate chairman Paley in considering *All in the Family's* acceptance, the involvement of network president Wood in day-to-day production issues regarding that show, and the general circumvention by Norman Lear of typical censorship lines of command were unusual for the time. In the case of another unconventional show, *Rowan and Martin's Laugh In,* Ed Friendly's involvement with the program at both the production and network ends, and the airing of a "pilot" special of the show (rarely done then with variety), took it, too, out of the typical development channels of the time. Additional illustration that shows perceived as unconventional take unusual routes to network airing is found in juxtaposing *Facts of Life,* the conventional NBC situation comedy of 1979, with *United States,* the bittersweet anomaly of early 1980. While *Facts of Life* was conceived through the suggestion and guidance of NBC's program development department (one typical development procedure), *United States* was created with NBC development people playing virtually no role from conception to taping (a rare phenomenon in 1980).

**United States**

The person with the unorthodox idea that became *United States* was Larry Gelbart, a writer-producer who had penned and (with Gene Reynolds) supervised the enormously successful 1972 television adaptation of the film *M\*A\*S\*H*. Around 1975, Gelbart had tired of the weekly TV production grind and had left the series to write for the Broadway stage and the cinema (very successfully, it turned out). Still, about a year after leaving television production, he began to conceive of a television series he felt would make it worthwhile for him to return to the medium. Believing that family situation comedies of the 1970s were simply stale "variations on originals I don't think anybody remembers anymore," Gelbart felt he wanted "to go back to basics. Simply to go back to a man and a woman, a husband and wife, and a family. And to treat it . . . like 1980, not 1950." During 1976 he suggested his idea "to some people at CBS" who were interested in creating a series for actress Linda Lavin. The executives expressed interest, but when Gelbart said he was not yet prepared to get more involved in a program than consult and perhaps write a pilot, they dropped the proposal. Some months later, Gelbart became more eager to pursue the idea, and he suggested it as a vehicle for actress Mary Tyler Moore, a friend who wanted to return to television after a hiatus. Moore and her husband, Grant Tinker (by then a successful independent producer), considered it seriously. However, when Gelbart said he wanted a year to write all the scripts for the series before starting production, they said they did not want to wait that long.

Gelbart brought his idea to NBC President Fred Silverman in December, 1978. The two had gotten to know one another when Silverman was head of CBS programming and Gelbart was supervising *M\*A\*S\*H*. Their paths continued to cross even after Gelbart had left television production and Silverman and had left CBS to become ABC's program chief. After a friendly clash with Gelbart about network program quality at a Writers Guild panel discussion, Silverman, acknowledging Gelbart's expertise and flair for originality, had publicly offered to allow him to program a block of time on ABC. However, Gelbart did not present concrete suggestions, and ABC program executives—riding high on the highest rated network—did not seem anxious to push him. It was only after he became seriously interested in creating the series about marriage that Gelbart approached Silverman, now at NBC, and reminded him of his offer. He wanted virtual autonomy to produce a series that would take a "witty," "honest," and unconventionally "adult" look at marriage. Moreover, he wanted NBC to allow him (as executive producer) and Gary Markowitz (his stepson, as producer) to have as much time as needed to refine an entire season's worth of scripts before production would begin.

Not even having received a "treatment" for the proposed new show, Silverman bought a season's worth of episodes. NBC was plummeting into third place in the ratings race in late 1978, and Silverman, appointed president of the network just a few months before, was hoping Larry Gelbart's track record would rub off on the network. Some people close to the situation also suggest that Silverman was at the time very aware of press accusations about his bringing "low quality" to CBS and ABC, and so wanted Gelbart's stage and screen prestige (notably for *Sly Fox* and *Oh God*) to help improve his image. Larry Gelbart, for his part, saw his primary mandate as developing an honest, witty show about "the state of being united." High ratings were not a concern. In planning the show, he, Markowitz, and Chuck Kalish (the supervising producer) took great pains to overturn many of the situation comedy conventions that had developed over the past decade. There would be no audience, no laugh track, no uniform floodlights, no proscenium perspective, no "three camera" set-up. The stars would not be television regulars; Beau Bridges and Helen Shavers, rarely on TV, were chosen.

An NBC censor was present on the show, but Gelbart took complaints about such interference (and there were several) to much higher levels in the network—to Perry Lafferty (head of NBC's West Coast programming activities), Jane Pfeiffer (NBC Chairman), or Fred Silverman. The program development department took no part in the show's evolution, and there were some disgruntled remarks in that corner as the series took shape. Some executives thought that it was too "high brow" for commercial television, that the central couple was too wealthy, that the show was simply not funny enough. An audience test of the initial episode confirmed their belief that the audience would not take to it easily. Nevertheless, none of these perceptions was relayed to Gelbart, and he asked for no feedback. Yet, when, after agreeing to a January 1980 start, NBC executives postponed the series until March, the *United States* company began to realize something was drastically wrong.

NBC did air the first episode in March, but in a time slot which seemed to reflect Fred Silverman's exasperation with Gelbart's final product. Not arguing with the show's literacy, distinctiveness, and ability to generate prestige, program executives felt the series did not have elements that would attract a huge audience. They decided not to risk placing the show at the center of prime time, where the network needed high ratings and "audience flow" badly. The place they found for the series was 10:30 Tuesday nights, after a new ninety-minute *Hollywood Palace*—like variety extravaganza, *The Big Show*. Opposing *United States* was an adventure series on ABC *(Hart to Hart)* that began at 10, and a two-hour CBS movie that began at 9. It seemed to Gelbart that the program's chance to grab an audience was, therefore, not from the other two networks (which would probably hold their viewers through the last half-hour of their programs) but from *The Big Show*. Gelbart feared an incongruity between *United States*'s probable audience (more sophisticated, older people, as he saw it) and the audience that would continue watching *The Big Show* past 10 o'clock. Silverman, acknowledging the problem, assured Gelbart the network would try to "lead" an audience into the 10:30 program by programming the last half-hour of *The Big Show* with sophisticated comedy. Gelbart was not convinced. On the contrary, to him the scheduling meant that NBC programmers' uncertainty about what to do with his show had led them to "electronic euthanasia."

## CONCLUSION

Much of this chapter has dealt with aspects of risk-taking—specifically with the circumstances in which producers and network executives risk suggesting, executing, and airing programs they recognize as unconventional. Several hypotheses were offered about these circumstances and about the differences which characterize the development of conventional and unconventional shows. The first hypothesis was that unconventional program innovations are most likely to be generated and accepted by organizations experiencing unusual changes or competitive pressures. As the previous pages have shown, that prediction was confirmed clearly regarding the networks. The networks that chose to accept the unconventional ideas (in two cases after another network refused) were lagging in the ratings (as in the case of NBC when it bought *Rowan and Martin's Laugh In* and *United States*) or (as in the case of CBS when it bought *All in the Family*) were perceived by top management as seriously deficient in ratings-related areas.

The hypothesis was not supported, however, regarding the producers who generated the shows in the first place. In the case of producers Norman Lear *(All in the Family)* and Larry Gelbart *(United States)*, at least, the motivation for tenaciously pushing an unorthodox program idea was not related to extraordinary changes or competitive pressures. Rather, it was related to the producers' awareness of having a power base outside the television industry which allowed them attractive alternatives to television work if a network did not accept their proposals.

This lack of support for the hypothesis at the production end is perhaps understandable when one realizes that while the networks are large organizations, that characterization does not fit the Lear-Yorkin association in the pre-*All in the Family* days, Larry Gelbart's status as an individual writer-producer, or, for that matter, George Schlatter's position at the start of *Laugh In*. Independent creative individuals heading their own small firms would seem to be free to pursue unconventional program ideas whether or not unusual pressures or changes are affecting the firms. Perhaps the prediction that unusual organizational pressures are particularly conducive to the generation of unconventional program ideas would hold in the case of large firms (such as Disney and Universal) that begin to falter. In this study, it seems that the hypothesis most relevant to the production firms is the suggestion that the members of unestablished firms are more likely than the staff of established firms to encourage and generate unconventional innovations, since the latter are much more likely than the former to be preoccupied with the need to protect and expand existing product lines.

That second hypothesis, and the four other predictions offered in this chapter, *were* supported quite strongly. Faithful to the second hypothesis, it was found that while all three conventional shows were developed by people or production firms enjoying ongoing work and comfortable success in the television industry, the three unconventional programs derived from people who were at moderate to low points in fitfully successful TV careers (as in the case of *Laugh In*) or who had been out of television work for some years and wanted to return only on their own terms (as in *All in the Family* and *United States*). The third prediction was supported as a corollary to the first two, since it suggested that the coming together of an unestablished production firm with a network experiencing extraordinary problems or changes most favors the development and airing of unconventional shows. Consonant with the fourth prediction, the acceptances of two of the unconventional shows *(All in the Family* and *United States)* at the network level were linked directly to the accession of new network presidents. The other unconventional show *(Laugh In)*, while not illustrating the consequence of a new president's arrival, did exemplify the case of an executive risking his current position to move to a more powerful one as a direct result of championing an unconventional program. Supporting the fifth hypothesis, all three unconventional shows moved through different network-related development routes than did their conventional counterparts; and, supporting the sixth hypothesis, the unconventional shows took a much longer time to move from the initial program suggestion to completion for network airing.

At the same time that the findings supported various hypotheses about the conditions encouraging unconventional innovation, they also implied that risk-taking under those conditions would only go so far. One recurrent theme was network reluctance to air unorthodox shows in favorable time slots. Larry Gelbart's comment about the euthanasic scheduling of *United States* echoed comments by the producers of *Rowan and Martin's Laugh In* and *All in the Family* about the unfortunate scheduling of their programs. Such statements might be dismissed as theatrical posturings by creators remembering anxious times. However, the comments of more dispassionate observers and the circumstances surrounding the airing of those programs do suggest that the unconventional series, much more than the conventional ones, evoked strong ambivalences in network schedulers. The programs were clearly unorthodox, and while key executives had taken the risk of buying them, those same executives and their program committees were hesitant about risking attractive—and valuable—time slots when airing them.

More important with respect to hesitations in network risk-taking was a feature of network program acceptance that implied severe limits on the range of unfamiliar approaches likely in unconventional shows on commercial television. That feature was the relatively small web of interpersonal relationships which dominated the process. Even in this study of only six programs, certain names—Grant Tinker, Perry Lafferty, Sam Cohn, Norman Lear, and others—recurred across time and across networks. Past activities and past acquaintances were keys to membership in the web—and to present potential. Professional friendships were often crucial to initiating or facilitating network interest or acceptance. It is, for example, important to recall that for both the conventional and unconventional shows, all of the principals involved at the production and network levels had considerable experience in the entertainment industry, and most had known one another prior to that program involvement.

This web of relationships serves an important function. Choosing producers from within it helps protect network executives from the ultimate risk—not having technically acceptable products delivered to them on time. One fairly new member of this web (brought in through friendship with a producer) voiced the accepted rationale for it:

> There just aren't that many people who have the experience of putting on a TV show with all of the complexities that are required: knowing whom to hire,

knowing whom to get to control the budget, knowing what studio to go to, what film house, what tape editing place—all the details that can get the work done on time, on schedule, and close to budget.

Yet, while this web of relationships does seem to allow network executives to rest easy about having a show delivered on time, it also seems to function (intentionally or not) to limit even unconventional "risk taking" to producers who have developed at least some track record within the entertainment community. Implicitly, these producers have indicated that, despite their unconventionality, they understand and follow many of the commonly accepted values and procedures of popular entertainment. By choosing people whom they consider, in some sense at least, "safe" producers of "entertainment," the networks imply a rather severe limit on the range of experimentation and unorthodoxy they will accept even in their unconventional shows.

This suggestion warrants a good deal more investigation. In fact, the findings and tentative generalizations of this comparative case study open a multitude of questions and research directions on the meaning of unconventionality in various mass media and the conditions that foster it. While the wellspring of unconventionally creative ideas is likely to be an individual (Wainwright and Gerlack, 1968: 12), the encouragement of such ideas, their development, and their implementation are likely to relate intimately to the social and organizational contexts in which those individuals exist. Understanding these factors and their interrelationships will move researchers a long way toward understanding the reasons for change and continuity in mass media.

# NOTES

1. The author gratefully acknowledges the following people who consented to interviews: Marvin Antonowsky, Jimmy Baker, Frank Barton, Al Burton, Dick Clair, Sam Cohn, Michael Dann, Ed Friendly, Larry Gelbart, Paul Keyes, Dianne Kirgo, Perry Lafferty, Norman Lear, Gary Markowitz, Dick Martin, Jerry Mayer, Glen Padnick, David Panich, Marty Ragaway, John Rich, George Schlatter, William Self, Stuart Sheslow, Danny Simon, Gary Smith, Ben Starr, Russ Stonam, David Swift, Grant Tinker, Sid Vinedge, Dighby Wolfe, and Robert Wood.

2. One finding, which might be expected in organizational research (see, for example, Spencer and Dale, 1979), was that different sources presented somewhat different versions of the same events. In some cases, factual contradictions arose. In others, different opinions about the meaning of events were presented. It is significant, perhaps, that most of these conflicts related to the unconventional shows that were successful—*Laugh In* and *All in the Family*. Despite these problems, the accounts of each program's genesis converged with respect to perspectives and incidents relevant to this study, and so allowed investigation of the hypotheses.

3. Unless otherwise noted, all quotations are taken from the author's interview with the person quoted.

4. Sheslow suspected that Silverman's reference to girls was to give the show a conceptual separation from *Different Strokes,* which dealt with boys.

# REFERENCES

ADLER, R. (1979) All in the Family: A critical appraisal. New York: Praeger.

BALDWIN, T. and C. LEWIS (1972) "Violence in television: the industry looks at itself," in G. Comstock and E. Rubinstein (eds.) Television and Social Behavior. Washington, DC: Government Printing Office.

BARNOUW, E. (1975) Tube of Plenty. New York: Oxford University Press.

BARTHEL, J. (1968) "Hilarious, brash, flat, peppery, repetitious, topical, and in borderline taste." New York Times Magazine (October 6): 154.

BROWN, L. (1971) Television: The Business Behind the Box. New York: Harcourt Brace Jovanovich.

BURNS, T. and G. STALKER (1961) The Management of Innovation. London: Tavistock.

CANTOR, M. (1972) "The role of the producer in choosing television content," in G. Comstock and E. Rubinstein (eds.) Television and Social Behavior. Washington, DC: Government Printing Office.

———— (1980) Prime-Time Television. Beverly Hills: Sage.

CRANE, D. (1976) "Reward systems in art, science, and religion." American Behavioral Scientist 19 (July-August): 719-734.

DIETZ, L. (1968) "Where TV comedy is at." Saturday Evening Post (November 30): 32-37.

DiMAGGIO, P. and P. HIRSCH (1976) "Production organizations in the arts." American Behavioral Scientist, 19 (August): 735-752.

DOWNS, A. (1967) Inside Bureaucracy. Boston: Little, Brown.

EVAN, W. (1976) Organization Theory: Structures, Systems, and Environments. New York: John Wiley.

HIRSCH, P. (1972) "Processing fads and fashions: an organization-set analysis of cultural industry systems." American Journal of Sociology 77 (January): 639-659.

JOHNSON, C. (1970) "Dying is not an option." Innovation 18: 40-45.

KHANDWALLA, P. N. (1977) "The design of invention and innovation," in P. N. Khandwalla (ed.) The Design of Organizations. New York: Harcourt Brace Jovanovich.

MARCH, J. and H. SIMON (1958) Organizations. New York: John Wiley.

MARQUIS, D. (1976) "The anatomy of successful innovations," in R. Rothberg (ed.) Corporate Strategy and Product Innovation. New York: The Free Press.

MELODY, W. (1973) Children's Television: The Economics of Exploitation. New Haven: Yale University Press.

National Industrial Conference Board (1967) The Challenge of Innovation. New York: National Industrial Conference Board.

Panel on Invention and Innovation (1967) Technological Innovation: Its Environment and Management. Washington, DC: Government Printing Office.

PERROW, C. (1980) Complex organizations. Glenview, IL: Scott, Foresman.

PETERSON, R. (1976) "The production of culture: a prolegomenon." American Behavioral Scientist 19 (July-August): 667-669.

_____ and D. BERGER (1975) "Cycles in symbol production: the case of popular music." American Sociological Review 40 (April): 158-173.

ROGERS, E. M. and R. ROGERS (1976) Communication in Organizations. New York: The Free Press.

ROTHBERG, R. (1976) "Product Innovation in perspective," in R. Rothberg (ed.) Corporate Strategy and Product Innovation. New York: The Free Press.

SCHON, D. (1966) "The fear of innovation." International Science and Technology 14 (November): 70-78.

SHANKS, B. (1976) The Cool Fire: How to Make it in Television. New York: Vintage.

SPENCER, L. and A. DALE (1979) "Integration and regulation in organizations: a contextual approach." Sociological Review 27 (Winter): 679-702.

STEELE, L. (1975) Innovation in Big Business. New York: Elsevier.

TUCHMAN, G. (1974) "Assembling a network talk show," in G. Tuchman (ed.) The TV Establishment. Englewood Cliffs, NJ: Prentice-Hall.

TUROW, J. (1980) "Television sponsorship forms and program subject matter." Journal of Broadcasting 24 (Summer): 381-397.

_____ (1978) "Casting for television: the anatomy of social typing." Journal of Communication 28 (Autumn): 18-24.

WAINRIGHT, C. and J. GERLACH (1968) Successful Management of New Products. New York: Communication Arts.

YOUNG, R. (1970) "No room for the searcher." Innovation 10: 50-56.

Chapter 7

# COPING WITH TELEVISION PRODUCTION

## Robert Pekurny

THE TASK OF THOSE who produce commercial television is, of course, to generate programming which can hold an audience for advertisers hour after hour, day after day, week after week. This is no easy task, due first to the difficulty of predicting the behavior of both the viewing public and competitors and, second, to the relatively nonroutine nature of the production process itself. In the language of organizational theory, the television industry exhibits environmental turbulence (Emery and Trist, 1965) as well as a relatively nonroutine core technology (Thompson, 1967; Perrow, 1967).

When organizations must contend with rapidly changing or otherwise unpredictable environments and nonroutine production processes, they may resort to "inspirational strategies" (Thompson and Tuden, 1959; Thompson, 1967) in which management "draws upon the residue of unanalyzed experience or intuition or relies upon chance and guesswork" to make decisions (Peterson and Berger, 1971: 97). Organization theory predicts, however, that organizations operating under the norms of rationality will attempt to develop mechanisms, structures, and strategies which render the environment more manageable or at least more predictable and the technology more routine (Thompson, 1967). Hirsch (1972), for example, has analyzed the mechanisms by which the recording industry has attempted to cope with its environment. These include deployment of "A and R" (artist and repertoire) men to locate new talent and the cooptation of those who determine radio stations' play lists. In the same vein, the television industry has developed such mechanisms as reliance upon track record producers whose past work has proven successful and ratings which monitor, if not predict, the public's viewing behavior.

AUTHOR'S NOTE: The research reported here was made possible by grants from the John and Mary R. Markle Foundation and the Northwestern University Office of Research and Sponsored Programs.

Still, such mechanisms may not—and often simply cannot—alleviate the problems facing an organization or industry. In comparing the recording industry to the pharmaceutical industry, Hirsch (1975) found that the latter was much more successful in coping with its environment than the former. The pharmaceutical industry, for example, has been more successful in coopting gatekeepers (that is, doctors) than the recording industry has been in coopting its gatekeepers due, in part, to differences in the legal and regulatory constraints upon each industry. The failure of coping mechanisms, then, may force an industry to fall back on inspirational or entrepreneurial strategies as the recording industry has, in fact, been forced to do (Peterson and Berger, 1971).

This chapter examines several coping mechanisms which the commercial television industry uses to help determine the continuation of existing programming (that is, ratings) and to help generate new programming (that is, reliance on track record producers and formulas). The focus is however, not so much on the mechanisms themselves as on the organizational and human factors which affect their success. The essay draws upon interviews with network executives, producers, and actors conducted since 1971 and upon three participant observational studies: a 12-week study of NBC's Broadcast Standards Department in 1974, a three-week study of NBC's *Saturday Night Live* series in 1977-1978 and a 12-week study of the ABC situation comedies produced by Garry Marshall in 1979. From these interviews and observations telling but not atypical examples illustrate the problems of rendering the production of commercial television predictable and routine. Implications for innovation in the industry are drawn to conclude the chapter.

## ORGANIZATIONAL CONTEXT OF TELEVISION PRODUCTION

It may be useful to begin with a brief overview of the organizations which together generate commercial television programming. Most network programming is produced by a limited number of production firms located in the Los Angeles area. Within these firms an executive producer is the overall manager and often the owner and/or "creator" of each series. Many executive producers have several series on the air simultaneously, hence their input into each series may be quite general. Responsibility for each series is, then, delegated to a supervising producer who oversees the writing, casting, preproduction planning, shooting, and editing as well as the budgeting and liaison with the network. Script writers, particularly for situation comedies, are usually members of a writing staff rather than freelancers, and the ranking member of the staff often holds producer-level rank.

The production companies which employ these individuals may be under contract to a studio/supplier such as Universal or Paramount or may be independent. The networks which, in turn, contract with these firms for series have divided their program management into two separate functions: development and current production. Ideas for new series, whether conceived by a production firm or within the network itself, are reviewed by development executives who decide whether or not to "pilot" an episode. Once a series is piloted and purchased it is transferred to the current section of the program department where executives see to it that the casting, writing, and production values of the series remain at the level expected by the network. The broadcast standards department also follows each episode through its various stages of production to be sure that sex, violence and controversial themes are handled within the standards of the network corporation. (For a more complete analysis of this network structure, see Pekurny, 1977.) Each episode of the series must be produced to the program and broadcast standard departments' satisfaction or the network will refuse to take delivery or to pay the license fee for that episode. This situation seldom arises, however.

Garry Marshall's Henderson Productions is typical of these organizational arrangements. During the study of this organization, Marshall had three highly successful situation comedies in production: *Happy Days, Laverne and Shirley* and *Mork and Mindy*. Marshall was the creator-producer of these series and, time permitting, did occasionally do some script rewriting. Each series' major creative activities were controlled by one or more supervising producers who also functioned as head writers. All three shows were licensed to ABC.

## THE RATINGS

Ratings are the basic mechanism which rationalizes the television industry. They organize and integrate the industry by systematizing the relationships among the advertisers, the networks, and the production firms. Specifically, the ratings organize the competition between the networks for the advertisers' dollars by providing both definition and measurement of program success and, more central to this study, the ratings also help regulate the creation and continuation of programming. With the ratings, at least, the industry has a reasonably well organized game to play—a game played with the life and death of shows. Still, the game is not always played by its own rules and realistically it cannot be because the ratings really do not provide very much information with which to play.

**THE LIFE AND DEATH OF PROGRAMS**

Contrary to the laments of stars whose series have been cancelled, the networks do not always make hard and fast decisions regarding program continuation and cancellation based on the ratings. The lowest rated shows are not all cancelled while some moderately successful shows are dropped. The decision not to cancel a low-rated series may be based on a contractual obligation to the supplier or other legal/financial criteria but it may also be based on an audience-related criterion about which the ratings can provide little information: the series' potential for audience growth. This is, in principle, a sound criterion for program continuation but it is, in practice, difficult to apply.

A case in point is the ABC series *The Hardy Boys Mysteries* which ran in 1977-1978 on an alternating basis with *The Nancy Drew Mysteries*. Despite the fact that Nancy Drew outrated the Hardy Boys, ABC combined the two series into *The Hardy Boys-Nancy Drew Mysteries* and eventually dropped the Nancy Drew episodes entirely. In addition, the series developed a sort of schizophrenia: some of the episodes fit the classic Hardy Boys mystery novel format while others featured the star, Shaun Cassidy, approximating his real life persona as a teen-idol rock star. When interviewed, a production company executive said that he was not aware of this pattern but after reviewing several episodes agreed that it was, in fact, present. The ABC programming executive in charge of the series also had not noticed the pattern until interviewed. He said, however, he was sure that the production company was purposefully experimenting with various directions for the series. Earlier, the production company member asked that the network not be told there was no purposeful plan and that things were just happening without design.

ABC renewed the series in part because it thought the supplier, Universal Studios, saw potential in it. ABC also felt that Shaun Cassidy, who was receiving a great deal of attention from the print media thanks to his singing career, would somehow deliver an acceptable share of the audience. This belief persisted despite the absence of any research to support it and despite the fact that an analysis of the size of his teenage audience would indicate that it was not sufficient to deliver that elusive 30 percent share of the audience (see Pekurny, 1979). Shaun Cassidy himself assumed that the production company had a game plan for the series which was also acceptable to ABC. In reality, the decisions that led to renewal of the series were based at least partially upon incorrect inferences and just plain wishful thinking—hardly the cold and calculating decision-making process so commonly assumed. Ratings do not, then, regulate the continuation and cancellation of series quite as mechanically as might be imagined, in part, because they offer no information about the potential of a series. "Inspiration"—of a sort—does play a role in the life and death of programs.

## RATINGS AS FEEDBACK

The popular, if not quite correct, image of ratings as the mechanical executioner of programs exists side-by-side with the network-promoted image of ratings as Feedback From The People. Ratings do indeed monitor the response of a cross-section of the public to programming. If, however, the notion of feedback implies the use of ratings to adjust or improve existing programming, then the ratings leave much to be desired as feedback. Ratings, first of all, can say no more about how to improve programs than they can about the potential audience for programs. Further, ratings are not synchronized very closely to the production cycle. A large number of shows are usually produced before the first of them is aired and ratings received. Finally, the procedures for making programming adjustments are not well defined. Together these factors make it very difficult to use ratings to fine-tune programs. From time to time the industry does try, however.

When beginning work on the second season of *Mork and Mindy*, the star, Robin Williams, as well as the producers and writers, desired more "meaningful" scripts than were done in that series' first season. Based on their own wishes to creatively explore new areas, the cast and staff consciously wrote and produced a different type of script. About 10 episodes of the season's total of 26 were produced in this new style by the time the first episode of the second season aired in September, 1979. Over the first few weeks, the series progressively lost ground in its week-to-week ratings battle with *Archie's Place* on CBS.

Panicked by the ratings slippage of *Mork and Mindy* and the other Marshall series on the ABC schedule, ABC programming executives got more actively involved in the scripting process. The network program department reduced the creative freedom previously granted and demanded story lines which were more "promotable." Guests such as Raquel Welch were booked and plot lines involving football cheerleaders, nude magazine photo layouts, and burlesque shows were developed for all three Marshall series. To get these "promotable" episodes produced and aired, the ABC program department had to prevail upon high level corporate executives to override the objections of the broadcast standards department. These shows did not improve the ratings, however, and the broadcast standards department reasserted itself. The program department retreated leaving the production company to find the proper direction for all three Marshall series, especially *Mork and Mindy*. At the end of *Mork and Mindy's* second season production cycle members of the production company and the program department executive involved said that they had learned their lesson and would make the third season more like the first.

This incident illustrates several of the problems which arise when ratings are used to "adjust" series content. Producers invariably claim that networks leave successful shows alone but meddle with a show "as soon as they smell blood." This does indeed seem to be the case. The creative freedom of even a proven producer like Marshall ebbs and flows with the weekly ratings of his series. Further, the network intervention often occurs in an atmosphere of panic. A number of shows are shot before the season begins and so the network must usually sit helplessly by watching the ratings as these shows are aired. The network may then overreact in attempting to "adjust" the season's remaining shows. In this case ABC veered violently away from the early "meaningful" episodes and when this did not work gave up and returned control to the production firm.

Another problem of using ratings to adjust content illustrated by this case is determining exactly what to adjust. Recently, the ABC program department, as well as that of NBC, asked production firms not for entirely new scripts but rather for the inclusion of "promotable" footage featuring "action" or suggestive situations which can be edited into promotional spot advertisements. Ratings are, then, more often used to adjust the sales pitch than the product for sale.

### THE REAL FEEDBACK SYSTEM

From the preceding discussion and examples it is clear that ratings do not offer very much information that is useful in creating or improving programs. Industry personnel do, however, have access to a rich source of feedback concerning their work. In interviews, network executives and producers have generally agreed that if in each season a series has one-third good episodes, one-third fair episodes, and one-third poor episodes then its producers and writers are doing well. The judgments of episode quality which allow these personnel to monitor their success in meeting this criteria are *not* those of the home viewing audience. Indeed, the home audience is seldom mentioned by industry personnel, particularly the producers and writers, as they go about their business. The real audience for producers and writers consists of the cast members, the executive producer, and network executives. The executive producer and network executives, in turn, are concerned with whether or not a script or completed show fits the series formula, duplicates a plot to be used on another series, contains material harmful to the commercial success or longevity of a particular character or the series itself, and meets network taste standards. Hazy notions of what the home audience will or will not like do loom behind these concerns but those notions are only the imaginary feedback postulated by DiMaggio and Hirsch (1976: 742).

> The etiology of conventions about what is and is not permissible (or, more broadly, 'commercial') remains one of the sociology of art's outstanding mysteries, for culture-producing organizations do remarkably little research on the taste preferences of their publics. Most decisions appear to be based on what might best be called 'imaginary feedback loops'—expectations about what a market, middleman, or federal or state agency *might* do if a certain line is crossed, a certain taboo violated.

The writers, producers, cast and network executives form a feedback system which is essentially closed to the outside. This is the real feedback system.

The sort of issues and concerns which flow through this internal feedback system are illustrated by exchanges between the network and the production firm concerning an episode of *Mork and Mindy*. The premiere episode of the series' second season featured Mork's descent into a parallel universe populated by characters similar to those in his earthly environment. The climax was the death of Mandy, Mindy's counterpart (played by Pam Dawber in a dual role). After the episode had been shot, the death scene generated extensive discussions between the executive producer, Garry Marshall; other producer-rank personnel; the star, Robin Williams; and an ABC program department executive. Williams and the producers who had written the script wanted the scene included as shot. The network executive, on the other hand, felt that the scenes had been played too powerfully by Williams, causing it to "lose its fantasy." The executive did not, however, want the scene eliminated because the footage of Pam Dawber's death would be valuable in promotional spots for the episode. In addition, he felt that it was necessary to kill off Mandy with whom Mork had fallen in love so that Mork's relationship with Mindy could fully resume in later episodes. Marshall himself decided the issue when he concluded that the scene was not only too powerfully acted but poorly shot as well. Marshall personally supervised the reshooting and editing of the scene in a toned down version.

In summary, the creative process which yields program content is one that is fraught with incomplete use of limited feedback from the ultimate home viewing audience. As Cantor (1980: 102) states, "The system as it exists may be the most efficient for reaching the audience desired, but it allows little direct input from the audience into the creative process." This void is filled by internal feedback loops which link the producer, writer, studio and network. Thus, a writer must satisfy the expectations of his producer, who must fulfill those of the creator-executive producer, who must fulfill those of the studio, who must fulfill those of network executives. Members of the production chain seldom think more than one step ahead of themselves on the organizational ladder, for the pressure to produce 22 episodes a season does not allow for—nor does the present system require—such an overview.

## TRACK RECORDS

Television's voracious appetite for new material is legendary. Only a few producers are, however, allowed by the networks to feed it. These are usually the producers with "track records." A track record is the history of successful shows which a creator or production company head brings with him when he "pitches" a new show idea to a network. While the past success of a creator is an eminently reasonable criterion for selecting programs when the audience appeal cannot otherwise be anticipated, the use of this criterion is not without problems of its own.

### TRACK RECORD AS RITUAL

Track records of producers are often used blindly or ritualistically by network program executives in decision-making. Fred Silverman, president of NBC, bought a series called *Who's Watching the Kids?* from the Marshall organization instead of another series from a different producer even though Marshall's offering was merely a retread of *Blansky's Beauties* which had already failed on ABC. It may have been that Silverman bought the series believing not that it would succeed but rather that it would give him access to a future Marshall series (that is, a future draft pick). While Silverman's judgment in this case may not have been entirely clouded by Marshall's track record, it is not uncommon for networks to buy a pilot or program in which they have little confidence but which is supplied by a track record producer. The rationale for this, according to Marshall himself, is that program failure is more easily justified to superiors if the program came from a track record producer.

Marshall's argument was compellingly illustrated in a brief conversation with an NBC program department executive who was in charge of a new Norman Lear series, *The Dumplings*. The executive said that he doubted the public would buy the premise of two overweight people who were madly in love with each other. The program had been purchased, however, because it was the only product which Lear had offered to NBC in a long time and the network could not afford to pass it up. The executive said that by purchasing the series he did not have to worry about the Wednesday 9:30-10:00 time slot for the next thirteen weeks and if the series failed as he expected, he would merely tell his superiors "How was I to know that Norman Lear would have a flop?" No matter what happened, the choice of a series from a track record producer would keep him out of trouble "career-wise." Programmers thus use track records much as journalists use the conventions of objectivity, according to Tuchman (1972), track records are ritualistic protection from future criticism and adverse consequences "career-wise."

### NEW TALENT

Several recent developments have further stimulated television's appetite for new material. The computerization of the ratings services which allow overnight results and the increased cost of network advertising time have led advertisers to demand—and get—faster replacement of series not garnering acceptable ratings. This has led to several television "seasons" each year with more new series than in the past and thus to greater pressure on the limited number of track record producers to provide more new material. And this, in turn, has helped to subvert whatever logic the extensive reliance on track record producers may contain.

Of course, the more programs a track record producer supplies the less time he has to spend with each program. The networks are, then, getting less of the producer's work and more of that of his proteges to whom production responsibilities have been delegated. At the same time, these proteges are getting less training from the executive producer who is usually the creator of the formula which the proteges must master. One young producer in the Marshall organization highlighted this problem:

> The one regret I have is the time I've spent here has been during the period when Garry has been busy doing other things. I haven't gotten to learn as much as I know I could have learned from Garry because every time he comes [to do work on *Laverne and Shirley*] I learn something. Basically the only time he would come to me is when we're in trouble or when we really don't feel too good about something. . . . We don't see him a whole lot [on *Laverne and Shirley*]. We saw him a lot when we worked on *Blansky's Beauties*.

Marshall and network executives as well as the proteges express regret about this situation, but the short-term concern of feeding television new series overrides the long-term concern of developing new talent.

### FORMULAS

Formulas help the industry cope with the problem of generating new material much as the use of track records do—what has worked in the past may work again:

The usual answer to this problem [chronic shortage of new material], of course, has been to re-use the same, basic artistic elements again and again, refurbishing and re-combining them so as to lend the newer versions the required appearance of novelty. . . . The creative task now becomes that of fitting these elements together (no doubt with the addition of some genuinely new components) into a satisfactory gestalt. . . . Saleability may also, of course, be more easily guaranteed if story elements already tested in the market are employed. Today, television series and serials probably embody the principle in its most obvious form [Brown, 1968, 617].

Garry Marshall's situation comedies, for example, all have certain general elements in common. First, the series are all meant to be viewed by children and adults together and so violence and other anti-social content is deemphasized while pro-social content (such as borrowing books from the library) are played up. Second, the plots are simple for the benefit of young children. Third, each series has at least one key character who is the messenger of pro-social values. Fourth, there is some "ticker," heart, or warmth in each episode among the characters. Finally, there must be a joke or bit of business at work about every minute or so.

Each of the Marshall series is a variation of these general elements with its own specific formula of characters, typical plot lines and standing jokes. For example, *Mork and Mindy,* which Marshall describes as "far out, off the wall" is also a social comedy which he has long wanted to do in prime time. The series examines such topics as emotions, death, politics, and fads through the naive yet insightful eyes of Mork from the planet Ork. Mindy provides a more normal frame of reference and together Mork and Mindy are the messengers of pro-social values. Still, the show is full of wild physical comedy, puns, topical humor, and running gags as well as catch phrases such as "shazbat" which are specifically intended to attract children.

The formula may well be the one coping mechanism reviewed here which operates much as is commonly supposed. Formulas do provide a theme which writers and producers can play out in slight but endless variations and they really do help routinize the task of generating television content. NBC's *Saturday Night Live* provides a good case in point because it set out to avoid reliance upon specific formulas. When it began, the show's general formula, if one existed, was simply to satirize society and the formulas of commercial television in particular. Beyond this, the producer, Lorne Michaels, the writers, and the cast deliberately set out to avoid specific formulas of their own. This intention was highlighted by Michaels' selection of writers and cast who had little television experience and by the aphorism: "if it might be done on the *Carol Burnett Show* we won't do it here."

In the middle of the show's third season Michaels and the writers said that they would probably leave the series at the end of the season. They expressed pride in not falling prey to the repetitiousness of formula television, citing as an example how they had boldly killed off their most popular characters. By the end of that season, however, the producer, writers, and cast had all negotiated deals with the network which gave them salaries not unlike those of their prime-time Hollywood counterparts. Not only had the staff returned but so had the popular characters.

Thus we once again saw Emily Latella misunderstand editorials on "Weekend Update," the Samurai warrior find new occupational roles, the Coneheads return from their planet, and the Nerds fail at yet another aspect of life. In a conversation, one of the writers reluctantly agreed that these characters and situations had, indeed, become the *Saturday Night Live* formula and explained, "We found it easier to write for familiar characters in different settings than to create new characters." The show continued for several more successful seasons operating under its proven and workable formula. (See Pekurny, 1980, for further discussion of the series.)

## IMPLICATIONS FOR CREATIVITY AND INNOVATION

It is clear that the mechanisms which make the generation of television programming more predictable and routine may be charged with inhibiting creativity and stifling the unconventional. The case against ratings in this regard has, for example, been made time and again. A key point of this study has been, however, that the ratings are not always mechanically applied in determining the life and death of shows. If unconventional shows are not likely to fare well in the ratings, at least initially, then this looseness in the application of the ratings criteria may occasionally allow unconventional shows to survive long enough to build an audience. While few would argue that the *Hardy Boys* series reviewed here deserved to survive because of its artistic merit, the history of television does offer a number of shows which survived low ratings and near cancellation to go on to both commercial success and critical acclaim. These include *Lou Grant, All in the Family, M\*A\*S\*H,* and the original *The Dick Van Dyke Show.* In the cases of *M\*A\*S\*H* and *The Dick Van Dyke Show,* the shows survived because their stars fought for them. Turow (in the present volume) argues that unconventional shows are generated outside of the normal channels. It may also be that the survival of such shows is determined outside of normal channels and the usual ratings criteria.

Like ratings, the track record syndrome may be credited with inhibiting the unconventional. Strict adherence to the use of track records certainly has led to a limitation in the number of program suppliers and perhaps also an inbreeding of program ideas. Yet this same mechanism can also lead to an occasional innovation. As ABC executives sat in New York plotting the 1978-1979 schedule, they decided to call Marshall to see what ideas he might have. Marshall pitched them an idea and without seeing a pilot, script, or even official proposal, ABC commissioned the series, passing over the pilots of other, less established producers. Marshall was thus able to get a "social comedy" which he had always wanted to do on the air. The series, *Mork and Mindy,* went on to both commercial and critical success in 1978.

A track record can, then, provide a producer the opportunity to get away with something a little bit different once in a while. Turow's argument that it is producers outside the mainstream of television production who are likely to develop unconventional programs, suggests that track record producers with programs currently on the air such as Marshall may not use this opportunity very often. Perhaps this is because the demands of producing the ongoing shows and developing an occasional spinoff occupy most of their time. Still, a track record can mean the power to innovate if the producer is able to use it.

Formulas, like the uncritical use of track record producers, are likely to simply give us "more of the same." But here too there is an alternative possibility which Brown (1968: 618) has cogently argued:

> By saying that the plots of film westerns or of television series tend to be "stereotyped," a negative note is struck immediately. However, the fact that a number of the necessary elements are provided for the writer when he comes to prepare the script for a new film or new programme may potentially be an artistic advantage. In one sense, the creative task is made simpler, since a number of constraints are already present: but this may allow the writer to concentrate more on the remaining tasks. Again, over time, it may be possible to explore all the permutations and combinations which the elements provided permit, and to discover which are artistically effective and which failures. Perhaps the position of the mass media artist working with already provided artistic elements is not so dissimilar in this respect to that of many hundreds of "serious" artists who have worked within established traditions in the past. Most artists, in fact, make use of established formulae, whether it is the structure of the Elizabethan sonnet, drawing in perspective, the sonata form, or the twelve-tone scale. . . . Popular culture has its traditions, just as much as the "high" arts: it is the way that the tradition is used which is all-important, not the fact that a tradition exists. And the popular work which explores beyond the bounds of the tradition perhaps gains force from the very tension set up between the conventions and the departures from it.

Writers—sometimes very good ones—must still create flesh to cover the bones of the formula and there is always the possibility that a particular embodiment of a formula will transcend that formula. Such scripts may not often survive to production but the use of a formula, as Brown argues, does not preclude the *possibility* that they will be written.

In summary, there is the possibility of creativity and innovation in commercial television because, thanks to both organizational and human factors, ratings, reliance on track records and the use of formulas do not—and, in fact, cannot—completely routinize the television production process. A certain amount of inspiration or entrepreneurship is still necessary. If reliance upon inspirational strategies represents an *organizational* failure of the industry, it also represents the opportunity for occasional *cultural* success. It is the sad, yet somehow sweet, irony of television that the industry produces these successes despite itself.

# REFERENCES

BROWN, R. L. (1968) "The creative process in the popular arts." International Social Science Journal 20: 613-624.

CANTOR, M. G. (1980) Prime-Time Television, Content and Control. Beverly Hills: Sage.

DiMAGGIO, P. and P. M. HIRSCH (1976) "Production organizations in the arts." American Behavioral Scientist, 19: 735-752.

EMERY, F. C. and E. L. TRIST (1965) "The causal texture of organizational environments." Human Relations 18: 21-31.

HIRSCH, P. M. (1972) "Processing fads and fashions: an organization-set analysis of cultural industry systems." American Journal of Sociology 77: 639-659.

———— (1975) "Organizational effectiveness and the institutional environment." Administrative Science Quarterly 20: 327-344.

PEKURNY, R. G. (1977) "Broadcast self-regulation: a participant observation study of the National Broadcasting Company's broadcast standards department." Ph.D. dissertation, University of Minnesota.

———— (1979) "How the media interact to create a star." Presented to the Speech Communication Association Annual Convention, San Antonio, Texas.

———— (1980) "The production process and environment of NBC's *Saturday Night Live*," Journal of Broadcasting 24: 91-99.

PERROW, C. (1967) "A framework for the comparative analysis of organizations." American Sociological Review 32: 194-208.

PETERSON, R. A. and D. G. BERGER (1971) "Entrepreneurship in organizations: evidence from the popular music industry." Administrative Science Quarterly 16: 97-106.

THOMPSON, J. (1967) Organizations in Action. New York: McGraw-Hill.

———— and A. TUDEN (1959) "Strategies, structures and processes of organizational decision." In J. Thompson et al. (eds.) Comparative Studies in Administration. Pittsburgh: University of Pittsburgh.

TUCHMAN, G. (1972) "Objectivity as strategic ritual." American Journal of Sociology 77: 660-679.

# Chapter 8

# PRINT OR BROADCAST
## How the Medium Influences the Reporter

**Lee B. Becker**

THAT THE MASS MEDIA differ in terms of the technologies employed for dissemination of messages is an obvious point. The implications of that observation, however, have not received the attention by journalism and mass communication researchers studying reporters and other news employees that they might. For the most part, the dominant view is that a reporter is a reporter is a reporter.

There are good reasons for challenging, or at least fully examining, that view. First, even casual observations of the training of journalists—particularly in the United States—and the career patterns these journalists follow suggest distinctiveness between the print and broadcast sectors. Most U.S. schools of journalism differentiate between career goals and designate partially distinct "sequences" or programs of study for print and broadcast students.

Some evidence suggests these students then go to industries producing rather distinct news products. In recent years, critics of television have argued that television news is more negative and conflictual than newspaper news, is more likely to focus on images and impressions at the expense of substantive data, and is more likely to be artificially balanced to present both sides of issues even when one side is clearly unequal to another. In short, print and broadcast news reports are seen as differing significantly in terms of structural and stylistic factors.

AUTHOR'S NOTE: The author wishes to thank John W. C. Johnstone, Professor of Sociology, University of Illinois at Chicago Circle, for making his data available for the secondary analysis reported here. The assistance of former doctoral students Idowu A. Sobowale, Robin E. Cobbey, and Jeffrey W. Fruit also is acknowledged.

## RELEVANT LITERATURE

The suggestions that print and broadcast reporters might behave differently or might have different views of the journalistic profession might well be treated as blase in Europe, where the broadcast media historically have played a different role from the commercial print industry. In the United States, however, the working assumption for many observers of the media is that journalists do pretty much the same thing regardless of whether they work for print or for broadcast. As members of a single profession, they deal with the common commodity of news in a similar fashion.

In fact, in the early days of broadcast news there was significant overlap between print and broadcasting, as owners of newspapers became involved in the broadcasting industry and some print newsroom employees moved to jobs in broadcasting. Some of the dominant news figures in U.S. broadcasting either started or spent significant amounts of time in newspaper work before moving to radio and/or television. Walter Cronkite, who worked for the Scripps-Howard organization and United Press before moving to CBS after World War II, is a prominent example. Eric Sevareid, a reporter for the Paris edition of the New York Herald-Tribune before moving to CBS in 1939, is yet another.

This interaction between print and broadcast, however, is a thing of the past. Federal regulatory pressures have limited print and broadcast joint ownership. And available data show that it is rare for news personnel to move from print to broadcast operations or vice versa today.

In fact, the national journalistic data gathered by Johnstone, Slawski, and Bowman (1976) show that although there is considerable mobility in journalism, only about 5 percent of the moves identified in the career patterns of journalists studied involved print/broadcast crossovers. And there are interesting differences among the divisions of the industry. Turnover is considerably higher in the broadcast sector than in the print sector, for example. And television news is much less likely to hire new employees without prior news experience than are other segments of the industry.

These findings suggest that it may be meaningful to view reporters working for the print and broadcast sectors as members of two rather distinct subgroups of the journalistic profession. This is a conclusion reinforced by a study by Becker and Dimmick (1980) of recruitment and personnel policies of selected media organizations. Scattered throughout the detailed interviews with persons in charge of hiring at the various organizations were references to the distinctiveness of the needs of the broadcast and print sectors. The print decision-makers were looking for applicants particularly facile in use of language, recognizing that the final product required of them is a detailed, written version of the news. Those in charge of broadcast personnel decision-making, on the other hand, were interested in persons capable of writing concisely in a way which would complement the oral or visual forms of the industry. Writing for the eye and writing for the ear, these managers said, are not the same. And while there was recognition that journalists share some common orientations to news regardless of medium, the differences in skills required were enough to make all wary of recruiting across media.

The news product of the broadcast industry, and particularly television, is distinct from the news product of the print news industry. These differences go beyond matters of simple style. To a considerable extent, these arguments about differences in the news products of the industries have been used to explain findings that persons dependent on television for their news, when compared with persons dependent on newspapers, are found to be less knowledgeable about public affairs (Wade and Schramm, 1969; Robinson, 1977a; Clarke and Fredin, 1978; Becker, Sobowale, and Casey, 1979; Becker and Fruit; 1979; Becker and Whitney, 1980) and, in some cases, more critical in their evaluations of government and its leaders (Robinson, 1975, 1976, 1977b; Robinson and Zukin, 1976; Becker and Whitney, 1980).

These differential effects have been attributed by some researchers to the tendency of television to focus on peripheral aspects of the news, often as a result of its search for exciting visuals (Harney and Stone, 1969; Lowry, 1971; Wamsley and Price, 1972; Epstein, 1973; Frank, 1973; Lefever, 1974; Carey, 1976; Patterson and McClure, 1976; Patterson, 1977; Robinson and McPherson, 1977; Hofstetter and Zukin, 1979). Robinson (1975) has been most pointed in his criticism. He argues that television news focuses on conflict, is impressionistic, forces balance in presentation of unequal viewpoints, and emphasizes problems at the expense of solutions. Weaver (1975) has argued that television and newspapers employ strikingly different organizational principles and styles in assemblage of the news. The former seeks a more unified presentation of the day's events than the latter. The television style also implies a personal style of journalism; newspapers employ a style of detachment emphasized by techniques removing the reporter and writer from the story being told.

It should be noted, of course, that the broadcast industry is not monolithic. The Becker and Dimmick (1980) analyses underscored differences between television and radio personnel needs, resulting primarily from the emphasis in television on visuals and the sole use of audio messages in radio. Powers (1977) similarly noted differences in the ways the national television networks and the local television stations handle news. And a recent study by Golding and Elliott (1979) has noted that cross-national comparisons of broadcast news operations can serve to illustrate similarities and differences in the ways news is handled by organizations.

Print news organizations, similarly, can differ quite strikingly. Johnstone, Slawski, and Bowman (1976), for example, note distinct mobility patterns for the national news magazines compared with both weekly and daily newspapers. And a separate analysis of these same data by Johnstone (1976) illustrated the significance of size of the organization in understanding newsroom attitudes and behavior.

## SUMMARY AND STATEMENT OF EXPECTATIONS

What, then, are the specific expectations which should guide an examination of potential differences between the personnel of the print media and those working for the broadcast media? What should these journalists have in common? In what ways should they differ?

First, if the news personnel in print and broadcast are really part of the same general profession, they should share general values and orientations toward that profession. In other words, the professional orientations the newspersonnel bring to their newsgathering task should be similar.

Yet, if the messages the news reporters and editors produce are different depending on sector of the media, then the reportorial and writing behaviors of these reporters and editors should differ depending on media type. In other words, the actual newsroom behaviors of the print and broadcast personnel might well be distinct.

## REANALYSIS OF THE JOHNSTONE ET AL. DATA

These two general expectations—of orientational consistency but behavioral distinctiveness—guided a secondary analysis of the national study of U.S. journalists conducted by Johnstone, Slawski, and Bowman (1976). The Johnstone data were selected both because of their availability and because they provide sufficient measures of the orientations of newspersonnel and their practices on the job. The national study, conducted in 1971 and consisting of lengthy telephone interviews with more than 1300 editorial personnel in daily and weekly newspapers, news magazines, wire services, and the news departments of radio and television stations and networks, is the most comprehensive study to date of U.S. journalists.

As noted above, Johnstone and his colleagues already have performed analyses examining differences in the print and broadcast sectors of the news industry. From the point of view of the research questions posed here, however, these analyses are limited in three ways. First, they are not organized to provide as full and complete of a test of the expectations as the data will allow. Second, they are limited to a certain extent by the lack of differentiation of responses by role. Direct comparisons across media type but within role (for example, reporters vs. reporters and editors vs. editors) should prove more meaningful than general comparisons which are confounded to a certain extent by the differences in the level of job differentiation in the industries. Finally, previous analyses have not always controlled for differences in organizational size while making comparisons between print and broadcast operations. Where the size of the organization has been examined (Johnstone, 1976), however, it has been identified as a significant factor in explaining reportorial behavior.

For the data presentations which follow, the decision was made to examine solely the responses of persons who engage in reportorial activity. Managerial personnel, oversampled in the study, and persons engaging solely in editing were excluded. This decision to exclude the managers and editors, rather than perform distinct analyses for them, was made for practical reasons. In general, the questions asked of these individuals were not so clearly relevant to the expectations posed above as those asked of reporters. Since reporters for both the print and broadcast sector actually do the initial writing or story compilation, this group is of prime interest here. The number of journalists interviewed who did news reporting at least once a week was 736.

The survey instrument used by Johnstone and his colleagues was examined and items were selected which might suggest whether reporters for the print and broadcast sectors actually differ in terms of their professional orientation (and therefore should more correctly be viewed as members of two distinct professions rather than a single journalistic profession) and the extent to which they differ in terms of actual reportorial practice.

## RESULTS

Responses to the items from the questionnaire thought to reflect orientations of the reporters to their profession and its role in society are presented in Table 8.1. In the case of newspaper reporters, responses are presented separately for those working for weeklies and those working for dailies. The latter classification is further divided according to the size of the editorial staff of the daily. Broadcast respondents are categorized according to staff size as well, while wire service employees are presented as a single group. The responses of the 11 newsmagazine reporters are not shown in the table because of statistical instability associated with so few respondents.

The categories used for classifying respondents according to the size of the editorial staff were arrived at by examining the distribution of responses in the sample. None of the broadcast respondents was working for an organization employing more than 50 editorial employees, while several of the print journalists worked for organizations employing five times that many editorial staffers. The categorization used here is responsive to the general nature of the distributions and maximizes to the extent possible the size of the key comparison groups. Any categorization would have clustered broadcast respondents at the lower end of the staff size continuum, indicating that comparisons of responses based solely on staff size would be misleading if significant differences between print and broadcast reporters exist.

It was not possible to differentiate in Table 8.1 between the responses of radio and television reporters. In several instances, reporters indicated they worked both for a radio and for a television outlet. Many network correspondents as well as reporters working for radio and television stations with overlapping staffs would fall into such a category. In general, however, since radio staffs are usually much smaller than those of television, the respondents falling into the category for broadcast organizations with from 1 to 10 editorial employees are more likely to be working for radio than to be working for television. Some of the employees in the category, however, may work on small television stations. Respondents in the 11 to 50 category are more likely to be working for television or a network than for radio.

Respondents working for the broadcast wires can write copy for broadcast, print, or both. The responses of wire service reporters are presented here more to fill out the range of possible responses to the criterion variables than for their relevance to the expectations presented.

Entries in the first row of Table 8.1 are based on scores on an index created by summing responses to several items in the questionnaire designed to measure the extent to which the journalists held attitudes generally viewed as consistent with a sociological view of a profession. The four items were similar to those suggested by McLeod and Hawley (1964) and indicated the extent to which reporters felt that autonomy and a chance to serve society were desired characteristics of their work. The items used to form the nonprofessional index asked what importance respondents assigned to pay, fringe benefits, and job security. Responses for this index are presented in the second row in Table 8.1.

Two additional indices were used to measure the respondents' assessment of the proper role of the mass media in society. The first orientation, labeled a "participant" orientation in Table 8.1, measured the extent to which the respondent felt it was important for the media to play an activist role in society, investigating government, providing analysis and interpretation of problems, and playing a role in policy formation. The "neutral" orientation measure indexed respondent acceptance of the view that the media should seek to entertain, avoid controversial content, and concentrate on news of highest interest to audience members. These indices are conceptually similar to those employed by Johnstone and his colleagues (see particularly John-

TABLE 8.1  Professional Orientations of Reporters (in percentages)

| | Newspapers Dailies, staffs of . . . | | | | | | Broadcast Staffs of . . . | | | Wire Service |
|---|---|---|---|---|---|---|---|---|---|---|
| | Wkly. | 1-10 | 11-50 | 51-100 | 101+ | TOTAL | 1-10 | 11-50 | TOTAL | |
| High on index of professional attitudes | 58.6 | 45.0 | 33.6 | 29.3 | 33.3 | 36.7 | 36.4 | 45.0 | 39.9 | 50.0 |
| High on index of nonprofessional attitudes | 31.5 | 47.5 | 34.5 | 27.5 | 34.4 | 33.5 | 46.6 | 36.7 | 42.6* | 33.3 |
| High on index of "participant" attitudes | 42.9 | 32.5 | 28.7 | 32.8 | 52.4 | 40.0 | 13.6 | 45.0 | 26.4* | 47.6 |
| High on index of "neutrality" attitudes | 45.7 | 60.0 | 56.6 | 42.3 | 36.9 | 45.4 | 45.4 | 41.7 | 43.9 | 35.8 |
| Thinking news media doing "outstanding" job of "informing public" | 28.6 | 22.5 | 16.4 | 11.3 | 10.2 | 15.2 | 31.8 | 13.3 | 24.3* | 19.0 |
| Thinking own organization doing "outstanding" job of "informing public" | 17.4 | 7.5 | 8.3 | 10.4 | 10.7 | 10.7 | 24.1 | 8.3 | 17.7* | 26.8 |
| Picking own medium as doing best job of "informing public" | 81.4 | 87.5 | 82.0 | 83.6 | 84.5 | 83.6 | 60.2 | 30.0 | 48.0* | NA |
| "Very satisfied" with present job | 57.1 | 45.0 | 36.9 | 46.5 | 46.0 | 45.4 | 48.8 | 38.3 | 44.5 | 47.6 |
| "Hoping to shift jobs in news industry in 5 yrs. | 20.0 | 27.5 | 32.0 | 25.0 | 16.0 | 23.0 | 33.0 | 40.0 | 35.8* | 14.3 |
| N | 70 | 40 | 122 | 116 | 187 | 535 | 88 | 60 | 148 | 42 |

NOTE: *The entries in the TOTAL columns are significantly different from each other at the .05 level.

e, Slawski and Bowman, 1973), though minor modifications were made in index construction.[1]

For two out of the four comparisons on these indices between responses of print and broadcast respondents significant differences appear. Broadcast journalists score higher on the index of nonprofessional values than print journalists and lower on the index of participant attitudes (see underlined values in the appropriate rows in the table). But these comparisons are deceptive, closer examination reveals.

In fact, the data suggest that broadcast and print reporters are remarkably similar in terms of nonprofessional attitudes when similarly sized organizations are compared.[2] In other words, size of the organization, rather than type of organization, is determinative. But in the case of professional attitudes, an interaction takes place between size and organizational type such that the reporters for the smaller broadcast organizations (probably mostly radio stations) are lower in professional attitudes than reporters for the smallest daily newspapers, while reporters for the larger broadcast organizations are more professionally oriented than reporters for the large dailies.

In a similar fashion, reporters for the small broadcast operations are less likely to accept a participant view of the mass media than reporters for the small dailies, while reporters for the larger broadcast operations were more likely to accept this view than reporters for any but the largest dailies. The neutral stance was more likely to be accepted by the print reporters than the broadcast reporters, when similarly sized organizations are compared.

Broadcast respondents seem to be less critical of the media in general, Table 8.1 shows, though the difference is primarily concentrated in the small organizations. The same is true for the assessment of the performance of the organization for which the respondent works. Broadcast respondents are considerably less likely to pick their own broadcast medium as the one doing the best job of informing the public than print reporters are to pick their own print medium. This is true regardless of size of the organization, though broadcast reporters for the smaller organizations again are less critical of their medium than those for the larger organizations.

There is no evidence that print and broadcast reporters differ from each other in terms of job satisfaction, though there do appear to be some slight differences between reporters of comparably sized print and broadcast organizations in terms of professional commitment. Broadcast reporters seem to be less committed to remaining in the industry than their print counterparts.[3]

In summary, then, the data in Table 8.1 show that print and broadcast respondents do differ from each other in certain ways. Reporters working for small organizations also differ from those working for larger organizations in several respects. This difference is most striking in the comparisons of responses of the broadcast reporters, where size may well be confounded with differences between radio and television news operations. Regardless of the origin of this within-broadcast difference, the data cast at least some doubt on the assumption that reporters for the various media are operating with a common set of attitudes and assumptions about their work, but the differences are striking only in the nonprofessional attitudes.

In addition, the data suggest that in at least some ways, reporters working for the larger broadcast organizations resemble reporters working for print organizations with much larger staffs more than they resemble reporters working for comparably sized print organizations. This is most notable in the comparisons of responses on the indices of participant and neutral orientations. In other words, in some cases, broadcast reporters seem to be thinking "big," despite the fact that their staffs are small. This would seem to make sense if one bears in mind that the larger broadcast organizations are likely to be located in communities which also house the newspapers in the larger size categories employed here.

The degree to which the discovered differences between print and broadcast reporters, as well as those differences among reporters for these two types of organizations, carry over to actual behavioral differences is examined in Table 8.2. Reporters for broadcast are considerably less likely to have specialized jobs, as represented by assignment to special news beats, than reporters for newspapers. The difference is consistent even when size of the respective employing organizations is held constant; specialization seems to reflect a true industry difference in use of personnel.

Overall, print and broadcast reporters do not differ in terms of the likelihood of working on hard news versus features.[4] But when reporters for comparably sized organizations are examined, the data suggest that a print reporter is slightly more likely to have this kind of assignment than a broadcast reporter. On the other hand, broadcast reporters seem to be slightly more likely to work on analysis and interpretation than print reporters for organizations similar in terms of size.

Overall, broadcast reporters are more likely to rely on more than one source in gathering news for a story than are print reporters, and this difference is even more striking when the comparison is made to the small newspaper organizations. There is a tendency for multiple source reporting to increase with the size of the organization, and this seems to be the dominant mode of work for wire service employees.

Such a finding is probably explained in several ways. First, since newspaper reporters are more likely to have beat assignments, they probably use direct observation and developed sources for stories more often than broadcast reporters, who are more likely to be generalists. In addition, the print reporter may be more likely to carry second perspectives or responses to events in related or second-day stories, while the broadcast reporter is under

TABLE 8.2 Indicants of Reportorial Behavior (in percentages)

| | Newspapers Dailies, staffs of . . . | | | | | | Broadcast Staffs of . . . | | | |
| --- | --- | --- | --- | --- | --- | --- | --- | --- | --- | --- |
| | Wkly. | 1-10 | 11-50 | 51-100 | 101+ | TOTAL | 1-10 | 11-50 | TOTAL | Wire Service |
| Having newsbeats | 30.0 | 52.5 | 56.6 | 54.3 | 63.1 | 54.6 | 30.6 | 30.0 | 30.4* | 33.3 |
| Working on hard news at least 80% of time | 22.9 | 42.5 | 32.2 | 31.6 | 26.3 | 29.6 | 35.2 | 20.0 | 29.1 | 52.4 |
| Working on news analysis, interpretation, in-depth reporting at least 26% of time | 30.4 | 17.5 | 19.2 | 29.2 | 42.3 | 30.7 | 20.5 | 27.6 | 23.3 | 17.1 |
| Relying on more than one source in gathering news for a story "most of the time" | 42.9 | 45.0 | 41.8 | 62.9 | 66.8 | 55.5 | 59.1 | 71.7 | 64.2* | 61.9 |
| "Frequently" working on stories which deal with topics of "public controversy" | 51.4 | 32.5 | 33.9 | 51.7 | 53.5 | 46.8 | 56.3 | 65.0 | 59.9* | 78.6 |
| "Frequently" working on stories of "little news value" | 22.9 | 35.0 | 19.7 | 14.9 | 15.9 | 18.9 | 14.9 | 13.3 | 14.3 | 4.8 |
| Feeling they do not have enough time to adequately prepare story at least 46% of time | 47.8 | 56.4 | 38.3 | 34.2 | 29.1 | 36.8 | 44.8 | 61.7 | 51.7* | 42.9 |
| Having "almost complete freedom" in selecting the stories they work on | 82.9 | 67.5 | 50.0 | 45.7 | 47.6 | 53.8 | 79.3 | 53.3 | 68.7* | 47.6 |
| Having "almost complete freedom" in deciding which aspect of story should be emphasized | 91.4 | 82.5 | 71.1 | 59.5 | 69.9 | 71.7 | 80.7 | 74.6 | 78.2 | 80.5 |

|  | | | | | | | | | | |
|---|---|---|---|---|---|---|---|---|---|---|
| Reporting that their stories get "great deal" or "some" editing by others in the organization | 44.3 | 62.5 | 73.8 | 81.1 | 83.4 | 87.3 | 46.6 | 50.0 | 47.9* | 85.7 |
| "Regularly" getting reactions or comments on work from superiors | 34.3 | 22.5 | 15.6 | 30.2 | 28.5 | 26.2 | 38.6 | 33.3 | 36.5* | 45.2 |
| "Regularly" getting reactions or comments on work from colleagues in organization | 15.7 | 27.5 | 26.2 | 39.7 | 32.8 | 30.1 | 34.1 | 44.1 | 38.1 | 33.3 |
| "Regularly" getting reactions or comments from readers, listeners, or viewers | 52.2 | 40.0 | 40.2 | 40.5 | 44.4 | 43.2 | 48.9 | 46.7 | 48.0 | 2.4 |
| N | 70 | 40 | 122 | 116 | 187 | 535 | 88 | 60 | 148 | 42 |

NOTE: *The entries in the TOTAL columns are significantly different from each other at the .05 level.

more pressure to integrate such multiple inputs into the same story. Finally, the broadcast reporter may be more likely to employ more than one source because the story is controversial, involving more than one point of view. Responses to the question posed to respondents indicates quite clearly that broadcast reporters more often report dealing with controversy than do print reporters, particularly those working for the small dailies. Reporting of controversy increases with size of organizations, as does use of multiple sources, and is very common for wire service reporters, who often use multiple sources. Regardless of the explanation of these differences, they are consistent with the view that broadcast—and particularly television— news is more conflictual and more likely to involve a presentation of balance than the average newspaper report.

Reporters for broadcast overall are no more or less likely to think they work on stories of little news value than reporters for print, but the broadcast reporters are less likely to hold this view than reporters for the comparably sized dailies. This difference is most striking when reporters working on organizations with 1-10 editorial employees are compared. On the other hand, broadcast reporters are more likely to think they do not have adequate time to prepare their stories than the print reporters. An examination of the relevant subgroups, however, shows that for broadcast reporters this feeling increases with size of the organization, while the feeling decreases for print reporters as the size of the organization increases.

Broadcast reporters seem to have more freedom in selecting stories they work on than print reporters, though the difference is accounted for almost entirely by difference between the smallest organizations. Any difference between the print and broadcast reporters in terms of freedom in deciding which aspects of a story is to be emphasized appears to be negligible, particularly when comparably sized organizations are examined. It also should be noted that the comparisons in Table 8.2 suggest that the interpretation by Johnstone (1976) that organizational size is a prime determinant of amount of reportorial autonomy (as indexed by responses to these two and related questions) is open to some challenge. Clearly, differences in the nature of the media need to be considered.

Such a conclusion is reinforced by examination of the data in Table 8.2 for the amount of editing reporters indicate their copy receives. The differences between print and broadcast reporter responses here is considerably more striking than the differences among the responses of daily newspaper reporters, for whom size of organization does seem to make a slight difference. Size of organization doesn't seem to matter much where broadcast reporters are concerned. That a true difference exists in the working arrangements of print and broadcast reporters also is evidenced by responses to the following item in the table. It seems that print reporters get a lot of feedback via the editing done to their copy, while broadcast reporters get feedback from their supervisors more directly. The print reporter's work is critically evaluated more often before it is printed; the broadcast reporter's work is evaluated after it has been on the air.[5] On-air presentation, of course, is crucial in broadcasting; feedback without examination of such presentation is of necessity partial.

There also is some suggestion in Table 8.2 that broadcast reporters get more feedback from their colleagues than print reporters, once size of organization is held constant. And there is a slight indication that the broadcast reporters may also get more audience feedback than print reporters.

It is interesting to note how isolated wire service reporters are from their audiences, as the response in the final row in Table 8.2 show. Such a finding serves to emphasize the general conclusion from these data that the organization influences the work of the reporter in many ways. It is extremely rare for the wire reporters to get audience feedback, though they appear to be not so different on the other feedback questions. Wire service reporters do report slightly higher levels of feedback from superiors than other reporters and extensive editing of copy. The hard news bias of the wires also is in evidence throughout the table.

## SUMMARY AND CONCLUSIONS

Broadcast reporters working for organizations with from 1 to 10 editorial employees were found to be somewhat less professionally oriented than their print counterparts, more likely to reject an activist role for the media, and less critical of the mass media and their own organizations. Reporters for the larger broadcast organizations, on the other hand, are higher in professional orientation than reporters for comparably sized dailies and more acepting of a participant or activist role for the media. Reporters for both sizes of broadcast organization are more likely to reject the neutral role of the press than print reporters working for comparable organizations in terms of size and more likely to be low in professional commitment.

Broadcast reporters also are more likely to be generalists than their print counterparts, the data suggest. Broadcast reporters seem to be somewhat less likely to report hard news than reporters for comparably sized print organizations, but more likely to do analysis and interpretation. Broadcast reporters say they are more likely than reporters for comparable print organizations to use more than one source in reporting and to deal with controversy. They also are more likely to feel the stories they cover are of news value and more likely to feel they don't have adequate time to deal with them. Broadcast reporters report higher levels of autonomy in selecting stories than comparable print reporters, less editing of their copy, and more extensive feedback from superiors, colleagues, and audience members.

These findings must be treated as tentative. Many of the differences identified are not large, and some may be due to chance error. The findings suggest, however, that reporters for the print media do differ from reporters for the broadcast media. They differ both in terms of their orientations to their jobs and profession, and in terms of the ways they go about their work.

As such, these data suggest it is important to begin to ask *why* reporters for print and reporters for broadcast differ. Are different values *and* newsgathering and reporting approaches being taught in schools? What are the relevant socialization processes, both prior to and after entry to the field? Some of the data presented here suggest that different professions are emerging. The important question is why.

In addition, it is important to discover what the ultimate impact of these differing orientations and differing newsgathering approaches is on the story presented to the reader. The data presented here show some support for a frequently voiced criticism of television news, namely that it frames stories to make them overly conflictual and controversial.[6] Broadcast reporters may create such an impression of conflict by dealing with controversy more often than print reporters and seeking out contrasting points of view in their newsgatherings. Resulting differences in the content of the news may help explain the findings that television audience members learn less about public affairs and, in some instances, seem to have more negative attitudes toward government than their print counterparts.

Journalists do not operate independent of the organizations for which they work. Unlike members of the medical and legal professions, journalists must ultimately submit their work to someone else if it is to be disseminated. What is needed now is a more systematic examination of the process of news production to determine what influence individual differences among reporters and what influence organizational and industry constraints have on news work. Each, most likely, plays a role.

## NOTES

1. Scores on the index of participant attitudes were correlated with scores on the neutral attitude index only slightly ($r = .06$). Similarly, scores on the professional index were correlated only $r = .01$ with scores on the nonprofessional index. For Table 8.1, respondents were classified as high on these indices if they scored above the median.

2. Statistical tests were not applied for these secondary comparisons primarily because of the small number of cases involved and the consequent lack of statistical power. As a rough

indicant, readers can interpret differences between print and broadcast in the 1-10 editorial staff size of 19 percent as significant at the .05 level, while differences between the print and broadcast in the 11-50 group of 16 percent meet this traditional level. In fact, of course, few of the differences are this gross, and readers may want to treat the inferences here as merely suggestive.

3. This difference between print and broadcast reporters in terms of occupational commitment is examined in more detail using these same data in Becker, Sobowale, and Cobbey (1979). Analysis of a rather complicated model of determinants of commitment suggest that influence of organizational type on commitment may be indirect, working through sentiments about the specific job.

4. For this and other questions reported in Table 8.2, respondents were asked to indicate the percentage of time they behaved in a specified way. A cut point was devised based on the actual distributions of the responses to the specific questions; splits near the median were used to the extent possible.

5. These findings are consistent with Tuchman's (1969) observations of a newspaper and a television station, and with those of Bantz et al. (1980), who suggest that at least in part the technological intensiveness of television gives television reporters more de facto control over the editing of their own work than that afforded to newspaper reporters; it is easier, faster, and cheaper for an editor to rework a newspaper news story than to re-edit a segment of television news film or tape.

6. The finding regarding the reporting of controversy should be viewed in light of research by Tichenor, Donohue, and Olien (1980) showing that all media in larger communities tend to report controversy more than media in smaller communities, a finding supported by the data in Table 8.2. In fact, as DuBick (1978) has shown, the environment of the media can have impact in various ways. Yet the findings here are that broadcast reporters working for organizations with reportorial staffs of 11 to 50 persons are more likely to say they report controversy than reporters for newspapers more than twice as large. Reporters for small broadcast organizations report levels of controversy in their coverage equal to those of reporters for the largest daily newspapers. Other comparisons in Tables 8.1 and 8.2, however, are not so robust, and size of community should be treated as a natural covariant of size of staff in interpreting these data.

# REFERENCES

BANTZ, C. R., S. McCORKLE and R. C. BAADE (1980) "The news factory." Communication Research 7, 1: 45-58.

BECKER, L. B. and J. W. DIMMICK (1980) "Selecting the gate-keepers: a market case-study of personnel decision making in media organizations." Report to the Communication Policy and Planning Project, East-West Communication Institute, East-West Center, Honolulu, Hawaii.

BECKER, L. B. and D. C. WHITNEY (1980) "Effects of media dependencies: audience assessment of government," Communication Research 7, 1: 95-120.

BECKER, L. B. and J. W. FRUIT (1979) "Television and the origins of Proposition 13: did the nightly news make tax revolt inevitable?" Presented to the American Association for Public Opinion Research, Buck Hill Falls, PA.

BECKER, L. B., I. A. SOBOWALE, and R. E. COBBEY (1979) "Reporters and their professional and organizational commitment." Journalism Quarterly 56, 4: 753-763; 770.

BECKER, L. B., I. A. SOBOWALE, and W. E. CASEY (1979) "Newspaper and television dependencies: their effects on evaluations of public officials." Journal of Broadcasting 23, 4: 465-475.

CAREY, J. (1976) "How media shape campaigns." Journal of Communication 26, 2: 50-57.

CLARKE, P. and E. FREDIN (1978) "Newspapers, television and political reasoning." Public Opinion Quarterly 42: 143-160.

DuBICK, M. A. (1978) "The organizational structure of newspapers in relation to their metropolitan environments." Administrative Science Quarterly 23: 418-433.

EPSTEIN, E. J. (1973) News from Nowhere: Television and the News. New York: Random House.

FRANK, R. S. (1973) Message Dimensions of Television News, Lexington, MA: D. C. Heath.

GOLDING, P. and P. ELLIOTT (1979) Making The News. London: Longman.

HARNEY, R. F. and V. A. STONE (1969) "Television and newspaper front page coverage of a major news story." Journal of Broadcasting 13: 181-188.

HOFSTETTER, C. R. and C. ZUKIN (1979) "TV network political news and advertising in the Nixon and McGovern campaigns." Journalism Quarterly 56: 106-115; 152.

JOHNSTONE, J. W. C. (1976) "Organizational constraints on newswork." Journalism Quarterly 53, 1: 5-13.

———— E. L. SLAWSKI, and W. W. BOWMAN (1976) The News People. Urbana: University of Illinois Press.

———— (1973) "The professional values of American newsmen." Public Opinion Quarterly 36, 4: 522-40.

LEFEVER, E. W. (1974) TV and National Defense. Boston, MA: Institute for American Strategy Press.

LOWRY, D. T. (1971) "Gresham's law and network TV news selection." Journal of Broadcasting 15: 397-408.

McLEOD, J. M. and S. E. HAWLEY (1964) "Professionalization among newsmen." Journalism Quarterly 41, 4: 529-39.

PATTERSON, T. E. (1977) "The 1976 horserace." Wilson Quarterly 1: 73-79.

———— and R. D. McCLURE (1976) The Unseeing Eye: The Myth of Television Power in National Politics. New York: G. P. Putnam.

POWERS, R. (1977) The Newscasters. New York: St. Martin's.

ROBINSON, M. J. (1977a) "Television and American politics: 1956-1976." Public Interest 48: 3-39.

———— (1977b) "Television news and the presidential nominating process: the case of spring, 1976." Catholic University, Washington, DC. (unpublished).

———— (1976) "Public affairs television and the growth of political malaise: the case of "The Selling of the Pentagon." "American Political Science Review 70: 409-432.

———— (1975) "American political legitimacy in an era of electronic journalism: reflections on the evening news," pp. 97-139 in D. Cater and R. Adler (eds.) Television as a Social Force: New Approaches to TV Criticism. New York: Praeger.

———— and K. A. McPHERSON (1977) "Television news coverage before the 1976 New Hampshire primary: the focus of network news." Journal of Broadcasting 21: 177-186.

ROBINSON, M. J. and C. ZUKIN (1976) "Television and the Wallace vote." Journal of Communication 26, 2: 79-83.

TICHENOR, P. J., G. A. DONOHUE, and C. N. OLIEN (1980) Community Conflict and The Press. Beverly Hills: Sage.

TUCHMAN, G. (1969) "News, the newsman's reality." Ph.D. dissertation, Brandeis University.

WADE, S. and W. SCHRAMM (1969) "The mass media as sources of public affairs, science and health knowledge." Public Opinion Quarterly 33: 197-209.

WAMSLEY, G. and R. PRIDE (1972) "Television network news: rethinking the iceberg problem." Western Political Quarterly 25: 434-450.

WEAVER, P. H. (1975) "Newspaper news and television news," in pp. 81-94 in D. Cater and R. Adler (eds.) Television as a Social Force: New Approaches to TV Criticism. New York: Praeger.

*Chapter 9*

---

# TELEVISION JOURNALISTS AND THEIR AUDIENCES

**John P. Robinson, Haluk Sahin, and Dennis K. Davis**

## INTRODUCTION

"Scratch a journalist and find a reformer" goes an old adage about the news profession. Scratch further to find out what makes the journalist tick and find an elaborate professional folklore, replete with examples from the muckrakers to the investigative reporters of the Watergate era, in which "informing the public" and "exposing the rascals" are declared to be the central accomplishments.[1]

Like so many occupational mythologies, this one tells us more about what journalists would like to think they do than what they actually do. The "rascals" who are exposed usually turn out to be none other than the journalists' main sources of information. Two decades of studies on newsgathering practices have shown what "exposing the rascals" actually involves. We know, for example, that the relationship between reporters and government officials on whom they report is more symbiotic than adversary (Sigal, 1973; Epstein, 1975). We also know that news organizations and newsworkers define at the outset which institutions and figures are "legitimate" sources of information; they thereby function to reproduce the status quo (Tuchman, 1978). Gans (1979: 116) points out that, more often than not, sources do the leading when journalists and sources do their tango. The growing body of research into the routines of the business of "making news" at least partially demythologizes the once hidden tangle of source-reporter liaisons.

What about the journalist's relationship to their audiences? How does the journalist's image of the audience affect the process of news production?

AUTHORS NOTE: We gratefully acknowledge the financial support of the John and Mary Markle Foundation and the British Broadcasting Corporation. We wish to thank the many British and American journalists who cooperated with us.

How informed are the journalists about the audiences they are trying to inform? The body of research on these questions is slim and the answers tend to be sketchy and impressionistic: earlier research suggests that few journalists have sharply defined conceptions of their audiences (Gieber, 1964; Pool and Shulman, 1959). More recent yet disparate pieces of research and observation reflect some surprise and disappointment over the extent of the journalist's ignorance on public opinion in general and the nature of their audiences in particular (Crouse, 1973; Bagdikian, 1971; Gans, 1979).

It could be argued that American television journalists in fact know their audiences quite well since they have easy access to data concerning the demographic properties of potential and real audiences. Indeed, the ratings system guarantees that basic audience data will be widely available to most television journalists. Yet, Gans (1979) reports that network journalists hardly pay any attention to such information.[2] There is, further, another type of information that seems to be in seriously short supply: information concerning the needs, knowledge levels, cognitive maps, and information processing capabilities of their audiences. Such information is directly relevant to planning how to structure news stories to ensure successful transmission of basic ideas and to evaluation of such transmission. How and why is the message getting across? If "informing the public" is really a sine qua non of the news profession, how much better informed does the public become as a result of the newscast? In this chapter, we will discuss these questions in the light of the television news audience comprehension research that we have conducted in Britain and the United States.

## PREVIOUS RESEARCH

Neither occupational ideologies nor their specific components, such as the journalists' perception of their audiences, can be studied in isolation from their societal and institutional contexts. The myths, ideas, and images that the ideology is composed of take shape over long periods of time. They reflect the historical experience of the society in which they are embedded. An understanding of American journalists' view of their audience, for instance, must take into account the conflicting ideologies of libertarian, popular, and participatory democracy in which journalists play a crucial role as watchdogs and more elitist conceptions which can be traced back to the days of the old partisan press (Schudson, 1978; Tuchman, 1978). The former is probably behind the high value assigned to "informing the public" while the latter may explain the paternalistic and cynical attitudes that come to the fore in times of disillusionment with the seeming inability of audiences to attend to and understand important information.

It is also necessary to be aware of the apparent contradiction between commercial imperatives and professional values. The flood of data gathered by commercial research firms is formulated for use and tailored to the needs of what is termed the "demand model." This model dictates that the market determines the content (Cantor, 1980). The ratings are accepted to be valid indicators of audience demand, and the manufacture of programs is by and large adjusted to its requirements. Of necessity, such an approach caters to *short-term consumer wants* rather than *long-term public needs,* and provides a purely economic rationale for programming decision. The demand model does ascribe great importance to "knowing" the audience—not as enlightened citizens, but solely as consumers of programs. The audience also needs to be known as a quantifiable commodity which can be sold to advertisers on a cost per thousand basis.

The traditional occupational ideology of American journalism rejects the demand model as an appropriate determiner of news content. Television journalists insist upon drawing a clear distinction between themselves and the producers of entertainment material in this respect. As William Leonard, Executive Vice President of CBS News put it (1978: 53): "We have an obligation to report what's out there and what's important by the standards of trained journalists, whether or not it is what people want." Yet, especially at the local level, news research is very much attuned to the requisites of the demand model. It is preoccupied with numbers not only as a criterion of popularity, but also format and content (Powers, 1977; Broadcasting, 1979; Newsweek, 1980). In the age of "news doctors" and "happy talk" formats, the fine line between the decision-making models of the news and entertainment sections has become blurred. With national news organizations more open to bottom line thinking, the cherished professional norms of the newsroom seems to be in increasing jeopardy.

This threat to professional autonomy, whether perceived or real, has made news professionals of the old school extremely suspicious of research. They view it as a handmaiden of commercial interests, an instrument of mercantile encroachment (Rubens, 1980; Gans, 1979). Increasing transfer of managerial control from journalists to sales executives indicates that this sensitivity is based on more than simple paranoia (Newsweek, 1980). When journalists refer to the "risk of being corrupted by research" (Rubens, 1980), it is not their soul that they are concerned about—it is their power to insulate their editorial judgments from external influences. "Corruption" refers to the threat to professional values posed by blatantly commercial directives. Research is feared as a Trojan horse, a subtle means of infiltration into the newsroom.

This is not to say that all journalists fail to recognize the difference between the manipulative "doctoring" of news programs and research which seeks to increase the amount of information comprehended by audiences. In response to our news comprehension project, the president of one U.S. network news operation commented in an internal memo that our approach "so clearly draws the line between the totally unacceptable kinds of research which fiddles around with cosmetics and, worse yet, dictates content and assignment of news personnel, on the one hand and [this] kind of research relating to comprehension, on the other hand" (Salant, 1980). This position was defended by referring to the social function of the news profession; *"Since we are in the business of informing viewers,* I think it is important that we not spin our wheels and do as well as possible" (our emphasis). On the whole, however, the suspicion of any kind of external evaluation appears to be prevalent. By and large, journalists either rely on feedback from their superiors or colleagues, or purposive "surrogate" audiences, made up of friends, neighbors, or whoever is available (Gans, 1979; Hood, 1976).

## GREAT BRITAIN

The institutional context of British broadcasting on the other hand places greater weight on public service. This is in keeping with the class structure and cultural traditions of Britain and brings about a less demand-oriented and more paternalistic view of the audience (Burns, 1969; Smith, 1973). In this context, the broadcasters are often reminded of their "obligation" to inform and educate their audiences. As Elihu Katz (1977) noted in his report to the BBC:

> If *the job of news and public affairs is to create an informed citizenry,* the most elementary obligation of public service broadcasting is to determine whether and what the citizens understand. At one level that means they understand the words and concepts used. At another, it means whether their understanding of their society, and the problems confronting it, has been enhanced by the particular program or by the particular mix of programs to which they have been exposed [our emphasis].

Yet, this emphasis on understanding the news has not created a hospitable milieu for systematic research feedback into the news process.[3] Katz (1977) has pointed to "a missing link between news producers and news consumers." Philip Schlesinger (1978) has reported in his study of the BBC news that British broadcasting journalists, like their American colleagues, prefer to rely on peer opinion, professional norms, and standards of performance. They believe that the mediation by research is not needed since they can anticipate audience comprehension as well as audience standards and tastes. As one television editor told Schlesinger: "we take it that if we can understand it, so can the public."

As part of our research we found some preliminary evidence that a significant gap in knowledge levels exists between television editors and their audiences. When 10 BBC news staff members were questioned about eight leading stories from the previous week, they averaged 7.9 out of 8 correct identifications. In contrast, not one person in a national representative sample of 510 persons scored that well on the same test items. Only 2 per cent scored 6 or 7 on the test. This suggests that the average news editor is more knowledgeable than 90 to 95 percent of the audience. Moreover, it is difficult for them to gauge the capacity of their viewers to understand their stories. They fail to provide necessary background information to help these viewers comprehend their stories because they assume that most people already know this information.

## OUR NEWS AUDIENCE COMPREHENSION RESEARCH

Our research is grounded in two existing research traditions. We have drawn from studies of news organizations like those discussed above and we have also followed previous research on media audiences, especially research focused on how much people routinely learn from news or information campaigns. There has recently been a resurgence of interest in what Becker et al. (1975) have labeled the "cognitive effects" of mass media. These authors point out that while direct media influence upon attitudes has been found to be quite limited, there is mounting evidence that people do routinely learn a great deal from media content. Research attention has been directed toward the conditions under which learning from media is enhanced or inhibited. Our research has been designed to identify the conditions which affect comprehension of specific news stories by different types of news viewers.

By combining these two research traditions we have sought to overcome the inherent limitations of each. Typically, research on the cognitive effects of media content ignores the objectives of communicators while research on communicators often neglects to determine whether communicator intentions are actually translated into effective influence on audience members. Much research on how well people recall television news suggests that people learn little from news (Katz, 1975; Neuman, 1976; Findahl and Hoijer, 1973, 1974, 1975, 1976). One of the first questions to be answered by future news comprehension research is whether television news serves any purpose at all. To what extent are the high-minded professional values of journalists guiding the creation of a product which has little social value beyond increasing industry profits? Perhaps television newsviewing is only a trivial pastime or fruitless ritual for most people. We have sought on the one hand to better understand how journalistic values lead to the creation of specific news stories and on the other to identify how well these stories could be understood.

The initial opportunity to initiate our research came as a result of an invitation from Elihu Katz to John Robinson to participate in a news research team being established by the BBC. Katz (1977) had just completed his report to the BBC on the types of research which the corporation should sponsor. This report put a high priority on research concerning audience comprehension of news. Professor Robinson spent the winter and spring of 1978 working at the BBC, and developed the research strategy described in detail below. This strategy seeks to integrate data drawn from audience members and journalists. Journalists are asked to judge how well audience members have understood their stories. In this way it was hoped that research findings might be of value both to journalists and their audiences. Such findings would provide the missing link between news producers and news consumers which Katz had identified in his report.

Our research would not have been possible without the cooperation of the BBC, which permitted Professor Robinson to participate in weekly editorial deliberations. BBC reporters and editors also evaluated how well audience members had understood their stories by rating the comprehension indicated by statements made by them. News program producers and editors at the three American networks also cooperated in a more limited way. In general, our access to newsrooms was quite restricted for a variety of reasons but we were able to discuss story construction and program format and make some useful observations of journalists at work. Our observations were consistent with those of earlier researchers (Epstein, 1973; Gans, 1979). News producers at two of the three networks assisted by going over the ratings of audience comprehension which we made and indicating their agreement or disagreement with our ratings.

## RESEARCH METHODOLOGY AND DATA COLLECTION

BBC journalists were instrumental in the development of our research methodology. We gradually evolved a strategy for obtaining self-reports from audience members which would both assess whether specific news stories were understood and remembered as journalists intended and assess the conditions under which this comprehension took place. Discussions with journalists revealed that they could normally isolate one or two main facts or ideas which they considered essential to a story. If these facts or ideas were not learned then the story failed to get its point across even if people learned minor details from it. Journalists tended to conceive of these central facts or ideas as "pegs" or "kernels" around which the rest of the story was constructed. The fundamental problem facing television journalists is somehow to subordinate the often intriguing but trivial details of their stories to the more significant ideas they seek to communicate. When these trivial details are contained in visually exciting videotaped coverage of events, it may be especially difficult to avoid losing the "peg" amid a flood of interesting pictures. We have discussed two examples of this below. Our discussions with American journalists suggested that their concerns and story construction problems were similar to those of the BBC producers. They too were frustrated by the apparent inability of audience members to sort out the details in complex stories and grasp the main points they sought to get across.

We implemented our research by developing a questionnaire based on our discussions with BBC journalists about their news stories. This questionnaire centered on 20 open-ended questions which required respondents to describe what they could recall from specific news stories. Recall of these stories was aided by our use of brief (two or three word) labels for each story. Respondents were told the label for a story and then asked if they could remember anything about it. In addition, the following types of questions were asked: (1) uses and gratifications of television news (Levy, 1978; Blumler, Katz, and Gurevitch, 1974), (2) perceptions of television news, (3) routine use of other media for news, and (4) demographic questions. In both Britain and the United States respondents were questioned in their homes within three hours about watching a specific news broadcast. In Britain two nationally representative samples of about 500 persons each were interviewed on five different evenings. In the United States 425 persons in nine different cities were interviewed. During a three-day period in June 1979 viewers of all three network news broadcasts were contacted. We decided that it would be prohibitively expensive to obtain data from a nationally representative sample in the United States. Therefore, we sought to maximize the range of responses we obtained by directing interviewers to neighborhoods which differed greatly in income and education, two factors which research on knowledge gaps has linked to news comprehension (Tichenor et al., 1970).

Because our interviews were conducted in respondents' homes immediately after news programs ended and because we aided respondents in recalling specific stories, we were not surprised to find that people could remember more than earlier research had indicated (Katz et al., 1977; Neuman, 1976). Our research does not invalidate this earlier research but rather complements it. We wanted to be certain not to underestimate communication of basic facts or ideas by news stories. However, our findings are not too encouraging for news professionals. In both Britain and the United States, we found that about half of our respondents could remember half of the news stories well enough to describe the main point(s) of these stories. Many could recall nothing or only trivial details from most stories. At the other extreme, we found that a handful of viewers could describe most stories almost word for word, often using the specialized terminology of news reporters. As expected, these viewers were among the best educated and wealthiest respondents.

Journalists assisted our analysis of our audience data by providing us with their evaluations of audience recall and comprehension. BBC editors read every statement made by respondents concerning their stories and then evaluated the comprehension indicated by these statements using a scale ranging from 0 to 7. On this scale a four was used to indicate that the main point of a story had been understood. A score of less than four indicated that additional useful details were remembered. In the United States we simplified the rating task in order to ensure cooperation of news producers. We did an initial rating of audience comprehension ourselves and then asked news producers to check the accuracy of our ratings. The producers at two networks cooperated and expressed agreement with more than 95 per cent of our initial ratings.

## REACTION OF BBC JOURNALISTS TO OUR FINDINGS

We were able to report our findings to BBC journalists immediately after our data were collected. In general, these journalists seemed disappointed to learn that they had effectively reached only half of their viewers. Some seemed threatened by this evidence of their failure to communicate. This may imply that they were working with naive notions about what they could reasonably expect audience members to understand. When questioned about the usefulness of this type of research, reactions varied greatly. Most journalists considered it a valuable professional learning experience, but others dismissed the results for varying reasons. One common reason for rejecting results was based on negative conceptions of the audience. Some openly admitted the audience was of no interest or consequence to them, espousing the stance that their job was to report the news as best they could and to let the audience cope with it as best they could. Along the same line, other news personnel felt that it was not their fault the audience was so ignorant or uncomprehending. They despaired of any remedy short of massive citizen reeducation.

The following two examples illustrate some of the reasons why specific news stories fail to communicate effectively and some of the reactions of journalists. On June 15, 1978, a story dealt with two Britons who had been flogged for breaking the strict Islamic laws on alcohol in Saudi Arabia, while another story on June 19 dealt with the killing of a policeman by the IRA in Northern Ireland. The placement and length of these stories should have increased the likelihood that each would be well comprehended. Both were lead stories and quite lengthy in comparison to other stories. But only 32 per cent of the audience was found to comprehend the main point of the first story and 13 per cent was found to comprehend the point of the second.

The reasons for such low comprehension were fairly obvious once the structure of the stories was evaluated in the light of the audience responses. In both cases, the main points which the editors intended to communicate were mentioned only once at the beginning and were followed by long, visually interesting filmed reports which dealt in detail with minor points that were only indirectly related to the main points. The Saudi Arabian story included a filmed segment which detailed the treatment of Britons in Saudi prisons while the Northern Ireland story had a long filmed interview with a priest who had been held hostage and then freed by the IRA.

The details recalled by respondents were predictable given the structure for these two stories. While what the journalists considered the main points were rarely recalled, there were frequent references to the fact that two Britons had come home that day, the number of strokes they had been given, the fact that two other men were scheduled to be flogged, and that the men had not talked to reporters because they planned to sell their story to a publisher. In the case of the Northern Ireland story, respondents recalled the experiences and character of the priest as well as the details of a separate IRA incident involving soldiers and a vehicle that had been blown up.

In both cases, then, too many elements had been introduced creating complex stories which had no overall point. The news editor had intended to communicate that the Saudis were enforcing their own Islamic laws and were sending a clear message to the outside world that they expected for- eigners to take these laws seriously. This point was lost in the flow of verbal and visual information dealing with specific events. Similarly, the point that the IRA had deliberately killed a policeman because he was "part of the British war machine" was blunted because of all the additional detail pro- vided. In both cases these main points were rather subtle and abstract and perhaps easily forgotten when followed by a rapid flow of detail.

The BBC editors' reaction to our findings was first one of disappointment and then of puzzlement over what to do about it. Some sought solace in noting that many respondents did recall many of the less important details; some of them were willing to redefine the main point of the story so that it conformed with what people could remember; others said they had already been informed about the inadequate structure of the stories through routine post-mortem critiques by colleagues. None of these reactions was especially constructive and confirms our overall conclusion that television journalists may have difficulty objectively diagnosing and solving the problems involved with effectively communicating with their audiences. For this reason, research on audience comprehension can be useful to journalists.

## IMPLICATIONS FOR JOURNALISTS

The research findings reported here are necessarily brief and lacking in detail. We are in the process of completing more detailed reports and interested readers will eventually be able to consult these. Several preliminary reports are available (Robinson et al., 1980; Sahin and Robinson, 1980; Sahin et al., in press; Dyer and Robinson, 1980). We have isolated what appear to be three factors which are strongly associated with people's ability to understand and recall television news; when they are present, people are much more likely to comprehend news stories. These factors are: (1) level of knowledge about what is being routinely reported in the news, (2) amount of skill possessed which enables effective use of television as a source of information, and (3) level of routine exposure to news in various media.

These factors tend to be interrelated. Some viewers are high on all of them. Most viewers, though, are low on one or more. In these cases, possession of one factor may compensate for low levels of others. For example, persons who lack useful information about current world events may be able to compensate by skillfully attending to specific news stories or through routine exposure to much news content in which a specific story is featured. People who already are in possession of much information about current events may not need to be skillful news viewers or frequent news consumers in order to learn about specific stories.

Perhaps the most useful conclusion which can be drawn from these findings is that to increase audience comprehension, television news stories should be structured to help people compensate for factors which they may lack. Audiences for television news can be characterized in terms of these factors so that useful decisions can be made about creating news stories which best serve these audiences. It seems likely that television has succeeded in increasing people's routine exposure to important news stories; that many persons now regularly hear and see coverage of events which they would not have read about in newspapers or might have ignored on radio. Television may have created new audiences for news because it is able to present news stories in attractive and interesting ways. But it is these audiences which are most likely to lack skill in using television as a medium for information and to lack information about most current news events.

James Barber (1979) recently discussed this problem in an insightful article in which he identified several barriers to comprehension posed by television news. He has argued that television news has the greatest responsibility in serving those persons who cannot be effectively reached through any other medium. He states that "we need to look at television news as the educational medium most promising for reaching and teaching the less informed what they need to know to do democracy well." Barber believes that to reach this goal may require significant changes in the values of journalists, which he argues are oriented toward the interest of persons who are already well informed.

Like Barber, we believe there are many relatively simple and quite practical steps which television journalists can take to help their audiences compensate for low skill in using television and gaps in background information. Elsewhere (Sahin et al., in press), we have detailed our advice. We have emphasized the need to structure news stories simply and to repeat main points often. The verbal information contained in a story should not be forced to compete with vivid, dramatic pictures which are only loosely linked to its main point. Too often, news producers include pictures solely to give a story a visual dimension. In the American stories we have analyzed, pictures of DC-10 airplanes landing, sitting, and taking off were endlessly repeated during follow-up stories about a DC-10 crash which had occurred several days earlier. Such pictures served little useful purpose and may have been quite distracting to viewers who were poorly prepared to make sense of television news. Journalists often seem impelled to squeeze as much unique and exclusive information as they can into stories even when such details are distracting. Insider gossip is routinely passed along to other insiders at the expense of most viewers.

While there are necessarily limits to what journalists can or should be expected to do to help audiences remedy deficiencies in background information, it is clearly possible for them to do more than they now do. It is not all that difficult for journalists to anticipate what events will be in the news and to prepare themselves better to communicate effectively about these events. For example, the Associated Press now routinely seeks to anticipate the most important events which are likely to occur each month as well as the issues which are likely to be featured in the news. National surveys could be conducted to assess how much information news audiences possess about these events and issues. News program content could be created which systematically seeks to develop people's understanding of relevant information. Many journalists might find such background information repetitious and boring. Since most of them already know these facts, they are likely to perceive little reason to communicate them. From their point of view, these facts are not news but rather history or civics lessons which people should learn in high school. But what our research makes quite apparent is that unless such facts are presented, most of the important news stories cannot be understood.[4]

## CONCLUSIONS

Television journalists' and other communicators' images and knowledge of their audiences are likely to be subjects of increasing social scientific scrutiny. Our work with television journalists suggests important ways in which they are unable adequately to conceptualize or understand their vast, diverse audiences. Many work with hazy and rather naive notions about the "mass" audiences which they profess to serve. Others refuse to acknowledge any responsibility to audiences and prefer to justify their performance entirely in terms of the norms of their craft. By and large, they are reluctant to pay attention to the evaluations of their work done by "outsiders." They perceive such efforts as a threat upon their editorial judgment and an infringement upon their journalistic integrity. On those rare occasions when they do cooperate with researchers, they are often disappointed with what they learn about the effectiveness of their work. They are inclined to believe that they are doing the best job they can do under difficult circumstances.

Perhaps, the journalists' reluctance to develop more highly defined conceptions of their audiences serves certain self-protective needs. When the audience remains a gray mass—a phantom public—it can be made to fit different organizational and professional exigencies. The insulation and isolation of bureaucrats from the people they are supposed to serve is a phenomenon widely reported by journalists about other bureaucracies. But that same phenomenon is likely to hold true for news bureaucracies as well. Altheide and Johnson (1980) have argued that news bureaucracies also create "bureaucratic propaganda" which serve to legitimize their work and shield it from criticism. Reporters rarely expose their own bureaucracy with the same enthusiasm which they reserve for the White House or City Hall. It could be that such "investigations" will need to be undertaken by outsiders. As Richard Hoggart (1976) put it in his forward to *Bad News,* "The sooner the newsmen and their superiors accept this starting-point, the better for them, us and 'the news.' In this they can after all learn something from outsiders, even if outsiders don't know all the jargon of their trade, even if the outsiders are those always suspect academics or, worse, social scientist academics."

## NOTES

1. Johnstone et al. (1976: 230, Table 7.1) asked 1300 practicing journalists from both broadcast and print media the importance they assign to various media functions. An overwhelming majority stated that "investigating claims and statements made by the government" was an important function (75.8%, Extremely important; 19.1%, Quite important). Functions

more strictly related to "informing the public" were also assigned heavy importance.

2. Local television journalists, and especially the anchorpersons, seem to pay a great deal more attention to cosmetic news research (Newsweek, 1980; Powers 1977). Lacking experience and credibility as journalists per se compared to their colleagues at the network news departments, they find themselves more subject to marketing considerations.

3. Richard Hoggart (1976) states that there are deep-seated reasons for the "hostility" that British television journalists show towards research on their work: "None of us like our professional practices to be scrutinized by outsiders; and television newsmen must be near the top of the league in this kind of defensiveness. Sometimes I think the strength of their defensiveness is in direct proportion to their refusal to take a good look at just what they are doing each day. One gets the impression of a trade which has hardly ever thought out its own basic premises but continues, come hell or high water, to rest its case on a few unexamined assertions."

4. In improving the comprehensibility of their news stories, television journalists might benefit from the insights of the information processing perspective. See, for example, Gunter (1980a, 1980b), Ortony (1978), Paivio (1971), Wodall, et al. (1980).

# REFERENCES

ALTHEIDE, D. L. and J. M. JOHNSON (1980) Bureaucratic Propaganda. Boston: Allyn & Bacon.

BAGDIKIAN, B. H. (1971) The Information Machines: Their Impact on Man and the Media. New York: Harper and Row.

BARBER, J. D. (1979) "Not the New York Times: what network news should be." Washington Monthly (September): 14-21.

BECKER, L. B., M. McCOMBS, and J. M. McLEOD (1975) "The development of political cognitions," pp. 21-63 in Steven Chaffee (ed.) Political Communication: Issues and Strategies for Research. Beverly Hills: Sage.

BLUMLER, J. G., E. KATZ, and M. GUREVITCH (1974) "Utilization of mass communication by the individual," pp. 19-31 in The Uses of Mass Communications: Current Perspectives on Gratifications Research. Beverly Hills: Sage.

Broadcasting (1979) "The Arledge differential at ABC News." (December 10): 70-80.

BURNS, T. (1969) "Public service and private world." The Sociological Review Monograph 13: 53-73.

CANTOR, M. G. (1980) Prime Time Television: Content and Control. Beverly Hills: Sage.

CROUSE, T. (1973) The Boys on the Bus. New York: Random House.

DYER, N. and J. P. ROBINSON (1980) "News comprehension research in Great Britain." Presented at the International Communication Association Convention, Acapulco.

EPSTEIN, E. J. (1975) Between Fact and Fiction: The Problems of Journalism. New York: Vintage.

––––––– (1973) News from Nowhere: Television and the News. New York: Random House.

FINDAHL, O. and B. HOIJER (1976) Fragments of Reality: An Experiment with News and TV-Visuals. Stockholm: Sveriges Radio.

––––––– (1975) "Effects of additional verbal information on retention of a radio news program," Journalism Quarterly 52: 493-498.

––––––– (1974) On Knowledge, Social Privilege and the News. Stockholm: Sveriges Radio.

––––––– (1973) An Analysis of Errors in the Recollection of A News Program. Stockholm: Sveriges Radio.

GANS, H. J. (1979) Deciding What's News. New York: Pantheon.

GIEBER, W. (1964) "News is what newspapermen make it," pp. 173-182 in L. A. Dexter and D. M. White (eds.) People, Society and Mass Communications. New York: The Free Press.

GUNTER, B. (1980a) "Remembering televised news: effects of visual format on information gain." Journal of Educational Television 6: 8-11.

_____ (1980b) "Remembering television news: effects of picture content." Journal of General Psychology 102: 127-133.

HOGGART, R. (1976) in Glasgow University Media Group (eds.) Bad News, Vol. 1. London: Routledge & Kegan Paul.

HOOD, S. (1976) "The dilemma of communicators," pp. 201-212 in C. W. E. Bigsby (ed.) Approaches to Popular Culture. Bowling Green: Bowling Green University Popular Press.

JOHNSTONE, J. W. C., E. J. SLAWSKI and W. W. BOWMAN (1976) The News People: A Sociological Portrait of American Journalists and Their Work. Urbana: University of Illinois Press.

KATZ, E. (1977) Social Research on Broadcasting: Proposals for Further Development. London: BBC.

_____ (1975) "The mass communication of knowledge," pp. 93-114 in Getting the Message Across. Paris: UNESCO.

_____ H. ADONI, and P. PARNESS (1977) "Remembering the news: what the picture adds to recall." Journalism Quarterly 54: 231-239.

LEONARD, W. (1978) "The history of electronic journalism is now in chapter one." U.S. News and World Report (November 20).

LEVY, M. R. (1978) "The audience experience with television news." Journalism Monographs 55 (April).

NEUMAN, W. R. (1976) "Patterns of recall among television news viewers." Public Opinion Quarterly 40 (Spring): 115-123.

Newsweek (1980) "Sex and the anchor person." (December 15).

ORTONY, A. (1978) "Remembering, understanding and representation." Cognitive Science 2: 53-69.

PAIVIO, A. (1971) Imagery and Verbal Processes. New York: Holt, Rinehart & Winston.

POOL, I. de SOLA and I. SHULMAN (1959) "Newsmen's fantasies, audiences and newswriting." Public Opinion Quarterly 23: 145-158.

POWERS, R. (1977) The Newscasters: The News Business as Show Business. New York: St. Martin's Press.

ROBINSON, J. P., D. K. DAVIS, H. SAHIN, and T. O'TOOLE (1980) "Comprehension of television news: how alert is the audience?" Presented at the Association for Education in Journalism Convention, Boston.

RUBENS, W. (1980) "Some rough notes on news vs. research." New York: NBC. (mimeo)

SAHIN, H. and J. P. ROBINSON (1980) "Is there light at the end of the flow? Audience comprehension of international news stories." Presented at the World Communications Conference, Philadelphia.

SAHIN, H., D. K. DAVIS, and J. P. ROBINSON (1981) "Comprehending television news." Irish Broadcasting Review (Summer).

SALANT, R. S. (1980) Memorandum to William Rubens. New York: NBC. (mimeo)

SCHLESINGER, P. (1978) Putting Reality Together: BBC News. London: Constable.

SCHUDSON, M. (1978) Discovering the News: A Social History of American Newspapers. New York: Basic Books.

SIGAL, L. V. (1973) Reporters and Officials. Lexington, MA: D.C. Heath.

SMITH, A. (1973) The Shadow in the Cave: A Study of the Relationship between the Broadcaster, His Audience and the State. London: George Allen & Unwin.

TICHENOR, P. J., G. A. DONOHUE, and C. N. OLIEN (1970) "Mass media flow and differential growth of knowledge." Public Opinion Quarterly 34 (Summer): 159-170.

TUCHMAN, G. (1978) Making News. New York: The Free Press.
WODALL, G., D.K. DAVIS, and H. SAHIN (1980) "From the boob tube to the black box: television news comprehension from an information processing perspective." Cleveland: Communication Research Center, Cleveland State University. (mimeo)

*Chapter 10*

---

# THE CONSTRUCTION OF ELECTION NEWS
## An Observation Study at the BBC

**Michael Gurevitch and Jay G. Blumler**

> "Considering the material we had, that
> was the best shape we could put on
> it."—*BBC news producer, in a*
> *postmortem discussion of an election*
> *news bulletin*

POLITICAL CAMPAIGN REPORTING for television news is double-masked. It wears both a face of chaos and scrambled responses to continual uncertainty, and a face of order, routine, shared understandings, and firm structure. It is at once a fluid and a highly constrained operation. Consequently, which electioneering slogans and events will finally get into the news is a far less predictable matter in advance than any post hoc analysis of the actually screened output might lead one to suppose.

Both features of election news preparation are fed in turn by many springs. The patterned consistency of the content reflects: the need to supply a daily bulletin, with its own long-established conventions of item length, speech excerpting techniques, and visual and verbal presentation styles; the institution of a tightly organized logistical routine for obtaining, and working up on a daily basis, the raw materials of eventual election items; obligations to respect externally set norms; for example, for party balance and to avoid editorializing; the keenness of campaigners to give television the nuggets of vivid comment they assume it demands; and the guiding presence in TV journalists' minds of certain criteria of a good campaign story.

Yet what appears on the screen also emerges from a more problematic process of genuinely sifting materials for use and of making decisions (sometimes remarkably swiftly, sometimes after much internal debate) between alternative ways of presenting what is at hand. Partly this is because, until the available offerings have been monitored and weighed against each other, nobody can tell exactly which materials will best combine into an effective campaign item. Partly it is because the journalists who engage in such work, however complete their training and socialization, are not singleminded creatures. Rather, they bring to election reporting a somewhat unresolved mixture of differing professional attitudes and dispositions, pulling them this way and that, both while performing on the job and when reflecting on what they have achieved afterwards.

This chapter presents some of the more outstanding impressions formed by the authors during an observation study of the production of television news at the BBC during the General Election campaign of April and May 1979. This study was the latest of a string of similar inquiries, stretching back to the 1966 General Election campaign, in which one or both of us explored the workings of the British political communication system from a variety of angles. Long-standing associations with news personnel at the BBC from these previous investigations, had helped to develop relations of mutual trust and confidence that were essential for conduct of the 1979 study. Consequently, we were given permission to be present at any location of our choice in the various news production areas; to sit in on discussions of news executives and producers, both those concerned with forward planning and those involved in postmortem analyses of recent output; and to discuss the implications of their work with any of the individuals engaged in campaign journalism.

## BACKGROUND

### THE CAMPAIGN ROLE OF BRITISH TELEVISION NEWS

Before the 1959 General Election, British news bulletins studiously ignored all campaign events. Nowadays the regular coverage they provide is a quite central vehicle of the campaign. Their centrality initially stems from the news programs' large audiences and credible reputation. That is why they are assiduously cultivated by party managers, who are anxious to plant their gems in the output, and hence become a prime electoral arena, in which the combatants daily parade themselves, make speeches, look authoritative, shake hands, and try to score points off their opponents. What viewers see of all this depends, however, on how the arena is constructed by the media professionals who are responsible for "reporting" and "covering" the campaign. In this respect television news is not merely a channel through which messages and images devised by the political actors are transmitted untrammelled to voters, like water flowing through a faucet. How editors and reporters go about their journalistic job of presenting or "staging" the contest is so formative that they become not just observers, but an integral part of the campaign itself.

In 1979, the role of television news in the elections was determined by at least four features of note. First, the calling of an election induces a subtle shift of gear: enthusiasm mounts but controls tighten. As one editor put it, "This is far and away the biggest kind of story that a TV news organization can be involved in covering." However, many of the rules that guide the journalists' work more flexibly in out-of-election periods are more rigorously imposed during a campaign, including a more strict interpretation of what impartiality and balance demands, a more faithful echoing of the issue and event initiatives of party spokesmen, and more circumspection when venturing comment on the politicians' activities. Though usually respected, the resulting curbs are also targets of resentment and resistance at times.

Second, election news is accorded a high status in British television, though its output has to be fitted into bulletins which must continue to cover each day's nonelection news as well. One sign of its special standing is the fact that at the outset of a campaign, many of the BBC's most experienced and trusted political personnel are assembled to work on the election news team. This may help to explain a major respect in which the thrust of British election coverage differs from its American counterpart: According to Patterson (1980), the American networks predominantly depict the presidential election as a horse race, paying far more attention to what he calls the election "game," defined as reports about winning and losing, strategy and logistics, appearances and hoopla, than to its "substance," defined as issues, policies, traits, records and endorsements. Although British television news does not ignore the campaign game, more of its output concentrates on party leaders' substantive remarks about issues and policies. In addition, election news takes up a sizable part of the available bulletin time, usually amounting to nearly half of the total. On a daily basis, however, the exact amount is negotiated in the light of circumstances, and on occasion the election news producers we observed were hard-pressed to squeeze what they had prepared into their alloted ration and to decide what to discard when they seemed likely to run over.

Third, the fashioning of election news for television is a continual struggle to reconcile two potentially opposed policy goals. Campaign coverage must be both newsworthy and fair. On the one hand, news personnel are supposed to behave like professionals, applying traditional news-values instincts to each day's crop of campaign statements and incidents. On the other hand, each party is supposed to receive that share of attention which is merited by its strength in the country (defined by a mixed formula of votes cast at the previous election and seats contested at the current one). In practice, news personnel take as their guide the share of political broadcasts that have been allocated to each party during the campaign concerned—which prescribed a 5:5:3 ratio for the Conservative, Labour, and Liberal Parties, respectively, in 1979.

Fourth, in advance of the 1979 campaign BBC policy makers had resolved to strengthen the analytical contribution of the election news output. In part, this was a response to criticisms of the 1974 coverage as unduly encapsulated and passive (Harrison, 1975). In part, it reflected a modified role of the main evening news report itself that had been introduced in the intervening period, moving away from a mere bulletin of record towards provision of longer reports on major news events which aimed to set them in an explanatory context. When the 1979 election was announced, it was therefore natural to decide that although campaign news should be predominantly "reactive" (distinguishing it in this respect from the Corporation's main current affairs and discussion programs), it should also make room for a modestly "reflective" element. One product of this approach was a decision to prepare a series of prefilmed items on the central issues of the election (such as, prices, industrial relations, taxes, agriculture) summarizing in each case the positions taken by the main parties and how they compared with each other. Another and potentially more significant idea was to give responsibility to the BBC's Political Editor for presenting all of each evening's election news package. As the Deputy Editor of BBC Television News explained:

> Last time we placed the Political Editor's piece somewhere towards the end of the newsreader's contribution. The election news might have consisted of a succession of speech items, precised by the newsreader, a bit of film, then the Editor winding up on how the campaign was going. What we all felt was that we should change this. What we badly need is not a two-line introduction or wind-up piece, but rather something that will set things, and indeed everything if possible, into their proper context. The idea is to get your senior political man also to be your anchorman, so that he is in a position to offer that. (The political editor), then, will be presenting campaign material early in every BBC1 main evening news bulletin. Thus he may well not only round off each day's substance of election coverage, summing up in his own way, but also insert interpretative comment inside the various items that are coming along as well.

## THE SETTING

The authors' observations were conducted on intermittent days in April 1979, spanning the four weeks of the election campaign. This was rather longer than the 2½ weeks that are usually set aside for campaigning in

Britain, because (a) the Easter weekend intervened and (b) rather longer advance notice of the election had been given than is customary. BBC coverage was based at its Television Centre in West London, where a special work area was set aside for this purpose. It was separate from the regular television newsroom, which continued to produce the nonelection portion of the various news bulletins transmitted during the day. The special area, or "the factory" as, significantly, it was called by the people working there, was manned by approximately fifty members of the BBC Television News staff, ranging from typists, copy editors, sub-editors and news organisers to the various reporters and analysts, including the then Political Editor. The executive producer in charge of the entire operation was the Deputy Editor of Television News.

The output of this "factory" consisted of three "packages" of campaign news, transmitted in the bulletins at 12:45 p.m., 5:40 p.m. and 9:10 p.m. The two daytime bulletins were fifteen and twenty minutes in length, while the evening bulletin lasted thirty minutes, an extension of five minutes beyond its usual nonelection length. Although the contents of the campaign packages varied from one day to the next, they most regularly drew on three forms of party-originated material: the press conferences held in London by all three main parties every morning of the campaign; feature material, such as shots of party leaders going on "walkabout" in the city streets, shopping centres and housing estates, chatting up ordinary voters on the way; and passages from politicians' evening speeches delivered to party rallies in large cities throughout the country, chiefly intended for use in the main evening bulletin. In addition, the packages might include the latest opinion poll results; politicans' reactions to events of the day, which, strictly speaking, were not campaign news but could impinge on election issues, such as publication of official statistics on prices and the state of the economy, or developments on some industrial relations front; notice of minor party manifestoes; and prefilmed items such as constituency reports or "day-in-the-life" profiles of the top leaders' campaign activities.

## CENTER AND PERIPHERY: LOGISTICS OF COVERAGE

During our periods of observation our attention was particularly drawn to three prime determinants of election news output. One of these concerned the near-umbilical relationship that obtained between the campaign "periphery," that is, the field where the political actors operated, and the production "center," where the news was compiled. At first this way of identifying the center and the periphery may seem odd, even a reversal of the "true" order, since in many ways the hub of campaign activity is where the politicians are performing. The most significant feature of the *periphery* is its highly concentrated character. That is, the places from which the news personnel secured raw campaign material were few in number and were repeatedly revisited on an almost totally predictable basis. They consisted almost entirely of the headquarters where the three main parties held press conferences every morning, the towns where party leaders chose to go on walkabout in the afternoon, and the halls in which they addressed party supporters at evening meetings.

In principle a wider range of evening speeches could have been covered, but this rarely happened, partly because of limits on the number of Outside Broadcast units that could be assigned to meeting halls throughout the country but mainly because the reporters felt obliged to keep close tabs on what James Callaghan, Margaret Thatcher, and David Steel had to offer. As one producer told us, "The trouble with the night-time material is that if you deliberately try to move away from a top party leader, he may well then say something significant." Thus, the attempt (in the words of another producer) "to bring the viewer as close in as possible to the way the election was going" was largely focused on a limited number of predesignated action stations. Even so, regarded from the perspective of the working journalist, the *center* of the campaign almost seemed to be located, not "out there" amidst the hurly-burly of speech-making and political posturing, but amongst the videotape machines and editorial discussions at the Television Centre.

The campaign day of the Television Centre began at 9 a.m. with a meeting of the executive producer and his senior editorial staff. This was devoted to a review of the previous day's production activity and news output, as well as a scanning of likely campaign developments in the forthcoming day. The meeting usually lasted about 45 minutes, after which most of the participants moved to the videotape area, where, joined by other colleagues, they observed the parties' morning press conferences. These were usually chaired by the top leader of the given party, who would be supported by up to half a dozen other figures, chosen according to the issues it hoped to develop on the day concerned. The conferences took place in party headquarters in central London and were transmitted directly to the Television Centre, where they were displayed on monitors and recorded for excerpting. Because the Labour and Conservative press conferences were scheduled simultaneously, some news personnel had to keep an eye on the Labour monitor while others watched the Conservative one. (The Liberal conference followed immediately afterwards.) Pen and notebook in hand, they took notes of the proceedings, just as they might have done had they been physically present at the conferences. This is not to say that the BBC stayed away from the conferences themselves. The Political Editor was usually present at one of them, while another reporter would attend the other. Both would then return to the Television Centre soon after the press conferences came to an end.

Similar procedures operated during the afternoon and evening. The afternoon walkabout material was piped back to the Television Centre, mainly in the form of a brief story written and fronted by the reporter on the scene. The likelihood of items from press conferences and walkabouts being used in the main evening bulletin depended, of course, on the availability and newsworthiness of other material. Decisions on these had to wait, therefore, until the next batch of statements by the party leaders arrived in the evening. Those which the parties hoped would be covered in the news were delivered at around 7-7:30 p.m. to take account of the deadlines involved. Since the BBC's evening news was transmitted at 9:10 p.m., its producers were at a slight disadvantage at this stage of the coverage in relation to their Independent Television News competitors, whose main evening bulletin went out at 10 p.m. Though "first with the news" of what the party leaders had said, the BBC staff had less time for excerpt selection and preparation of surrounding comment, and the Political Editor was sometimes observed still working on his script only 20 or 30 minutes before air time.

Advance releases of key passages of politicians' evening speeches usually arrived at the "factory" shortly before they were due to start. These were quickly skimmed to identify the main themes being stressed and to help locate illustrative passages that could be pulled out for inclusion in the bulletin. Nevertheless, the speech as delivered was shown on monitors in the "factory" area and listened to through headphones by several members of the production team, who would often exchange terse remarks about striking and useable quotes. Although a BBC reporter was always present at the meeting hall, the shortage of time, and the fact that the producers at the "factory" were in possession of the raw material, meant that they could, and were obliged to, prepare items on the evening speeches with little if any help from reporters on the spot. Having everything in hand by 8 p.m. or so, they could then put the various stories of the day into that sequence which best reflected their relative importance, edit the extracts so as not to exceed the total amount of time allowed the election segment within the bulletin as a whole, and finalize the links that would move the viewer from one story to the next.

We have described this daily routine in some detail to illustrate a crucial feature of the process, namely the extent to which the coverage of the campaign was conducted from the "center," as it were, rather than from the "periphery" in the field. Although in newspapers the newsroom is the place where the final shape is given to the news product, the materials with which editors usually deal are complete stories, filed by reporters in the field, who witness events or talk to sources and base their reports on first-hand experiences. But in constructing news of the campaign, the personnel at the Television Centre regarded everything that flowed in as "raw material" and were in a position themselves to observe the events to be reported as they unfolded. Only on rare occasions were such experiences mediated by a reporter before they reached the Centre. At one level, all this might be regarded simply as a technical matter: Electronic technology has enabled personnel at base to be linked directly to the events of the campaign, or rather it has brought those events directly into the newsroom. But changing technologies also tend to alter the working habits of the employees concerned, as well as the products that emerge from them.

Many consequences seemed to us to flow from a "center-dominated" coverage routine, which processes materials regularly received from only a few repeatedly visited stations at the periphery. First, the role of the reporter in the field was considerably reduced in importance, if not yet totally eliminated. What has been directly affected is the dependence of the editor in the newsroom on the judgments and impressions of reporters. Of course press conferences cannot be held before camera crews only; someone must be present to ask questions. Yet the Political Editor who attended one of the conferences almost every morning did not, on his return to base, file an account of the event. Instead he exchanged views with the Centre editors and producers, who were also eyewitnesses, though at a distance. His aim in attending the conferences was not to report on what had transpired but to "experience it at first-hand," to familiarize himself with the reactions of the other attending reporters, and to "soak up the atmosphere." Admittedly, the reporter assigned to a party leader's entourage was more actively engaged in fashioning certain stories later in the day. But these mainly dealt with the more gimmicky part of the campaign, devised by party publicity advisers to furnish broadcasters with attractive pictures. As the Deputy Editor pointed out in describing the reporters' role, "They prepare the film reports, adding a certain amount of color to the campaign coverage, but they are not expected to offer political comment."

Second, the atmosphere at the Centre seemed subtly but powerfully to strengthen the influence of what in our field notes we termed "TV news presentation requirements" at the expense of "political significance judgments" when decisions were being made about which comments of campaigners to pass on to the audience. When summing up what those presentation requirements seemed to be, we noted them down at the time as follows: a need for crispness of expression; suitability of length (neither rambling nor unduly brief); a need for vivid and pithy phraseology; ready comprehensibility (not requiring an unduly extended exposition or elaboration); emanation from the activity of "our own correspondent"; compatibility with a preconceived view of what the dominant election story or theme of the day might be; continuity with the previous day's theme or story; vigor of attack on the opposition; and the provision, when two or more such items were being taken from different party sources, of a complementary form of thrust and counterthrust or point and counterpoint.

Moreover, we were impressed with the subordination to such criteria of certain actors who might otherwise have been expected to inject more solidly political criteria into the selection process. For example, the Political Editor, in discussing his part with us, continually played it down, treating himself as no more than one voice in a chorus, where others had at least as much right to consideration of their impression as he himself. This is not to imply that political judgments counted for nothing. They noticeably affected many decisions, particularly when choices had to be made between excerpts from politicians' remarks that seemed more or less equally suitable on other grounds. But it was as if even a figure like the Political Editor had become socialized to the characteristic demands of television news and accepted their legitimacy and overriding necessity. On one occasion he told us that on that particular day he had attended two party press conferences and listened to portions of a third. It struck him, he said, that the person with the clearest view of what was happening that could be newsworthy would be somebody "back here, watching the process, rather than somebody attending one of the conferences in person." At any rate, he went on, "my usual way is to try and find out what someone who has been away from the scene sees as the most interesting set of options for extraction from it."

Third, in "coverage from the center" relations between broadcasters on the one side and politicians and their campaign managers on the other side become rather *distanced*. News personnel working at the Centre seemed to be relatively insulated from the hectic and heady atmosphere of the campaign trail, and to regard events with the more detached perspective that could be maintained in the sheltered environment of their "factory." This could explain why it was surprisingly difficult at times for some of them to become fully involved in what was taking place. Even though party differences were arguably sharper in 1979 than at any election since 1945, throughout the campaign individual reporters would tell us that, "It all seems very low-key today"; "It is still unriveting." Perhaps it should be noted in addition that the lack of direct contact with politicians could reduce the latter's opportunities to exert an influence on the broadcasters. Except for the occasional telephone call or telegram, the work environment we observed was relatively free from direct pressures or attempted intervention by the parties. In such circumstances, the shaping of campaign content may strongly reflect the influence of broadcasters' professional standards, however they may be conceived and interpreted at the time.

Nevertheless, fourthly, the limited number of periphery sites that television regularly taps makes the broadcasters highly dependent on whatever materials the politicians happen to provide at those particular places. This enhances the campaigners' chances of getting the message they want to drive home into the news, not through overt pressure but indirectly by manipulating the situation where the journalists are working and by playing on their professional predilections and preferences. Several strategies are open to them for this purpose:

(1) To relate the message to some issue that is being treated as dominant at the time in the ongoing news flow.

(2) To couch it in terms that score high on a cumulation of "TV presentation requirements."

(3) To put it in the mouth of someone thought likely to be highly attractive to the broadcasters as a personality at the time.

(4) To keep all *other* material in the speech of a party leader likely to be followed by television as dull, quiet or repetitious as possible.

(5) To take some step that will signal the likely importance of the passage concerned in some extraordinary way.

It so happens that on one evening we observed a quite dramatic example of the effective use of one of these ploys. In the late afternoon it was announced in the "factory" that a telephone call had just been received from one of the political party's headquarters about its leader's evening speech. No advance release would be available, but the message was conveyed that, "The bit you want is 3½ minutes long and will commence some 4 minutes after the Leader has got up to speak." As one of the assembled producers remarked to us immediately afterwards:

Why don't they say that it's on prices or whatever the subject is going to be? They have left us in a position where we don't know what the content will be. They are trying to condition us. They are making us wonder if the leader is rewriting his speech so as to take account of something that has already appeared in early news bulletins. The psychology of this message is that it tends to make us get keyed up to look for the piece that we are now expecting to hear, and to look forward to it in some more heightened anticipation than might otherwise be the case. With a printed advance you can check up on the different pieces that you might want and compare them with each other. But now he has got us excited by telling us that thus and such is the bit you want. This might encourage us to give it more importance that it might justify. Also, we may listen with less attention to the other bits of the piece. And very probably he will pause in order to give us a clean edit on the passage that he has in mind.

When we asked the Editor of the Day how the speech would be handled, he told us that he and several colleagues would listen to its entirety and then choose that clip from it which most deserved selection on newsvalue grounds. Nevertheless, as the time approached for the speech to start, and they began to put on their headphones to listen to it, a keen air of expectation built up in the "factory." At the start of the meeting the leader was introduced by a local party dignitary and then began to speak in quiet terms about the area of the country he was visiting and the fine candidates who were fighting seats there. Then quite abruptly he plunged into what was obviously the passage to which the Television Centre had been alerted. It recalled a comment on industrial relations issues made by his rival at a press conference that morning, and vigorously attacked it as misguided, risking industrial peace and reneging on promises that had previously been made to many groups of workers—a blunder that, unless retracted, could cause "untold damage to the country." From that moment onwards, there was no doubt in anybody's mind that the originally pinpointed passage would be prominently highlighted in the evening news package. Indeed, as soon as it came to an end, all headphones in the "factory" were laid down—except those of the authors.

In sum, it is clear that election coverage by television news has become a heavily routinized operation. It consists in the main only of what has passed from a few favored stations on the periphery to the center for processing and transmission. This is a far cry from the more "old-fashioned" notion of election coverage in which alert reporters roam the field to see where the action is and send back stories of the most interesting and important developments they can find. Such a routinization must be highly convenient for the broadcasters, and it presumably eases the parties' tactical problems of publicity planning as well. Yet significant campaign material may be missed simply because it is out of reach of the umbilical cord. And the needs of voters for illumination and reasons to become involved may also be short-changed as a result.

## THE ELECTION BALANCING ACT:
## DISTRIBUTION OF NEWS ATTENTION

A Chief Assistant to the Director-General of the BBC once rounded off an account of the Corporation's election coverage policies by proclaiming that "fairness is all!" (Hardiman-Scott, 1977). The reality, of course, is more complex: Other principles also apply, and the commitment to fairness is not without a recognized and sometimes regretted cost. Even so, it highlights the second formative influence on campaign news construction that we noticed in 1979: the producers' determination to achieve an appropriate "balance" when reporting the activities of the principal election contenders.

This was an ever-present source of concern to the news makers we observed, guiding their efforts in a host of selection, presentation, and timing decisions. Their preoccupation with balance was only partly traceable to their legally defined responsibilities. The obligation to present controversial issues with "due impartiality," which is inscribed in the Independent Broadcasting Act, and which after its passage was also accepted by the BBC, is couched in quite general language and spells out no specific duties. A more urgent incentive to be even-handed lies in the broadcasters' pragmatic awareness that when the chief parliamentary forces, to which they are ultimately accountable, are locked in a struggle for power, they must not be open to the charge of having influenced the outcome. Indeed, an alleged lack of balance is the most often-cited ground of complaint that is leveled against broadcasters in the political field, even forming the basis of an official accusation by the Labour Party in the aftermath of the October 1974 election. Moreover, many British broadcasters have internalized the fairness principle as well. In the words of a television news reporter we interviewed in an earlier study (Blumler, Gurevitch, and Ives, 1978):

> When I see all that bias blatantly emerging from how the newspapers cover political affairs, then I am grateful that our broadcasting system does at least have that marvelous quality of striving to be unbiased. What is left, after all, if somewhere among the numerous approaches taken to political coverage, you don't find some form of neutrality?

But what does "balance" mean, and how is it to be maintained? Hardiman-Scott (1977) provides a classic statement of BBC policy on this matter, including revealing hints of the dilemmas faced by the news personnel who have to apply it:

> In reporting an election campaign, both in television news and current affairs programs, there remain the problems of achieving a fair balance between the parties contesting the election. Should one rely solely on the editorial judgment of what is news? Or should you superimpose upon that judgment a requirement to give equal time to the parties? That, unfortunately, is not the end of the question. Should equal time apply also to minor parties, to extremist parties and to individual cranks? We do, after all, live in a Parliamentary democracy.

> The BBC has answered these questions with a compromise. . . . In reporting the election and the party campaign, the BBC applies its traditional journalistic news values. It reports, in other words, what seems to its professional editors to be of interest, of importance and of significance to its viewers. . . .

> So news values *are* the basis for reporting the election in television. But—and this is our compromise—if we are using recorded extracts of speeches by politicians in television news bulletins, then we say we must achieve a fair

balance between the political parties. Thus, in the course of the campaign, we would expect about the same amount of television time to have been used in news bulletins for extracts from speeches by Labour and Conservative politicians, and rather less time for speeches from Liberal politicians. We use the share of the total vote obtained by the parties at the previous General Election as a guide to the share of time devoted to extracts from their speeches in our news bulletins.

This passage graphically summarizes the professional aspirations of BBC journalists, the constraints under which they work, and the presumed "solution" to their dilemma. News is governed by "news values"; the need for "balance" is introduced as an extra requirement that forces a "compromise"; and the "solution" is found in the adoption of a stopwatch approach to the allocation of timed coverage shares to the competing parties, based on "objective" measures of their relative strengths in the country.

This quantitative interpretation of fairness, it should be stressed, is not legally prescribed. It results from formulae that have been devised by the broadcasters themselves, though the parties now expect them to be observed with complete fidelity as well. Their main function is presumably defensive, to protect them against accusations of bias. Indeed, impressions of some party's supposed dissatisfaction with how they were being covered occasionally were exchanged among the reporters, who would also mention certain countermeasures that could be taken in response. In these circumstances the great strength of balance by the stopwatch comes from its calculable specificity. Of all possible operationalizations of the principle, it is the most measurable and therefore the least challengeable.

Admittedly, the policy did allow for one element of flexibility: Quantitatively balanced news attention was to be achieved across the campaign period as a whole, not invariably within each individual bulletin. The precision with which this particular target was met in 1979 is illustrated by these figures (taken from Pilsworth, 1980):

*Party Shares of Election News Coverage in 1979*

|  | Conservative | Labour | Liberal | Other |
|---|---|---|---|---|
| BBC1 | 34.8 | 34.7 | 21.9 | 8.5 |
| Independent Television News | 36.6 | 37.4 | 20.6 | 5.3 |

Nevertheless, the necessity to come out with an almost exactly balanced election-period result eventually played back onto the BBC journalists' daily routines. One member of the "factory" team had the task of calculating the cumulative amount of time given the different parties in the news as the campaign proceeded, and the Editor of the Day and other producers often consulted the up-to-date version of this "tot," as it was called, to see how they stood when putting that day's election package together. In fact, there were at least three reasons for trying to be quantitatively balanced on a daily basis. First, it would look better; the day's product would be more defensible if attacked. Second, an imbalance favoring one party on a certain day would only create a corresponding (and possibly difficult to meet) need to overbalance in favor of its rivals on some subsequent day. And third, day-by-day balance was a way of avoiding involvement in an unfortunate last-minute scramble to get back into overall balance in the closing and arguably decisive days of the campaign. The flavor of some of these considerations is well-conveyed by the remarks of an Editor of the Day, who had been observed agonizing over whether to include a marginally useful Labour excerpt in the day's election package:

> I decided to accept it in the end partly because when we went over the timing we discovered that we were balanced all right in Labour vs. Conservative terms. But the problem is that Labour will be holding press conferences over the weekend, and James Callaghan will be out speaking tonight and on Saturday afternoon, while Margaret Thatcher will not. Also Callaghan started campaigning earlier this week, and I am worried. I am worried about being out of kilter in the presentation of Labour vs. Conservative material over a longer period of the campaign overall. So the question arose in my mind whether to drop the [Labour] piece, which was interesting but not riveting, so as to give us more leeway for achieving a major party balance later on. I decided not to do this, and to wait and hope that there will be more things I can put on the air from the Conservatives later in the campaign. I am supposed at the end to come out in a strict 5:5:3 balance so far as the three parties are concerned. But I don't want to be in a position of having to redress the balance between the parties drastically in the last few days of the election, when whatever happens may be particularly influential so far as voting is concerned.

"Balance by the stopwatch" is relatively easy to effect, even though news values sometimes have to be sacrificed to achieve it. But both broadcasters and politicians realized that there were other dimensions to the problem as well. One issue raised by the Labour Party in 1974 concerned the order of battle in which leading politicians appeared in election packages. Party managers are keen to win the "initiative" in campaign news coverage as often as possible and to appear to dominate the argument by pushing "their" issues to the fore and by putting their rivals on the defensive. "Leading off" in the news may seem one way of gaining such an advantage. For their part, the BBC producers aimed to concoct a running order that would flow smoothly and would reflect the political significance of what had been said on the particular day. But the need to "ring the changes" over which party's message would front the news also weighed with them. When out of balance in this sense they soon looked for ways of redressing the situation.

Fairness of treatment also involved sensitivity to the kind of image of the party leaders that was being projected in the election packages, though of course this was more difficult to assess. To illustrate such a concern, during one discussion the Executive Producer told the Editor of the Day that he should

> look at some of the shots of David Steel which have been used. The Liberals have complained that Steel looks ill-shaven. See if we can get a more closely-shaven one. They are also complaining that the extent of Steel's audiences wasn't shown. . . . We probably need a few more reaction shots of the audience.

Balance could also be sought by ensuring that the number of news appearances of each party leader was more or less equal. In fact, the Labour leader rarely appeared in a bulletin without being preceded or followed by a clip featuring the Conservative leader. On this count the Liberals seemed to have fared better in 1979 than they could have expected through a strict application of the 5:5:3 quota.

*Number of Appearances of Party Leaders in Election News*
(Adapted from Pilsworth, 1980)

|  | *BBC1* | *ITN* |
|---|---|---|
| Labour (Callaghan) | 39 | 44 |
| Conservative (Thatcher) | 40 | 45 |
| Liberal (Steel) | 38 | 42 |

This criterion particularly exercised the broadcasters early in the 1979 campaign, when it was understood that Margaret Thatcher intended to keep a low profile, in contrast to Labour's expected strategy of heavily promoting James Callaghan as their strongest vote-pulling asset. As a BBC news executive remarked at the time, "This will present us with some 'statutory problems' of how to ensure balance between the party leaders." They feared having to "overstate" the Tory case in order to maintain balance and having "to distort news values for purely technical reasons." The Executive Producer added a wry note of his own, musing about

> what would happen if the Tories did not campaign until the last two days before the election. In that event would one try to cram all their allotted time into those last two days?

Note how this executive regarded Tory appearances in the news as something "allotted" rather than, say, something to be "earned" through application of news values. Fortunately for the broadcasters, however, after a somewhat low-key start, the Conservatives soon plunged vigorously into the fray and eventually gave Thatcher as much of the limelight as Callaghan enjoyed on Labour's behalf.

How shall we weigh, in the "balance sheet" as it were, the British broadcasters' scrupulously fair approach to campaign reporting? Though it shelters the political parties from blatantly slanted coverage and ensures attention to most of their pet themes, it also constrains the construction of election news in at least three major respects. First, the balance principle is in tension with the criterion of objectivity. Even if one side happens to be making far more of the running than the other, television will tend to do its best to ignore and conceal the fact. Second, it circumscribes the role of news values in the selection process—more so even than the official policy language of "compromise" acknowledges. The newsmen cannot afford to be predominantly guided by what would be most interesting and significant to viewers. Instead their point of departure must be the need to derive from the Labour, Conservative, and Liberal activities of the day that particular even-handed mixture which can be most readily combined into an easily followed overall package. Third, balance inevitably moulds the *form* of election reports. Since election stories have to be built up from Labour, Conservative, and Liberal messages, producers continually face the problem of deciding how to *juxtapose* the multiparty ingredients that they are regularly obliged to present: in other words, how to wrap them into a professionally satisfying package.

## PUTTING IT TOGETHER: PACKAGING, AGENDA-SETTING OR WHAT?

This last concern is closely related to a third major determinant of election coverage that repeatedly came to our attention: the "factory" team's concern to fashion a set of items which, by virtue of excerpt complementarity, incorporation into some overall theme, and the provision of suitable connecting links, would seem to "hang together." It was as if the flow of raw campaign materials presented dangers to be shunned and professional goals to be achieved. The former stemmed from the multiplicity of comments and incidents which in principle could be used. Viewed in that light, the cardinal sins to be avoided were randomness and disconnectedness of presentation. Viewed more positively, however, the art of editing the campaign news was regarded as one of producing a coherent package. Indeed, much of the editors' time and effort was spent in pursuit of a unifying story line, on which the day's election events could be threaded. Thus, as each new campaign day dawned, the search was on for some overarching theme around which the packages of the several bulletins could be constructed, and to which clips of politicians' remarks could be related.

On the days of our observations, this preoccupation with thematic story-building took many forms. For example, it provided the centerpiece of a sustained interview with a leader journalist who, when asked at the outset to describe what election coverage should aim to do, replied that it should portray:

> the issues that are arising, the ones that rise of their own accord because of external events, those brought up by the parties because that is part of their strategy . . . and to follow this day by day and to try and discern and convey *some pattern in this* [our emphasis].

This, he went on, was "a difficult thing to do," because "on one day there are possibly ten issues raised by various people, maybe 20 or 30 different ones." Yet somehow they had to "try to establish a pattern" in what was being communicated. To illustrate this problem, he pointed out that earlier in the day the month's unemployment figures had been released. It followed that

> one gives rather more attention to those and to points being raised in speeches about those figures than some of the other things. But today we've also had housing, we've also had some references to other aspects of employment and a whole host of things. You can't get them all in; the viewer wouldn't be able to absorb and digest them even if you did.

And when asked to explain how the pattern of the day was typically formed, his reply vividly conveyed the picture of a professional communicator whose antennae were all attuned to the expectation of somehow managing to find one:

> You rely very much on your own instincts, and lights of one color come on when certain things are said. Sometimes no lights come on at all; they don't register on your scale. Sometimes lights of quite exceptional color come on, and you realize that they fit exactly into patterns, or they are new, or they are better ways of saying something which you've been waiting to be said. You know that you are waiting for a Conservative response on a certain aspect of unemployment or a certain aspect of their attitude towards the National Health Service, and you remain within yourself dissatisfied while that response is not given. You've been listening to a speech about something else perhaps, and suddenly the thing that you've been waiting for, which hasn't to do with one's own political preconceptions, but the answer comes. It's right, it's the right

length, and this is perhaps the thing we should go into, and it fits neatly into your pattern. You seize it and you put it in. It's right; you've got no doubt about that.

This was not merely one person's way of rationalizing his own part in the production process. According to our observations, such packaging concerns surfaced at every stage of the campaign day. In the morning, for example, frustration over the simultaneous timing of the Conservative and Labour press conferences was expressed on one occasion in this manner:

> This is not just a matter of having to split our attention between them. Rather it is that simultaneous press conferences deprive us of the chance to secure that cut and thrust that stems from a newsman taking something said at one conference and putting it in the form of a question at the other, a matter of them "bouncing off each other."

In fact, to counter this difficulty, a BBC reporter attending one of the conferences would sometimes wear a miniature earpiece, transmitting the proceedings of the other one. This enabled the reporter to put charges being made by one party in the form of a question to the leader of the other party—so as to obtain, as he told us later, "matchable excerpts on the same theme."

Again later in the day, when editors had a number of items to hand and were perusing various running order options, they would often pass such remarks as: "Let's see how things might fit in with each other"; "Things are beginning to shape up"; "We'll do it on the prices theme—with challenge and counter-challenge between the parties." But since no single theme was likely to apply to all the available stories, close attention had also to be paid to the integrative wording of sentences and phrases linking the various items. As one producer remarked after a particularly time-consuming involvement in such an exercise:

> We newsmen tend to operate a special form of logic when working out sequences between items. I don't really know whether it means anything to the viewers. Sometimes I go home, and my wife exclaims to me, "What a crazy way you ran on from one thing to another tonight!" It's the syndrome of, "Speaking of kangaroos, in Australia today . . ."

Finally, the postmortems that were held after viewing the finished product, as broadcast on the "factory" television set, often centered on packaging successes and failures. On one such occasion, for example, a producer complained that "there was still no theme to the election package. It was presented well, but it was all bits and pieces." The Political Editor also confessed, "It was the bittiest edition I've taken part in so far." The Executive Producer was not so bothered: "We should not beat our breasts too much. We had no theme, and a lot of obligatory items to make room for, but tomorrow is another day." But the Political Editor would not be consoled: "There *should* be something there, even despite all that. One should be able to search for it and find that overarching theme."

As many of these remarks show, "good packaging" was defined by certain norms that were not always achieved in practice. But in aiming to edit the election news to such standards, what exactly were the television journalists trying to do to, or for, the campaign? This question is difficult to answer because their role is at once passive and creative. The bulk of the materials they process originate, not in their personal priorities, but from partisan sources. One experienced political reporter even told us that

> we are really in the business of pushing party propaganda. If they want to emphasize a thing like [here he mentioned an issue stressed at one of the party's press conferences that morning], then that is something we ought to take account of.

Yet they also strive to impose a structure on the materials flowing into the "factory," which reflects *their* perception of how the most outstanding elements can be fitted into the day's election jigsaw.

Does this amount to a role of "agenda-setting" by the television news producers? They would deny it, presumably because in their eyes this term has an active interventionist meaning, as if they were being accused of promoting issues they personally deemed significant, despite or even in contradistinction to those the parties wished to press for. Yet the packaging functions they perform may have formative consequences, both for how the campaign is communicated to the public and for how the political parties devise their campaign strategies.

First, the editorial process of selecting, collating and juxtaposing statements, which may have been made independently of each other, often yields a severely "boiled down" version of the campaign. At a time when the team may have witnessed numerous initiatives and monitored many arguments, it allows the newsreader to open an election package with some terse statements like, "Prices were a key issue in today's party press conferences." Such a decision to lift "prices" out of the numerous issues being voiced, and to underline it as the day's central theme, stems from the journalists' need for a viable "hook," "peg," or common denominator, not their own political values. But it undoubtedly shapes the campaign, if not via independent agenda-setting, then in the twofold sense of (a) *pruning* it by cutting out material that cannot be fitted into a tight story, and (b) *crystallizing* it by bringing it to a convergent focus.

Second, one of the more important consequences of election news packaging is the *amplification* of the extracts chosen for transmission. A traditional view of the selection process in the mass media interprets it as a gate-keeping operation. In that view, selection merely involves decisions about which viewpoints ought to be allowed through the media gates and which are to be shut out. Yet this ignores the resulting amplification of a small portion of a speech into the total message. It is not just that the spotlight is focused on the broadcast extract, but that the extract comes to represent the essence and centerpiece of the originating party's message to the viewing audience for that day.

Third, in continually counterposing one party's stand on an issue with that of its rivals, the journalists appear to be *promoting interparty communication*. When we asked one producer why it was important to strive for some degree of "meshing" between the clips of rival party spokespersons, he answered:

> Because otherwise one party will be making its statements on Smith Square [the address of both the Labour and Conservative headquarters at the time] independently of what the other side was doing, with neither of them relating what they had to say to each other. If neither of them gets to grips with the other's points it would be a very arid campaign.

And when he was then asked whether he and his colleagues were helping in effect to bring about a confrontation between the parties, he replied:

> Not exactly. It is rather for the sake of the coherence of the argument. We want to try to say, not just that this is going on and that is going on. That would turn out to be rather shapeless and formless.

It is as if the news personnel are trying to create a dialogue between the parties, where it otherwise might not have existed, and to trigger the politicians into comments and actions that might not have been forthcoming otherwise. Television journalists thus help to *orchestrate* the campaign, even if they did not write the original score.

Fourth, the campaign tends to be served to the audience in the form of an *"issue a day"* —since today's most "presentable" materials are unlikely to be shaped by the theme that would have dominated the previous day's package. Elsewhere, we have ascribed this feature of the modern campaign to party publicists' efforts to capture the attention of the mass media with a new issue each day (Blumler, Gurevitch, and Ives, 1978). From the foregoing analysis it may be concluded, however, that the issue-a-day approach to electioneering is a subtly composite outcome of the mutual adaptation of politicians and media personnel in the conduct and communication of the campaign to the public (Blumler and Gurevitch, 1981).

Fifth, it is evident from much of the above that the broadcasters regard coherent packaging as an expression of their responsibility to serve the campaign communication needs of their viewing audience. The production of thematically unified stories, unfolding a pattern in events, should help audience members to follow the campaign more easily and to find more meaning in it. As one journalist told us:

> You're always acting on behalf of your audience. At least that's the way I see it. It's much more intelligible if you pull out this fact, that fact and that fact and use them in quite a different order from the original one because they illustrate your representation of the argument.

But if, he continued, "you just reported everything as it happened, the audience would become terribly bored with it, and it wouldn't communicate. I mean we are in the business of communication."

Of course the claim that election argument would be more difficult to follow if it was not carefully ordered is impossible to refute. Yet this justification ignores two essential features of the journalists' work situation. For one thing, operating from their "factory" base, they are far removed from viewers' real communication needs. They have no means of telling whether the packages they are fashioning are actually being received by viewers as having helpfully clarified the election issues. For another thing, due to tight timing constraints that are inseparable from the news bulletin format (on speech extract lengths, item lengths and overall package length), any "dialogue" they manage to create will almost inevitably be brief and unsustained and will run the risk of reducing complex issues to a rapid-fire and tense exchange of vivid slogans, one-liners, metaphors, allegations, and ripostes.

The news professionals tend to see themselves, then, as knowledgeable and skillful packagers, sifting through the raw materials provided by the politicians, selecting those extracts which, in their view, are significant and lend themselves to being linked and juxtaposed with other remarks, preferably oppositional ones. Through these connections and juxtapositions they try to tell a story and construct a coherent package. Media academics sometimes come in at this point and label the results of the process as "agenda-setting." Editors and reporters, however, find it difficult to view their work in such terms. Perhaps their hesitation is simply an example of the difficulty all social actors have in identifying the latent functions (or unintended consequences) of their behavior. But if the broadcasters were designated "co-orchestrators" of the campaign rather than "agenda-setters," perhaps they would be willing to acknowledge responsibility and accept the honor.

## IN CONCLUSION: ASPIRATIONS AND CONSTRAINTS

In this chapter we have sought to identify certain salient features of the production of campaign news for television as we observed the process at the BBC during the British General Election of April and May 1979. Schlesinger (1980) has recently outlined several advantages of "ethnographic" studies of news-making in terms which partly coincide with, though they do not fully explain, our own attraction to this approach. First, he argues, the theoretically informed observation of journalists at work should clarify the origins of recurrent patterns of mass media content: "All forms of external analysis of cultural products face intractable problems of inference concerning the production process as such, and therefore contain an explanatory *lacuna."* Second, he maintains, observation studies should cultivate a more "sophisticated appreciation of the complex and ramified nature of editorial systems," in particular highlighting "the crucial elements of *routine* in the production process." In drawing attention to the "mediatedness" of news output, such a focus counters simplistic "conduit" theories of the news, which depict it as a readily available relay system for dominant ideologies. It also sensitizes the observer to sources of stability and change in the production routines, which are continually open to external challenge and internal review and revision. Third, Schlesinger points out, "direct observation may act as an important corrective to conspiracy theories." Such a corrective is particularly apposite in election conditions, when the political parties' anxieties about their portrayal on television are at their height, even though, ironically, the broadcasters' endeavors to be balanced could not be more fully and rigorously sustained than at such a time.

"Ethnographically" derived insights served two further purposes in our own case. One had to do with the relationship of journalists to their *sources* in the election news field. Much of our theoretical interest has focused on interaction between politicians and broadcasters, regarded as joint and mutually adaptive producers of political communications. In that context observation facilities helped us to note how election news-making both reflects and impinges on the interplay between television journalists and party campaigners. In addition, we were moved by a policy-based interest in the kind of campaign that is projected to viewers as a result of the routines that these two types of communicators jointly operate. Having committed ourselves a few years ago to the proposition that, "More weight must be given [in campaign programming] to what voters would find interesting, informative and geared to their needs" (Blumler, Gurevitch and Ives, 1978), observation offered first-hand impressions of the feasibility of such a goal—of the organizational constraints that may impede its pursuit and of the prospects for relieving them.

In fact, much of the story of the production of election news, as we witnessed it, could be told in terms of aspirations and constraints. During the observation period we frequently heard expressions of concern to take certain steps which in the end remained largely in the realm of promise. For example, considerably fewer prefilmed items of issue analysis actually appeared in the news than were originally planned. Difficulties of length and scheduling frustrated this policy. To do justice to a designated issue more time was needed than a jam-packed bulletin could afford. And because editors preferred to screen such items on days when campaign events made them topical, they then created for themselves a professionally unwelcome duplication of themes and speakers between other election stories and the special issue analyses. In this event, responsibility for their presentation was transferred to a late-night current affairs program.

Similarly, the broadcasters resolved at one of their nightly postmortems to cut down the number of party leader walkabout films they were showing, realizing that they had little inherent news value. Their intention was eroded, however, by the daily availability of such stories, manufactured by the politicians and their media consultants in forms that proved difficult to resist. Despite their lack of news value, they at least offered moving pictures, capable of relieving the heavy verbal diet that otherwise threatened to dominate the campaign packages. Yet another concern the producers occasionally expressed was to broaden the range of political personalities appearing in the election news: "We don't want to have Callaghan on the box six nights a week." Yet the 1979 campaign on television turned out to be "much more presidential than had been the case in October 1974," with over 60 percent of the total coverage of the two major parties being relayed through the utterances of Callaghan and Thatcher, while in the Liberal case the share of attention paid David Steel was as high as 69 percent (Pilsworth, 1980).

However, the central innovation that was intended to improve news coverage of the 1979 campaign was undoubtedly the proposal to embed the election packages in a more firmly defined surround of analysis and interpretation. Such a policy decision probably emerged from many influences, including the evolution of news philosophy in a more analytical direction since the previous election; BBC research into audience reactions to the coverage, which is carried out after every election; and the criticisms of those academics who had deplored the overly snippety approach of television news to campaign reporting (Blumler, Gurevitch, and Ives, 1978; Harrison, 1975; Pateman, 1974). But the outcomes of lengthy postmortems, held by news and current affairs policy makers in the aftermath of each campaign, would have played a part as well. Bicker's (1978) account of policy discussion in the American television networks in advance of the 1976 presidential campaign could probably serve equally well to characterize the climate of opinion at the BBC in 1978-1979:

> Executives, producers, writers and correspondents alike joined in agreeing that things had to be done better than they had been in the past. Few of the outside critics were more concerned or articulate than those in the media in general and in television news in particular.

Consequently, the task of fronting and presenting the election news package was assigned to the Political Editor, the most senior journalist covering the political scene for the BBC, in the hope that he could inject a form of commentary that would be interpretative without being opinionated.

Though we are in no position to pronounce this venture a success or failure, from observation we can state, first, that it was continually beset with difficulty, and second, that those involved rarely seemed satisfied with how it was working out in practice. At an early stage the core group of editors and producers chiefly responsible for the coverage pondered the problem of providing election news analysis in our presence. "Are you happy with your role?" the Executive Producer asked the Political Editor. "It has been a rather scrappy campaign so far," the latter replied at first, though he then went on to wonder whether he would have much to say even in different circumstances: "I am sometimes faced with a blank sheet of paper and am uncertain what to put on it. It is as if sometimes I have run out of things to say." Some of his colleagues suggested that he was being distracted by the need to compose introductions to, and links between, items and advised him to hand that job back to others, concentrating his own efforts on provision of analytical remarks at the end of packages. The Political Editor, however, was reluctant to relinquish this task. He preferred to write whatever he was going to say to camera. In any case, such a step would have been retrograde, reinstating the very version of the Political Editor's role they had been trying to transcend.

But the problems of achieving a more "reflective" form of election coverage are probably rooted in certain working conditions and procedures of the news producers, including those determinants of their campaign output that have been examined in previous sections of this chapter. At a quite particular level, the difficulties of providing effective campaign analysis arose from severe time constraints in two senses. There was acute deadline pressure on the Political Editor, who an hour or less before the evening bulletin was due to go on the air could be seen still composing links between speech extracts and the other items in the election package. There was also a shortage of available time, in the ration negotiated for the election package inside the day's bulletin, for accommodating analytical remarks after the various stories and actuality clips had consumed whatever minutes and seconds they needed.

In addition, strict adherence to the norm of balance may have had an inhibiting effect on the supply of interpretation. Analysis often had to be reduced to what could be couched in a more or less impartial terminology, along such lines as: "On the other hand, Labour is faring well in promoting its theme of . . ." "On the other hand, the Conservatives are fighting back by emphasizing . . ." When forced into such an even-handed mold, campaign interpretation may lose its analytical punch.

Similarly constraining effects may have flowed from the team's preoccupation with *packaging* desiderata. These put a premium on the weaving of various campaign events, pledges and speech clips into a coherent story line, which emphasized in turn the need for suitable passages linking the day's several items. As we have seen, the Political Editor was keen to write these sequences himself. But when immersed in such tasks, it seemed to us that he lacked time to "brood" at leisure on the more reflective demands of his contribution. In addition, his socialization to a traditional BBC view of the reporter's role, which valued the presentation of political events in a relatively factual and straightforward manner, may have militated against his emergence as more of a "star" commentator.

Finally, the atmosphere of the workplace that was described in our account of *center-periphery relations* may have worked against the adoption of a fully analytical approach to campaign coverage. The concentration of the process in the "factory" at the Television Centre meant that a large number of highly skilled people were brought together in a confined space to fashion, under urgent deadlines, a polished and professionally acceptable product. This required closely meshed teamwork, the avoidance of unduly prolonged discussions of rival selection and story options, and rapid-fire decision-making. The conditions needed to sustain the smooth flow of such a production process could have been quite different from those that would have supported the emergence of a prominent analyst, given his head to rise above the routinely generated output and to impose his interpretative stamp on it.

It should not be concluded that the impulse to innovate in election programming is invariably *bound* to be thwarted. The record shows that it has made significant contributions to campaign broadcasting at each successive British election between 1959 and October 1974 (Blumler, 1975). Nevertheless, this case study does suggest that attempts to transform the election role of television news are likely to encounter at least four formidable sources of constraint, ones that are rooted respectively in: (a) the bulletin format; (b) the organization's prevalent working routines; (c) socialization to a corporate ethos, favoring straightforward approaches to the presentation of campaign events at the expense of more adventurous ones; and (d) the need to avoid anything that might upset the delicate balance of the broadcasters' relations with the political parties.

This account of the construction of election news has depicted the broadcasters' contribution to a subtle and largely undeclared division of labor between television journalists and party spokesmen in the political communication process during an election campaign. We have found that the role of the broadcasters, even when construed mainly as "packaging" and deprived of much analytical thrust, still serves certain vital functions of identifying and crystallizing the themes of the campaign, as well as promoting an interplay dialogue on the issues of the day. These are important functions in their own right, and they underscore the role of the mass media in general, and of television in particular, in nourishing the political debate in society and in focusing it more coherently than the political competitors could achieve if left to their own devices. Ironically, broadcasters often seemed reluctant to accept credit for this, preferring a more narrow definition of their contribution in terms of "reflecting" and "mirroring" the debate. To that extent they fall prey to a blinkered view of their societal role, emphasizing its more technical-professional aspects while obscuring its political consequences. Such a neutered view of television journalism needs to be unpacked and critically examined, not least for the broadcasters' sake, but also to continue the difficult quest, with their involvement, for ways of enhancing their political journalism.

# REFERENCES

BICKER, W. E. (1978) "Network television news and the 1976 presidential primaries: a look from the networks' side of the camera," in J. D. Barber (ed.) Race for the Presidency: The Media and the Nominating Process. Englewood Cliffs, NJ: Prentice-Hall.

BLUMLER, J. G. (1975) "Mass media roles and reactions in the February election," in H. R. Penniman (ed.) Britain at the Polls: The Parliamentary Elections of 1974. Washington, DC: American Enterprise Institute for Public Policy Research.

————— and M. GUREVITCH (1981) "Role relationships in political communication," in D. Nimmo and K. Sanders (eds.) Handbook of Political Communication. Beverly Hills: Sage.

————— and J. IVES (1978) The Challenge of Election Broadcasting. Leeds, England: Leeds University Press.

HARDIMAN-SCOTT, P. (1977) "Some problems identified," in RAI/Prix Italia (eds.) TV and Elections. Torino: Edizioni Rai Radiotelevisione Italiana.

HARRISON, M. (1975) "On the air," in D. Butler and D. Kavanagh (eds.) The British General Election of October 1974. London: Macmillan.

PATEMAN, T. (1974) Television and the February 1974 General Election. Television Monograph 3. London: British Film Institute.

PATTERSON, T. E. (1980) The Mass Media Election: How Americans Choose Their President. New York: Praeger.

PILSWORTH, M. (1980) "Balanced broadcasting," in D. Butler and D. Kavanagh (eds.) The British General Election of 1979. London: Macmillan.

SCHLESINGER, P. (1980) "Between sociology and journalism," in H. Christian (ed.) The Sociology of Journalism and the Press. Sociological Review Monograph 29. Keele, England: University of Keele.

*Chapter 11*

# BY PEN OR BY POCKETBOOK?
## Voter Understanding of Congressional Contenders

### Peter Clarke and Susan H. Evans

POLITICAL COMPETITION for seats in the U.S. House of Representatives is stifled by weak and preferential newspaper journalism. The public's awareness of challengers for political office suffers. Processes that link journalistic performance with voters' understanding of candidates magnify the need for large campaign treasuries.

Our study comes to these conclusions reluctantly. We did not set out to prove them, although many students of the press (such as Roshco, 1975; Gans, 1979) have drawn attention to routines of journalism that favor prevailing social and political arrangements. We offer the following report because details of our findings break new ground, even though underlying themes may sound familiar to some.

Much of the story appearing here is told in the language of effects research about mass communication. But while analyzing the impact of journalism on political understanding, we stress implications for how the press could organize its actions to help sustain political competition in American life.

One can hardly dispute that treasure is required in increasing amounts for election to Congress. Congressional Quarterly, from its studies of Federal Election Commission reports, reveals that expenditures in the general election for the U.S. House topped $88 million in 1978, up 44 percent from 1976. While there are differences in the cost of running campaigns in rural, suburban, and urban districts, the average candidate in a contested race spent approximately $120,000 in 1978.

AUTHORS' NOTE: This research was supported by the Howard B. Marsh Center for Journalistic Performance, Department of Communication, University of Michigan. The authors gratefully acknowledge the cooperation of Warren Miller and the staff of the National Election Study and the Center for Political Studies, Institute for Social Research, University of Michigan.

A substantial and growing share of this money, 25 percent in 1978, comes from Political Action Committees (PACs). These groups dispense largess from distant board rooms in New York, Chicago, Washington and other centers where corporations, unions, trade associations, and health professionals have their headquarters. The largest investments are made by groups of realtors, automobile and truck dealers, and unions, especially the United Auto Workers. The number of oil industry PACs multiplied from 12 to 128 groups between 1974 and 1978.

Money—in general and from PACs—flows most freely to incumbents.[1] In all, 106 of them received $50,000 or more of PAC money, while only 33 of their competitors fared as well in the 1978 election. Challengers were even less well endowed than candidates in open races, where 37 individuals exceeded the $50,000 mark.

It is against this backdrop that we view press performance. As another national study makes clear, newspapers are the mainstay of information that voters use to reason about political choices (Clarke and Fredin, 1978). Newspaper journalism is particularly crucial in House races, where geographic boundaries stray so widely from broadcast signal reach. Print may seem old-fashioned in an electronic age, but newspaper reporters and editors fill the primary roles delivering nonpartisan political information.

This study includes a national sample of reporters, matched with eligible voters to whom their newspapers circulate. We link journalists' writing to public knowledge about contenders. Races where incumbents face challengers are distinguished from open contests for vacated seats. We describe the independent effects of campaign funds; these, of course, finance a torrent of partisan communication that competes with journalism for the public's attention. Results are examined with an eye toward the increasing role PACs play in electoral financing and the narrow agenda for public policy these groups maintain.

Critical appraisal of press performance requires more than measurement of gross journalistic output. So many of the words written and the political stories published deal with mechanics of campaign events, such as meetings or parades; other coverage is preoccupied with gladiatorial topics, who is ahead and size of the campaign crowds. We look past these details in order to examine more fundamental ingredients of campaign reporting—candidates' personal and political characteristics that might help voters make purposeful choices on election day. Desire to gauge the depth of journalists' work is guided by our view of a major requirement in public information: political choices that sustain representative society demand having reasons for preferring one candidate, party, or policy over another.

Current research on learning and impression formation demonstrates that affective responses to people often precede cognitions or beliefs about what they are like (Zajonc, 1980). It makes sense, therefore, to retrieve what the public knows about political figures by asking what they like and dislike about them. This storage system for information squares nicely, of course, with the task voters face at the polls.

Many choose not to vote; only 35 percent of eligible adults participated in the 1978 congressional elections. And, some of the things people "know" about candidates may not survive the test of independent validation for accuracy. But articulated likes and dislikes are surely a necessary, if not sufficient, condition for calculated decision-making by the public.

We demonstrate four features of press performance that bear on opportunities for political competition. Two findings encourage one's faith that newspapers are a significant American institution:

(1) News coverage of candidates affects public awareness about them, even when level of partisan campaign expenditure is held constant.
(2) Press performance is especially crucial in races with close outcomes, where incumbents face strong and reasonably well-financed challengers.

Beyond these conclusions, however, stand two ominous discoveries:

(3) In the closest incumbent-challenger contests, news reporting is imbalanced; attention to office-holders outpaces challengers by a wide margin.
(4) And, in open races, the political system's most obvious chance to nurture competition, the press virtually ignores candidates. These contenders' ability to capture public attention depends on how much they can raise and spend for partisan messages.

## METHODS

This survey of journalists was coordinated with the 1978 National Election Study sample of eligible voters. The design called for selecting one-quarter of the congressional districts in the coterminous United States. These 432 districts were partitioned into 108 strata, each containing four districts with comparable characteristics—geographic area, urbanization, and recent voting behavior. From each of the 108 strata, one was randomly drawn.

Of the 108 sample districts, 86 had races with two major party candidates on the ballot. Our study was conducted in these contested districts. We identified the newspaper with largest daily penetration reaching the Primary Sampling Unit (PSU) where Michigan's Center for Political Studies conducted interviews with voters.[2]

Results are based on responses from 82 political reporters,[3] 71 of whom covered the most common type of race—where incumbents seek reelection. The sample also includes eleven open contests, where the incumbent was defeated in the primary or had left office. These latter campaigns feature two relative newcomers to the political scene.

Through phone contacts we reached political reporters assigned to cover our selected congressional races.[4] During two weeks prior to the election, 40- to 60-minute interviews were conducted by trained staff at Michigan's Survey Research Center.

In addition to the survey data, newspapers were collected from all sites where reporter interviews had taken place. News stories, editorials, opinion columns, advertisements, and letters were clipped from September 27 through election day, November 7. This analysis examines only the news articles (N = 653). Coding guidelines called for the inclusion of each of the 4071 paragraphs where the candidate's name or reference appeared.[5] Within each paragraph, we coded the presence or absence of each of five content themes of political communication.[6] The scheme links incumbents to copy specifically associated with them and challengers to their images conveyed in the news.

Finally we examine results from lengthy personal interviews with an average of 25 eligible voters in each district. These comprise the data base from the National Election Study postelection investigation.[7]


## CAMPAIGN REPORTAGE

We start with an overview of types of themes found in congressional campaign coverage. Figure 11.1 shows incumbent, challenger, and open candidates; the chart illustrates the percentage of news articles which carried at least one mention of each content theme.

We read news stories, noting five themes of information that could be associated with either candidate. First is political characteristics—experience in office, name recognition, legislative skills, and the like. Second is personal features—appearance, family, and trustworthiness, among others. The third category embraces a pair of items—mentions of issue positions and affiliation with electorally significant groups. Fourth is party mentions, the frequency of which may be exaggerated by our coding rules requiring the recording of even perfunctory references to "Rep." and "Dem." Our final category is organizational themes—chiefly the level of campaign funding and quality of a candidate's staff.

Political information is clearly the most common type of copy appearing about incumbents during the general election period. For instance, in articles where incumbents were mentioned, 77 percent included recent votes in the House, committee work, or some other political attribute. Not surprisingly, neither challengers nor candidates in open races have much political

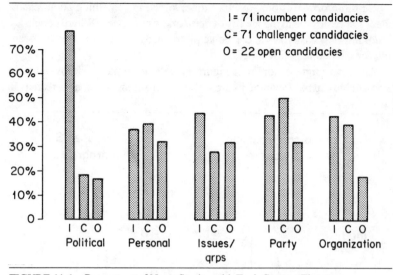

FIGURE 11.1    Percentage of News Stories with Each Content Theme

experience to attract reporters' attention. Incumbents receive fairly uniform coverage across the other content categories of political information.

For challengers, personal mentions and organizational prowess or liabilities command most of the journalistic ink.

Issues are poorly reported; evidently vows of future legislative action are not particularly newsworthy.[8] Avoidance of issue and group mentions is especially apparent in coverage of challengers.

Surprisingly, open races are covered differently from challenges to sitting office-holders. Personal and issue articles appear in equal numbers for open contenders. Organizational copy is less frequent for open candidates than for challengers.

## REPORTERS' ACTIVITY, NEWS COPY, MONEY, AND VOTERS' AWARENESS

We disentangle four major elements in House elections with the aid of Figure 11.2. Separately for incumbents, challengers, and open candidacies, bar graphs show four averages:

(1) how vigorously reporters pursued the candidates;
(2) how many paragraphs of news copy papers ran about each contender;
(3) the amount of campaign money each candidate spent in the primary and general election; and
(4) average levels of public information.[9]

Being informed is our Rosetta Stone; knowing something about candidates is a basic clue to the vitality of democratic processes. Where people are ignorant, they cast votes and execute preferences that are stripped of meaning for the public policy process.

The lower right quadrant of Figure 11.2 demonstrates just how variable knowledge can be. Incumbents are well known among newspaper readers in

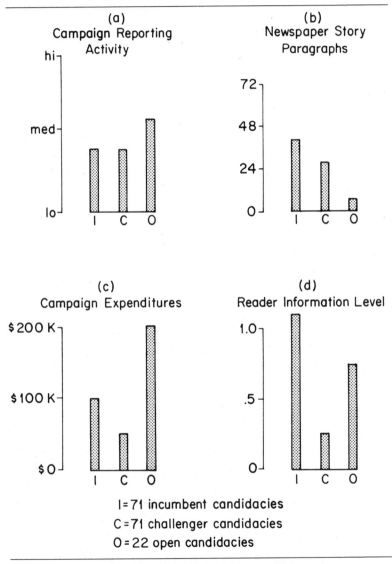

FIGURE 11.2    Averages for Activity, News, Money, and Information

their districts.[10] The mean score, slightly greater than one, indicates that eligible voters who read papers have at least one piece of information stored about the House member representing them. This impression may be fragmentary—perhaps the candidate's experience in office or reputation for trustworthiness—but it is something to anchor choice.

Challengers are comparatively invisible. One quick but unwise interpretation: challengers have made less of a dent in the public's mind because they are new to the public scene. A glance at the mean information score for candidates running in open races casts doubt on the "new faces" explanation. Most open contenders are babes on the congressional stage, too, but they have managed somehow to make themselves known. We will shortly see how they accomplished this feat, and how small a role professional journalism played in the process.

We turn to forces that can influence public understanding. In the upper-left quadrant of Figure 11.2, we see that reporters exerted about equal energy traipsing after incumbents and challengers—talking to the candidates, phoning their managers, digging in the library or newspaper morgue, and the rest (for further discussion of this activity index, see Clarke and Evans, 1980). While their efforts were evenly divided, there are sharp differences in quantity of news copy published. Coverage of incumbents is greater, by a margin of 40 paragraphs to 28. In addition to preferential treatment in news articles, where papers endorsed a congressional candidate, 95 percent of the editorials supported the incumbent.

Incumbents outspent challengers by a 2-to-1 margin, as Figure 11.2 also makes clear. But, this financing, with its yield in visibility for candidate or in credibility for campaign, does not directly explain the gap in news coverage. We shall return to these issues below.

Open races present a democracy with its most obvious test of political competition. Two candidates, usually unmatched against each other in previous races, vie for public attention on relatively equal footing and the outcomes of these contests are generally closer, by congressional standards.[11] The press should be drawn to matches with these fresh contenders and their lavish spending.

The data tell a different story. Reporters pursue open candidates with more effort than they expend in following incumbents and challengers. But this produces a disappointingly thin file of published stories. Open races are almost invisible in public print. An unmistakable political story fails to command news space.

But if editors and publishers are indifferent, eligible voters are alive to open campaigns. The average information score across 22 candidacies is three times greater than found for challengers, and approaches the level for incumbents. How can we account for this public interest? Easily, by noting the campaign dollars spent promoting the interests of open candidates.

As Figure 11.2c makes clear, open contestants invested twice as much money as incumbents and four times that of challengers. These data offer presumptive evidence that paid advertising reaps dividends.

We test this suspicion directly. The 22 candidacies can be arrayed by size of budget and level of public information. This relationship is steep and linear, with only four deviant cases. In two districts in Texas and California, competitors spent huge amounts of money and gained little public awareness for their efforts. Aside from this quartet, there is little room for any factor except money to explain public information.[12] If journalism were to boost the public's awareness, we would find candidacies spending small sums, but achieving high levels of information. There are no cases of this kind in our 1978 sample.[13]

So, journalism loses again. The stage was set for political change; an incumbent had died, resigned, or had been driven from office in the primary. New faces were at hand, stimulating reporting activity. But what came of this effort? Almost nothing in the way of published news. The 22 candidacies garnered a total of 30 news stories between late September and election day.

Meanwhile, PACs and other interested parties were pumping money into the districts with great effect: public attention was won. Candidate preferences were formed without the aid of independent and dispassionate press reports.

In each of the 11 races, an incumbent was born. The next time out, that candidate will be sustained by all the journalistic perquisites we have already documented. The challenger, a newcomer who tries to unseat the one-term officeholder, will suffer the same invisibility and lack of endorsement support demonstrated here in 1978. Political competition will suffer its second journalistic blow.

## JOURNALISM VS. MONEY

A more finely textured arrangement of our findings is needed to grasp fully how journalism affects public information about incumbents and their challengers. Averages shown in Figure 11.2 are not enough. And, as we shall see, it is important to distinguish races by their level of competition. Few elections are settled by close margins in the absolute sense, but some are closer than others. We separate contests that resulted in lopsided margins from less settled outcomes.

To start, however, it is clear that voters have accumulated information about incumbents before campaigns start, growing out of years of service. Correlations between public information and two predictors—volume of news reporting and size of campaign war chest—are low for incumbents;

journalistic output and dollars spent in 1978 added only marginally to what the public already knew.

Voter information about challengers never catches up to knowledge about incumbents.[14] But levels of public awareness are quite tightly linked to amount of press coverage and campaign dollars invested, as we should expect. How else, except through news reporting and advertising enabled by contributions, would eligible voters learn about challengers, most of them visible for the first time in late 1978?

Two details need to be added, however. The first compares the informing power of journalism against the blare of campaign advertising: Which trumpet accounts for most of what the public knows about incumbents and challengers?

The second refinement is to ask this question separately for close elections and for shoo-in victories. Like the open races, close contests stand apart as an opportunity for political change. Participants often anticipate a narrow outcome, leading to a greater effort in campaign tactics and coverage in the news.

Figure 11.3 compares predictive strength of journalism (number of paragraphs published with candidate's name) against the sheer weight of campaign dollars spent to buy public attention and support.[15]

A rich literature deals with campaign financing (Jacobson, 1975, 1978; Goldenberg and Traugott, 1979; Glantz, Abramowitz and Burkhart, 1976; Wanat, 1974). Our data show that news articles exert an independent effect on public awareness, especially in elections with the closest outcomes. Correlations between paragraphs of news copy and the public's information level survive statistical controls for dollars the candidates spent. Only in the case of incumbent coverage in lopsided races do we fail to find evidence for the reporter's voice.[16]

An additional point about press coverage hinges on the wide range of journalistic output found where reporting correlates with public information. The average for paragraphs runs from a high of 55 for incumbents in close races, to 41 for challengers they face, to 13 for challengers who were hopeless losers on election day. Nonetheless, all partial correlations between news coverage and public information are large and significant. Press coverage helps shape public awareness.

But we should not forget that the press' attention fastens most on incumbents. In the close elections, they attract almost 40 percent greater coverage than their competitors. At the same time, these incumbents are outspending challengers by a slightly greater margin and enjoy more than double the level of public information.

Part of an incumbent's edge in news coverage results from the ease with which officeholders can create news pegs. The signing of bills, release of

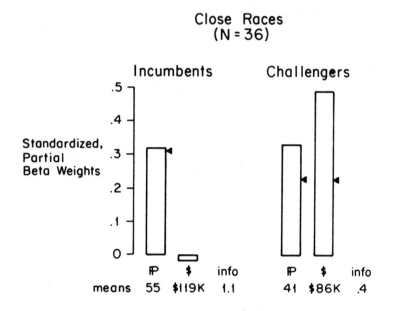

## Close Races
## (N = 36)

### Incumbents          Challengers

Standardized, Partial Beta Weights

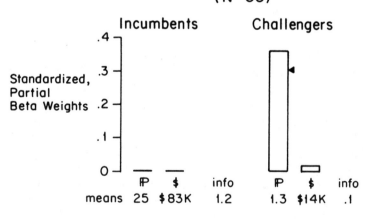

## Lopsided Races
## ( N = 35)

### Incumbents          Challengers

Standardized, Partial Beta Weights

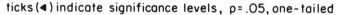

ticks (◄) indicate significance levels, p = .05, one-tailed

FIGURE 11.3    Journalism Versus Money

committee reports, and award of federal grants and contracts carry headline potential. Challengers have to scramble for story ideas.

But the press's preference for incumbents is more deepseated than quick salivation to the sound of obvious and official news releases. In the final seven days of the campaign, well after Congress had adjourned and while candidates were at the peak of electioneering, newspapers continued to play incumbents more prominently than their opposition. In the close races, office holders were mentioned in 91 percent of news stories, compared to 77 percent for challengers. In the lopsided contests, challengers sank even lower; they appeared in 58 percent of stories, compared to incumbents' score of 97 percent visibility.

## DISCUSSION

Our findings paint a side of journalism that cramps opportunities for political competition. Preferential treatment favors incumbents in precisely those races where they might be unseated. Avoidance of open-race coverage forces candidates to rely on the lubricating flow of campaign dollars, many of them awarded by PACs and other calculating parties.

But why do newspapers act in these ways? It seems that journalism shrinks from uncertain outcomes in the political realm, as though three rules were being followed:

When the outcome is in doubt, support the traditional winner;

When the outcome is a foregone conclusion, be evenhanded, and gain a reputation for fairness;

When the electoral prize will be won by a newcomer, stay away from the contest; don't risk identifying with a loser.

These commandments stand as a dark translation of our findings, an uncheerful interpretation of press performance in congressional coverage. Safety and timidity is their unifying theme.

## CONCLUSIONS

Other parts of this research address reporters' and editors' perceptions, decisions, and behavior covering elections. Here we cast light on press performance indirectly, with the mirror of effects analysis. We conclude with some modest suggestions for how journalism might more successfully nurture political competition, without indulging in partisanship.

Most obvious, perhaps, is the lack of news attention to open candidates.

These races may occur without premonition, as when a seemingly popular incumbent falters in the primary. Or they may be anticipated.

Any newspaper should immediately recognize open contests as a special opportunity to inform voters and to counterbalance leverage exerted by large campaign contributions. The task of building public awareness should not be lightly abandoned to PACs and other special interests.

Reporters could be reassigned from more conventional political races—at local or other levels—and newspace could be reserved in amounts that would not be justified in more familiar electoral frays. Attention to other elections or news might be sacrificed in order to capitalize on heated contests and heightened reader interest.

The problem of covering challengers is even more vexing. Poorly financed candidates often lack skills in arranging press access; their managers, if they have such staff, may fail to return telephone calls, miss chances to build news events, and generally stumble through the campaign. This discourages media attention and undermines the candidate's credibility.

Journalists faced with these candidates are forced to manufacture their own news priorities, rather than waiting for story leads to drop in their laps. This requires an initiating attitude, a willingness to structure the press's educational role from inside journalism, instead of outside. Studies of reporters' behavior (such as Cohen, 1963) have noted a continuum stretching from "self-starting" to "conveyor-belt" habits. At one end, reporters seize chances to fashion the agenda of public attention (MacKuen in MacKuen and Coombs, 1981); at the other end we find journalists who prefer a more stenographic role, responding to news "created" by sources.

Reporters and editors may find their preferred niche on this continuum out of personal values or temperament. But we should recognize a consequence from favoritism shown incumbents, so vividly documented here. The press forfeits many of its chances to participate in consciously weighed political choice by the electorate. We can assume that the ambitions of potential candidates for office are also stifled, as they view the bleak correlation between journalistic interest and their capacity to mount well-funded assaults on the status quo.

Occasional efforts by newspapers to pursue more obscure challengers might refresh the political community's belief in competition. To report a contender's issue stands, personal characteristics, and method of campaigning need not propagandize or support; attention does not equal partisanship.

Without more journalistic self-consciousness about staff assignments and their importance to political competition, the electoral stage will continue to require increased campaign funding. Whether this trend is sinister or not depends on one's values. But this trend, in our view, forecasts a weakening press role.

# NOTES

1. This enlarged flow of money coincides with stability in House elections. Since 1970, except for the year of Watergate reaction in 1974, no fewer than 92 percent of incumbents seeking reelection have been returned to office.

2. For other analytic purposes, we interviewed at newspapers with the largest daily circulation in the district. Sometimes both district and PSU criteria were met by the same paper, other times they were not. Data from the voter-linked newspaper sample are used here, since our interest is in the connection between press performance and public information.

3. The three New York City newspapers were on strike during the preelection period and were not included. One respondent refused to be interviewed.

4. We expected that our interview with the political reporter would satisfactorily represent the newspaper's commitment to coverage of the congressional race. As reassurance, we inquired whether there were any other reporters at the paper who covered the same campaign. The correlation between our designated respondent's journalistic activity and the number of times candidates' names appeared does not vary between newspapers with one or more than one reporter. This confirms that our primary respondent at each newspaper serves as an adequate informant about the organization's election coverage.

5. Three coders averaged 91 percent agreement in assigning content codes to individual paragraphs.

6. The five content themes are political references, personal characteristics, issue stands and group mentions, party, and organization. For examples and analysis of the themes, see Clarke and Evans (forthcoming).

7. Ideally, within-district household sampling would have distributed voter interviews across each district; this specification was impossible to satisfy within cost constraints. When the congressional district was part of a major city, its sample of eight to ten interview clusters was distributed across the district. But, with lower population density, the sample was confined to a part of the geographic area which was randomly drawn; this was the Primary Sampling Unit (PSU). Selected households were spread within the PSU according to probability sampling procedures—with the understanding that such selection could never mirror within-district heterogeneity or serve as a basis for precise district estimates.

8. The path these content themes follow—from candidate through journalistic interpretation, and on to newspaper readers—highlights many more incumbent-challenger differences than this figure reveals. For more details see Clarke and Evans (forthcoming).

9. For each congressional candidate, interviewers asked: Was there anything in particular that you (liked/disliked) about [name of candidate], the (Democratic/Republican) candidate for U.S. House of Representatives? Up to four open-end likes and dislikes were coded for each candidate.

10. We filtered nonreaders from the district samples in calculating averages for public information.

11. On average, the margin of victory in races which pit an incumbent and challenger was 36 percent. In open contests, the margin was 24 percent.

12. The rank-order correlation between money and public information equals .84 without the four deviant candidates. When we include them, the correlation drops to .54.

13. To reassure ourselves that these results are not the product of some quirk in the sampling frame, the open races were examined on a number of standard criteria. Encouragingly, districts span geographically from north to south and east to west, and include newspapers with daily circulation ranging from 6,000 to 550,000.

14. One hardly needs to document that challengers' success at the polls rests on impressions citizens gain over the campaign. In this 1978 sample of 71 races, public information about challengers correlates (rank order) at .62 with share of two-party vote won on election day.

15. Statistically, the bars in Figure 11.3 stand for standardized, partial beta weights. These were obtained from multiple regressions—entering public information as the dependent measure against two predictors, news paragraphs about the candidate and size of campaign war chest. Margin of electoral outcome, the contingent variable, has been divided at the median; close races are those with results in the 33-to-67 percent range.

16. Public information scores reveal that voters know as much about these incumbents as about their more threatened colleagues in the House.

# REFERENCES

CLARKE, P. and S. EVANS (1980) "All in a day's work: reporters covering congressional campaigns." Journal of Communication 30: 112-121.

———— (forthcoming) The Broken Quill: Journalism in Congressional Campaigns.

CLARKE, P. and E. FREDIN (1978) "Newspapers, television and political reasoning." Public Opinion Quarterly 42: 143-160.

COHEN, E. (1963) The Press and Foreign Policy. Princeton, NJ: Princeton University Press.

GANS, H. (1979) Deciding What's News. New York: Pantheon.

GLANTZ, A., A. ABRAMOWITZ, and M. BURKART (1976) "Election outcomes: whose money matters?" Journal of Politics 38: 1031-1038.

GOLDENBERG, E. and M. TRAUGOTT (1979) "Resource allocation and broadcast expenditures in congressional campaigns." Presented at the annual meeting of the American Political Science Association, Washington, D.C.

Inter-University Consortium for Political and Social Research (1979) The American National Election Study, 1978. Ann Arbor, MI: ICPSR.

JACOBSON, G. C. (1978) "The effects of campaign spending in congressional elections." American Political Science Review 72: 469-491.

———— (1975) "The impact of broadcast campaigning on electoral outcomes." Journal of Politics 37: 769-793.

MACKUEN, M. and S. COOMBS (1981) More than news: two studies in media power. Beverly Hills: Sage.

ROSHCO, E. (1975) Newsmaking. Chicago: University of Chicago Press.

WANAT, J. (1974) "Political broadcast advertising and primary election voting." Journal of Broadcasting 18: 413-422.

ZAJONC, R. (1980) "Feeling and thinking: preferences need no inferences." American Psychologist.

# Chapter 12

# NEWS AND NONEVENTS
## Making the Visible Invisible

### Mark Fishman

SOME HAPPENINGS in the world become public events. Others are condemned to obscurity as the personal experience of a handful of people. The mass media, and in particular news organizations, make all the difference. This study examines a crucial part of the newsmaking process—the routine work of beat reporters—which determines what becomes a public event and what becomes a nonevent. I will show that reporters' "sense of events," their methods for seeing the newsworthiness of occurrences, are based on schemes of interpretation originating from and used by agency officials within the institutions beat reporters cover. Nonevents are specific happenings that are seen as "out of character" within the institutional settings in which they occur. They are treated as "illegitimate occurrences" because they violate or challenge the procedural basis upon which all routine business is transacted in the setting. To seriously entertain these occurrences as potential news events would force journalists to question their own methods for detecting newsworthy events. In short, what routine newswork systematically excludes from public view are just those occurrences which might challenge the legitimacy of the institutions reporters depend on for news.

## THEORETICAL BACKGROUND

Borrowing from ethnomethodological, phenomenological and symbolic interactionist perspectives,[1] several studies within the last ten years have taken a fresh look at news and the work that produces it (Molotch and Lester, 1973, 1974; Lester, 1975, 1980; Tuchman, 1972, 1976, 1978b; Fishman, 1980). What sets these studies apart from earlier approaches is their primary focus on news as a practical accomplishment. The practical accomplishment perspective says that journalists' routine methods for producing news—that is, the very process of "newsgathering"—constructs an image of reality. In this view, news is neither a reflection nor a distortion of reality because either of these characterizations implies that news *can* record what is "out there." News stories, if they reflect anything, reflect the practices of the workers in the organizations that produce news.

Some time ago Walter Gieber (1964) made the point that "news is what newspapermen make it." What he and most of the traditional literature argued was that journalists, operating under newsroom norms, professional standards, and the deadlines and story quotas of their news organization, make crucial decisions involving the selection of which events to cover and which stories to print (Breed, 1955; Gieber, 1956, 1964; White, 1964; Stark, 1962; Galtung and Ruge, 1973; Epstein, 1973; Sigelman, 1973).

But the idea that news is a practical accomplishment implies much more than this. In recent years several studies have made the point that prior to any selection of events or stories, journalists must determine what constitutes an event, where events can be found, and how they can be told as stories (Molotch and Lester, 1974; Tuchman, 1978b; Fishman, 1980). All these matters, too, are accomplishments. Something must be done in order to see and to say that an event "happened" and that it was "timely" or "important." The world is not already organized into discrete events waiting to be noticed and selected by reporters. Nor do events have intrinsic qualities (such as "newsworthiness," "importance") which tell journalists how to deal with them (Lester, 1980).[2] Rather, events, and the qualities associated with them, are constituted in the process of their being noticed (Molotch and Lester, 1974). "What's going on here" or "what happened today" are things formed in the process of making an account (Tuchman, 1976; Fishman, 1980).

Molotch and Lester (1974) make the point that happenings in the world become potential events for the news only insofar as there is someone with an interest in noticing them, someone with a practical concern about telling a story. In this context, Molotch and Lester make a useful distinction between "mere occurrences" and "public events." Mere occurrences are happenings which participants or observers attend to during an ongoing activity. But they are not necessarily happenings about which one is interested in formulating an account for outsiders to the scene. Public events, however, are those occurrences about which accounts are constructed for the consumption of some wider public, the widest public of all being the audience of mass media news. The news media transform mere occurrences into public events, thereby making them "a resource for public discourse" (Molotch and Lester, 1975). The world outside an individual's first-hand experience is a "public reality" constructed by those who have the power to promote mere occurrences as public events. Occurrences not so promoted are lost to public consciousness: they remain either the "private troubles" of individuals powerless to make news or the little-known workings of the powerful who choose not to make certain things news.[3]

To be sure, events are formulated and accounts are made for strategic purposes. But Molotch and Lester's analysis passes over a fundamental question for the practical accomplishment perspective: How are journalists first able to perceive something as an event? Newsworkers must have ways of seeing meaningful chunks of activity in the happenings going on around them. They must have ways of delimiting the boundaries of events. How journalists routinely do these things is the subject of this study.

To examine the issue of how journalists see events, we must first consider what an event is. Events are interpreted phenomena, things organized in thought, talk, and action. People employ schemes of interpretation to carve events out of a stream of experience. Any scheme of interpretation, if it is to be useful in newswork, must allow reporters to pick events out of some ongoing activity and allow them to see events in relation to one another. That is, any scheme of interpretation that will be useful to a professional story-teller must enable that person to structure their experience in terms of a beginning, a middle, and an end. It must enable them to see a "chain of events"; that is, to see the overall action in terms of its phases with one phase leading into the next. Schemes of interpretation which do this will be called "phase structures."[4] Shortly, we will examine the specific phase structures that beat reporters use.

When we examine journalists' routine methods for perceiving news events we also discover what they routinely do not or will not see as news events. In other words, nonevents are by-products of schemes of interpretation (or phase structures). By a nonevent I do not simply mean any happening or "mere occurrence" which goes unpublicized. We can think of nonevents as a special class of mere occurrences, that is, those which are or could be conceived as events worthy of public attention.

Since events are interpreted phenomena, an event is always an event *for* somebody or some collectivity who has come to define a complex of activities as a meaningful entity. Because events are part of actors' definitions of the situation, and because these definitions are not always harmonious, all parties to some ongoing activity can differ considerably over "what's happening here," that is, what are the "real events." Nonevents are born in such a conflict.

Individuals or collectivities who do not share the same schemes of interpretation can see different events in the same displays of behavior. From one point of view, a behavioral display can be "obviously a significant event," while from another point of view it can either go unnoticed or be noticed but deemed "trivial" or "a fragment of something else." Moreover, one can notice that others who were present did not see an event; that is, for them it was a nonevent. The term nonevent, then, denotes that which can not be seen under a certain scheme of interpretation, but can be seen under a different one. It is a relational concept referring to a discontinuity between perspectives.

The concept of nonevent should be distinguished from the notion of "news selectivity" which is frequently employed in the literature on news bias (Lang and Lang, 1953, 1958; White, 1964; Gieber, 1956, 1964; Oestgaard, 1965; Robinson, 1970) to explain why journalists do not report some events. While that too is my purpose, I part ways with the latter concept in its assumption that all events (both the reported and unreported) are objective, unformulated entities "out there" in the world, and that they are given in perception and available to any competent, clear-headed observer. Consequently, most sociologists studying news bias have assumed that they (and perhaps a few other select social scientists) are objective enough to recognize all the "really real" events, against which they can measure the extent and pattern of selective reporting.

I am arguing that nonevents are not the "pure" events screened out by journalists. It makes no sense to speak of a "pure," unformulated event. Molotch and Lester (1973: 1) term the assumption that news can (or ought to) reflect some "pure" reality "out there" the *objectivity assumption*. As a methodological strategy Molotch and Lester (1974: 111) advocate dropping this assumption in order to study news not as a distortion of a reality that could be reflected, but as a document which reflects the work of news promoters and journalists, those who have the power to construct reality for a public (see also Tuchman, 1978a). Following that strategy, this study examines the practices of beat reporters and the practices of those they depend on for their "raw data" for news stories. These practices are viewed as methods for constructing public accounts. These methods ought to tell us why journalists and news sources formulate some mere occurrences as news events, while other occurrences, although formulated by somebody as an event, become nonevent.

## METHOD

The data for this study come from research conducted in a small California city in 1973-1974. Two kinds of participant observation were done. First, I worked for seven months on an alternative weekly newspaper reporting about the affairs of city hall and county government. This, my first experience as a journalist, allowed me to observe beat reporters working for other media in the community. More importantly, my experiences as an apprentice journalist provided data that no veteran newsworker could have told me and that is only clear to the novice: the invisible background knowledge one has to know in the first place to determine "what's going on" in a setting in order to "see" news in it. Thus, my fieldnotes from that period were, in part, a kind of diary reflecting not only what I saw of the work of other beat reporters, but also my observations of myself learning to report news.

The second phase of my research was conducted inside the city's major newspaper. Over a three-month period I observed the daily work routines of three journalists who covered the city hall, county government, and police-court beats. I shadowed each of these reporters as they moved through their work days, tape recording wherever possible their interactions with other reporters, editors, and news sources. Interviews were also conducted both before and after observations of their work.

### EXPOSURE TO OCCURRENCES: THE NEWS NET

To understand how nonevents arise in newswork we must first examine just what part of the world journalists come in contact with, and then we must look at the schemes of interpretation newsworkers employ in order to identify newsworthy events.

Happenings which become news must first become objects of experience to journalists. Journalists do not look for news everywhere at all times, but follow routines of coverage which locate reporters spatially and temporally in a determinate pattern, what Tuchman (1976, 1977, 1978b) terms a "news net." News organizations favor coverage of occurrences taking place during weekday business hours, since that is when the media allocate the vast majority of their newsgathering resources (Tuchman, 1977: 46, 1978b). Moreover, they favor coverage of prescheduled activities (news conferences, trials, legislative sessions) because these allow news personnel more control over their work (Tunstall, 1971: 24-30; Bagdikian, 1971: 97; Epstein, 1973: 103-105; Tuchman, 1973: 123-124).

News organizations also spatially allocate their newsgathering resources according to a system of beats and bureaus which locates reporters almost exclusively in legitimated institutions of society (Sigal, 1973: 119-30; Roshco, 1975: 62; Fishman, 1980; Tuchman, 1978b). Elsewhere (1980: 27-53) I have shown that the beat system includes within it a routine round of coverage activities that routes reporters through a small number of governmental agencies. Inside these agencies reporters follow a path which takes them to a few "key" locations which are seen as focal points of information (such as master files, press officers, and meetings). Thus, on the newspaper I studied this meant that crime was covered through the police and court bureaucracies. Local politics were covered through the meetings of the city council, county board of supervisors, and a host of other commissions, committees, and departments. Even nature was covered through a formally constituted organization (the U.S. Forestry Service). Whatever the sphere of human activities or natural occurrences (as long as it was covered through a beat) the newsworker knew it through officials and authorities, their files and their meetings. The round systematically exposed reporters to settings in which only formally organized transactions of official business appeared. Thus, the temporal and spatial organization of the news net is institutionalized in a beat round which steers reporters away from collectivities which are not formally constituted or bureaucratically organized (Fishman, 1980: 32-46). Community organizations and other informal groups, with members who have other jobs during normal business hours, meet on evenings and weekends when most reporters are off work. Grassroots social movements who lack the resources of press agentry, have few if any meetings, no formal leadership structure, and no "headquarters" are virtually impossible to cover according to standard news practices (Tuchman, 1977, 1978b; Gitlin, 1980).

Following the round insures that reporters will be in a position of exposure to occurrences on a beat. But it is quite another matter for reporters to know what to make of the activities to which they are exposed. Things going on right under a reporter's nose may not be noticed and thus not become news because the reporter does not have the means to see them as "something," as an event.

## SEEING EVENTS: PHASE STRUCTURES

What kinds of schemes of interpretation do reporters employ on beats in order to understand what is going on and in order to find events in complicated displays of activities available in talk, gestures, and documents? My ethnographic evidence indicates that journalists see events by using the same phase structures that beat agency officials use to formulate their own and others' activities as events.

Within organizational settings (whether or not there is a reporter covering them), complexes of activities are organized into events on the basis of a few specific phase structures. When stepping into a new beat, the novice reporter is confronted with an established domain of "typical events." For example, on the police beat, which included the city and county police and felony court, typical events were such things as "arrests," "sentencings," "preliminary hearings," "plea bargains," and "arraignments." These typifications were not encountered as a loose collection of event categories. They were seen as interrelated in a highly structured scheme: typical events were organized along a timeline or career path. Thus, the police reporter saw crime news events as organized around "legal cases," each of which progressed through a fixed sequence of phases: "the arrest," "the preliminary hearing," "arraignment," "readiness and settlement hearing" (plea bargaining), "probation review," and finally "the sentencing." The entire sequence of events is a phase structure, each phase defining a possible news event. A phase structure portrays streams of interwoven activities as an object moving through a series of stages, or as a case moving through a career.

This manner of picturing events and reporting on them is not restricted to formally organized collectivities. In everyday conversation one can present a complex of activities (for example, "What I did on my summer vacation") in a similar mode ("First I went to Boston and saw some close friends, then I flew to . . ."). The formulation of phase structures in everyday (nonbureaucratic) settings tends to be open-ended, something that can emerge in conversation. The names of each phase of action (the terminology of events) and the number of phases (how far back the chain of events begins, how recently it ends, and how much "detail" goes in between) can be formulated in a variety of ways, depending on the purposes of the speaker, what the speaker thinks hearers already know, the dynamics of the conversation, and a number of other contextual matters.

However, phase structures that reporters encounter in the agencies that they cover on their beat are formally fixed and prespecified. In these bureaucratic phase structures the sequential order of phases, the number of phases, their names, where they begin and end, the duration of time between each phase—all these are standardized because they are *made to happen* by bureaucrats following "proper" agency procedures. Bureaucratic phase structures are organizationally produced and organizationally enforced. For agency workers, a bureaucratic phase structure is not merely a scheme of interpretation; it is used to produce the case and to move it through a sequence of stages. It is a scheme for doing as well as a scheme for seeing. It continually informs workers "what the case looks like when it is done right" and "what I have to do in order to make it look like I have done it right." A bureaucratic phase structure is employed like a road map to produce the proper career of a case, and it is used as a scheme of interpretation to see the results of that work as the proper career of the case it was supposed to have been all along.

Despite the power and authority of legitimated institutions to impose an official scheme of interpretation on the activities taking place within their jurisdiction, it is important to note that bureaucratic phase structures are but one perspective on the chain of events associated with any actual case. For example, an individual taken into the criminal justice system as a "suspect" would most certainly organize their own experiences differently than the way an agency official or a journalist would. Events for the "suspect" could include such matters as their betrayal to police by a friend-turned-informer, the whole gamut of experience in jail, their formulation of a legal defense with an attorney, and so on. These kinds of "personal" or nonbureaucratic phase structure have received considerable attention in the sociological literature on "careers," both deviant and nondeviant. Most notably, Goffman's studies of "moral careers" (1961, 1963) and Roth's work on "timetables" (1963) show the way in which clients, patients, and prisoners organize a set of experiences under institutional and non-institutional conditions.

Although alternative formulations of activities may abound in the places reporters cover, the journalist's sense of events comes not from clients' oral histories (as it did for Goffman and Roth), but from official case histories. Journalists simply do not regularly expose themselves to "unofficial" interpretive schemes. For example, the police reporter steered clear of suspects, victims, and their families on his round. The only routine occasion in which the reporter was exposed to the suspect's version of events was during formal court hearings. But these are settings in which the suspect's version necessarily has been reformulated through an attorney to fit the legal-bureaucratic definition of events. In general, reporters in courtrooms will seek out lawyers, not their clients, as news sources. Why, then, do newsworkers so readily adopt a bureaucratic definition of events?

As already pointed out, beat reporters systematically and exclusively expose themselves through their rounds to formally organized settings which present them with bureaucratically packaged activities. Officials produce these activities so that they are seen as events composing some larger bureaucratic phase structure. Without reference to this intended phase structure no observer could understand what agency personnel were doing at any given moment of producing the case and its movement through a career. Thus, reporters must learn bureaucratic phase structures when they learn how to cover their beats. They employ these idealizations as schemes for interpreting bureaucratic activities, just as the officials they observe employ these idealizations to produce what the reporter sees. If the reporter does not have cognizance of the specific phase structures of the beat, the reporter cannot understand at the simplest level what is happening there, what officials mean by what they are doing. Lack of understanding this basic could be seen as serious journalistic incompetence. After a few stories betraying this "ignorance," the reporter would be transferred off the beat. For the journalist, bureaucratic phase structures are socially sanctioned schemes of interpretation.

## THE USES OF PHASE STRUCTURES

Bureaucratic phase structures are of much wider use to journalists than the mere passive understanding of "what's going on" within the agencies covered on a beat. In particular, bureaucratic phase structures enable newsworkers routinely to solve two practical problems in their work: (a) How is the reporter to know when something "new" is happening? and, (b) how is the reporter to distinguish "important" from "trivial" events? Let us consider each of these.

## Seeing "Newness"

News is considered a highly perishable commodity (Park, 1940: 676; Tuchman, 1973: 118; Roshco, 1975: 10-11). One aspect of the newsworthiness of stories is their timeliness. News must be published recently with respect to the occurrence of an event. But what is meant by "the occurrence of an event"? After all, most objects of news coverage are "occurring" all the time. A defendant in the criminal justice system is an "active case" whether standing before a judge, sitting in jail, or conferring with a lawyer. Antitrust suits develop over a period of several years through a succession of investigations, private negotiations and court hearings. Legislative issues can continue over months and years of public debate, backroom agreements, and official voting. Even so-called "spot news events" like floods, plane crashes, oil spills, and nerve gas leaks can take months before a "full" account of what took place surfaces. How does the journalist know at what points in time these continuing activities warrant a story?

Bureaucratic phase structures solve this problem because they provide the resource for reporters to sense when something "new" is happening. That is, an event "occurs" when a case crosses a boundary between phases, when it moves into a new phase of its bureaucratic career. This movement provides the occasion for writing a news story, although by no means does it guarantee that one will be written. When a case enters its next phase a news story is warranted only in the sense that the case's official change in status justifies for reporters and their superiors the coverage of the story at that point in time. Consider this routine crime story which I saw formulated on the police beat:

## WOMAN PLEADS IN SHOOTOUT CASE

Martha Mungan pleaded guilty today to a charge stemming from a pre-dawn shootout last December that left her wounded and her common-law husband dead from police bullets.

Mrs. Mungan pleaded guilty to one count of threatening and interfering with police officers, and a second count was dismissed.

Her sentencing was set for March 22 in the court of Superior Judge Lloyd Bennett.

> Police were called to Mrs. Mungan's home at 410-B Oceano Ave. last
> December by Rodney Charles Harvey, her common-law husband, during a
> family fight. In the ensuing gunfight, Mrs. Mungan was wounded and Harvey
> was killed when he retrieved the pistols and shot at police.

The reporter who was to write this article had been sitting in a courtroom looking for news. He suddenly knew that the court proceedings he had been viewing constituted "an event" as soon as he recognized that the defendant was Martha Mungan, that a plea bargain was being discussed, and that "this must be the Martha Mungan case in its next official phase" (the readiness and settlement hearing). On returning to the newsroom, he told his city editor what happened and said he preferred to wait until the sentencing in four weeks to write about the case. The city editor, however, told him to write about it now, because by doing a piece on her guilty plea the future story on her sentencing would be a "follow-up story."

The Martha Mungan case was only "an event" each time it resurfaced in the courts to enter a next phase in its judicial career. For all practical (journalistic) purposes, the case was invisible in between these resurfacings. Reporters will not write about a case at any point in time; they need a "news peg" or "news hook" to hang their story on (Crouse, 1974: 115, 240; but see Goldenberg, 1975). Bureaucratic phase structures provide these pegs and hooks. The agencies covered on a beat establish for journalists their very concept of timeliness.

Moreover, journalists can plan the reporting of future news stories around bureaucratically defined news pegs. With the publication of successive stories about a case newsworkers establish for themselves and for their audience a sense of continuing news and follow-up stories. Bureaucratic phase structures create the possibility of continuing news and, at the same time, enable preplanned coverage.

### Seeing "Importance"

Over and above the use of phase structures to occasion news stories, reporters employ these interpretive schemes in another important way. Once journalists have adopted a bureaucratic frame of reference, they possess a convenient means for spotting the highlights of events. That is, bureaucratic phase structures contain implicit *schemes of relevance*. A "scheme of relevance" is a scheme of interpretation which is used for deciding the relative importance of various perceived and interpreted objects. Two such schemes of relevance emerged from my observations of beat reporting in local government: the police, the courts, city hall, and county government. One scheme focused journalists' attention on the official dispositions of cases;

the other focused their attention on policy (as opposed to administrative) deliberations among officials.

One of the striking features of bureaucratic phase structures is their consistent orientation toward "the disposition of the case." Each official phase of a case is procedurally organized around some decision to be made or action to be taken which "settles" the case for the time being; that usually means sending it to its next phase, if there is one. This disposition of the case is seen as the "key" or "central" activity within each phase. The reason for this is not hard to understand. Insofar as journalists (or bureaucrats) see something as a case moving through a phase structure, then their interest is bound to focus on the official outcome of the case since bureaucratic cases only exist so that they can be properly settled.

The Martha Mungan case illustrates this. After encountering the case in court, the police reporter told me he was "very interested in what would happen to her." His primary interest was couched in terms of her "ultimate" disposition in the court system, that is, the future sentencing. His immediate practical interest was defined by her most recent disposition in the plea bargaining stage, that is, the results of the bargaining. In classic journalistic style, the lead sentence of the reporter's article stated, along with some background information, the "most important" aspect of the event, namely, its disposition. It was only at the end of the story that something other than the disposition of the case was mentioned.

The phenomenon of focusing on the dispositions of cases was not restricted to the police beat. On the city hall and county government beats the key activities reported were the formal legislative dispositions of issues, which usually meant the results of voting in meetings. Pleading guilty to interfering with a police officer, getting sentenced to two years in prison, voting down a raise in the property tax, and passing a new loitering ordinance are all bureaucratically appropriate dispositions *and* they are the stuff of which routine news stories are made.

All other features of these kinds of events are of secondary importance. They become the "details" which are defined by and revolve around the "central" fact of the case's actual disposition. The bargaining process that produced the guilty plea, the judge's lecture to the sentenced prisoner, the defendant's reason for "interfering" with the police, the arguments for and against the legislative issue, the behind-the-scenes lobbying which arranged the voting—these are all "details" which embellish the "basic event." By focusing on bureaucratically appropriate dispositions in their everyday reports, journalists' stories leave invisible the agency procedures and social conditions which give rise to these dispositions. In this sense routine news stories implicitly support the status quo by taking for granted these "background" factors. The report of Martha Mungan's guilty plea renders the procedure of plea bargaining unproblematic by obscuring it. Even less visible are the social conditions of Martha Mungan's life (as a ghetto resident) which surrounded the incident that made her into a judicial case in the first place.

The point is not that such "background" factors are never reported, but that they are rarely given attention. When they are highlighted, they are not published as routine news but "human interest stories," "news analysis," and "editorial opinion." In short, what is written outside a bureaucratic scheme of relevance is "soft news," not "hard news."[6]

Besides the dispositional aspect of cases, there is another, equally important bureaucratically defined scheme of relevance based on an orientation toward "policy" vs. "administrative" matters in bureaucratic work. The policy-administrative scheme of relevance derives from a fundamental "political division of labor" in governmental work: legislative or executive bodies deal with ("ought to deal with") policy matter, while an administrative staff deals with ("ought to deal with") administrative matters. Policy matters are considered "political decisions" (matters of opinion) of widespread importance which provide guidelines for the conduct of bureaucrats in the form of work instructions and the conduct of citizens in the form of laws and taxes. Administrative matters are considered "technical decisions," matters of professional problem-solving, which are made in the implementation of policy decisions.

Bureaucratic work is self-consciously organized in these terms. The policy-administrative distinction provides an orientation principle by which decision-making authority and bureaucratic work is distributed or delegated. As such, it provides participants in bureaucratic settings with procedures for organizing, displaying, and recognizing "proper" governmental work. These procedures include:

(1) If the business before us is an administrative matter, and this is a policy-making setting, then "rubber-stamp" the matter.
(2) If the business before us is a policy question, and this is an administrative setting, then refer the matter to a policy-making body.
(3) Serious questions about administrative matters should be taken up outside policy-making settings.

The distinction between policy and administrative business is so well known around institutions of government that it is normally taken for granted. Both the individuals who produce formal governmental business, in files or in meetings, and the journalists who cover these files and meetings employ the distinction as a means for deciding what matters of business are "important" and what are "trivial." For example, on every formal agenda for city and county meetings there were items of business which reporters would know in advance to focus on as potential newsworthy policy matters, while other agenda items were known in advance to be "merely" administrative matters on the agenda for technical reasons. To distinguish the newsworthy from the trivial agenda matters these reporters were relying on the bureaucratically defined policy-administrative distinction. The actual determination of whether any given agenda item was "policy" or "administrative" was an ad hoc decision for reporters, primarily depending on the way the item was presented in the agenda, any previous experience the reporter had with the matter, and the way local officials were talking about it prior to the formal meeting. Shortly, we shall see an example of how the policy vs. administrative distinction can lead to nonevents.

## NONEVENTS

Bureaucratic phase structures serve as schemes of interpretation and relevance which are definitive of news events. By implication, these schemes also define what activities within the reporter's beat territory are nonevents. To explicate the nature of journalistic nonevents, I will present two rather typical cases in which reporters "saw" no event, while others within the same setting were clearly trying to formulate such an event. Both cases reveal that nonevents are happenings which are seen as "out of character" in the social settings in which they occur. Reporters, and others familiar with the routine business transacted in a given setting, ignore a nonevent because if it were attended to as a reasonable occurrence, the nonevent would call into question the procedural basis upon which all routine business is transacted and would make problematic reporters' routine methods for identifying "important" events. Because they disrupt the "normal" flow of business-as-usual, nonevents reveal the taken-for-granted background features of social settings which reporters depend upon for their sense of events.

### ILLUSTRATION #1: THE INVISIBLE CRANK

In the course of their annual budget hearings, the county board of supervisors were considering next year's budget for the sheriff's department. This agenda item followed a prescribed sequence of activities: first, the chief administrative officer and the auditor-controller read their recommendations, then the board questioned the two bureaucrats, then the floor was opened to opponents and proponents, and finally the supervisors debated and voted on the issue.

During the "public input" phase, the speeches focused on whether the administrator was justified in recommending fewer new deputy sheriff positions than the county sheriff had asked for. The Sheriff's Department argued for a larger force so as to keep up with population increases. A taxpayer's group argued that new positions were unnecessary if one correctly calculated a "service ratio," the number of officers per 1000 inhabitants. Then a young woman took her turn at the public podium to say that she felt any consideration of funding the Sheriff's Department was "shameful." She recounted an incident in which she had been selling wares from a pushcart when a sheriff's car pulled up to her. Two deputies stepped out and asked what she was doing and if she had a license. She protested that she did not know she needed one.

At this point in the story the chairman of the board of supervisors interrupted and told the woman to come to the point or give up the floor. She simply continued: The sheriff's deputies had ordered her into their patrol car, and when she refused she was handcuffed and pulled in. When she insisted on knowing why she was being accosted, she was subjected to verbal abuse. At the sheriff's station she was bound hand and foot and left in a room for several hours. Once again, the chairman interrupted and asked the woman to please leave the podium. She ignored him and went on to say that the sheriffs finally released her with no explanation, but that they would not accept complaints she tried to lodge afterwards. By this point in her presentation, the woman was upset and angry. Again, the chairman broke in, said that they had heard enough, and told her she would be removed from the room if she insisted on staying at the podium. The woman quietly left.

From the point of view of those present the woman's talk was so out of character with the budget proceedings that her presentation could only be "bizarre." Throughout her speech no one in the room maintained eye contact with her; some people demonstrably showed their uninvolvement by doodling, reading, or conversing with others, and others clearly indicated their impatience by rolling their eyes, smiling, or making jokes. At the press table all the reporters acted as if the woman's talk signalled a "time out." Reporters stopped taking notes; soon one journalist left the room, while others started up conversations about unrelated matters. Attention to the meeting returned as soon as the woman left the podium.

The incident was not reported in any news medium. It was a nonevent, not in the sense that it was never seen, but in the sense that journalists considered it "not worth seeing." It never occurred to reporters that it could be a newsworthy event. It could only be an uncomfortable time out, a "snag" in the flow of the meeting. Why?

After all, the speaker was not incoherent, nor was her argument, taken on its own terms, senseless or irrelevant. But instead of speaking to the issues of "service ratios" and "tax cuts," the woman spoke of a corrupt law enforcement agency unworthy of any public support. What she proposed was "unreasonable" because it was not among the set of alternatives procedurally prescribed for the board to entertain in budget hearings. Moreover, the woman was not, and made no pretense to be, speaking from a structural position of interest: She represented no formally constituted group which fit into the constellation of interests appropriate to the issue. To entertain her talk as appropriate to the occasion, those present would have had to break the procedural bounds of the budget session in order to take on a wider political perspective from which one could render as problematic the issue of any funding for the Sheriff's Department.

### ILLUSTRATION #2: THE INVISIBLE CONTROVERSY

At a city council meeting a "routine" agenda item came up entitled "Recommendation for contract award: Bid No. 943—one three-wheeled street sweeper, diesel powered, to lowest bidder, Boulder Beach Machine Company, in total amount of $17,623.20." The public works director had placed the item on the agenda. Matters of this sort, in which a department head requests approval to purchase equipment after competitive bidding, are normally rubber-stamped by the council.

A council member began by pointedly asking the public works director why he was replacing the old gasoline street sweeper with a more expensive diesel one. The director responded that the more expensive vehicle would last longer and consume less fuel. Two other council members joined with the first to press the original question. In doing so, they also seemed to be implying that the director's motives were suspect. Soon a controversy had taken shape, with three council members defending the director, three questioning him, and one refraining from the debate.

It was apparent to the four reporters at the press table and to others present that this was not merely a dispute over a street sweeper. One side was implying incompetence or venality on the director's part; the other side was asserting that the whole matter was overblown and that it was not the council's business to embroil itself in the details of staff operations. The longer the controversy was kept alive, the more the issue became a question of confidence in a department head. After 20 minutes of increasingly bitter debate, the council voted four to three that the director should return next week with more information.

During the debate the four members of the press showed increasing signs of impatience with the proceedings. At first the reporters stopped taking notes, then they began to show disapproval to each other, and finally they made derisive jokes about the controversy. This was considered a "stupid debate" over a "trivial matter" unworthy of everyone's time and energy.

Although the incident did not go entirely unreported, one city hall reporter gave it only a brief mention. It was placed towards the end of a long story which cited several "miscellaneous" items of council business: "In other matters . . . the City Council voted 4-3 to continue until next week the recommendations of Public Works Director R. D. Dolan to purchase a diesel-powered street sweeper." This one sentence report, the only mention of the incident in any news medium, rendered the controversy invisible.

Even though at the time of the incident I was sitting at the press table as a reporter making derisive comments about the "foolishness" of the Council along with the other journalists, later it occurred to me how this controversy could be seen as an "important event" in city hall. The controversy explicitly dealt with whether it was appropriate for the council to embroil itself in the "details" of its staff's "administrative decisions." That is, *the controversy rendered problematic the policy-administrative scheme of relevance* discussed earlier. This was a debate over whether or not the council was going to abide by that traditional distinction. Three council members were challenging the underlying political analysis of government embodied in the policy-administrative scheme: that power is held by elected policy makers who, in turn, delegate authority to a professional staff to implement their decisions. Such an analysis contrasts with alternative views that power is held by an economic elite which manipulates official decision-making, or that power is held by bureaucrats and technicians who form a technocracy which runs government. By reference to these alternative schemes I could see the debate as "significant," "relevant," and "newsworthy."

But the controversy was a nonevent for the newsworkers at the press table. The incident was "a waste of time" because it was "an administrative matter" which "ought to have been rubber-stamped." It prevented other "more important policy matters" on the agenda from being considered. Thus, reporters could not see the controversy as a sign of the council's brewing dissatisfaction over who, in fact, was running city government (elected officials or technocrats). This was invisible because the means by which reporters oriented to the meeting in order to sort out the "important" from the "trivial" was also the very topic of the controversy. For the journalists to have taken that topic as a serious issue would have meant calling into question some of their basis procedures for interpreting routine governmental activities. Newsworkers do not readily part with their familiar methods of event interpretation—methods which make coverage of the beat territory possible in the first place.

**DISCUSSION**

There is a good deal of similarity between the two cases I have described. In both nonevents the reporters noticed things going on, but ignored them by taking a time out and pointedly showing their disapproval. Even though they literally "saw" something, all they saw was a moral character: These were occurrences that "did not deserve reporting." They were unnewsworthy in the strongest sense. The reporters never considered them as candidates for news. It is not that the journalists weighed their relative newsworthiness against other events, and then rejected the nonevents as not newsworthy enough. Rather, the two incidents were events that never had a chance. As soon as they were encountered the reporters knew to cease paying attention to them as serious candidates for news. They were unpublishable because they were "illegitimate events" which did not belong as topics in the territory (setting) in which they occurred.[7] To publish an illegitimate event would be "unprofessional." If the City Council becomes embroiled in a dispute over an administrative matter, it would be "misleading" to cover it "as if" it were another plausible argument in the debate. In short, to the reporter nonevents have the quality of being morally seen but professionally unnoticed.[8]

In both these nonevents their morally seen and professionally unnoticed character derived from the fact that they were occurrences that stood outside the procedurally provided-for alternative courses of action possible in the bureaucratic setting. Bureaucratic procedures organize activities within formal settings. To follow these activities—to understand "what's happening" and "what's important"—reporters rely on these same procedures as schemes of interpretation and schemes of relevance. Incidents which defy, ignore, or question the procedural foundation of the setting, if taken seriously by journalists (that is, entertained as potentially newsworthy events) would bring them to question the very methods they have come to rely upon in doing their work. Nonevents are possible because, ironically, reporters are blinded by their own methods for seeing events.

Nonevents are violations of the bureaucratic procedures which organize beat settings. If, from a bureaucratic point of view, something is not a legitimate occurrence, then, from a journalistic point of view, it can not be a genuine news event. News events and bureaucratic events are tightly bonded, and nonevents are the consequence of this union, the illegitimate offspring, as it were. Thus, nonevents are not primarily the result of reporters' personal biases, nor of their attempts to protect friendly bureaucratic sources, nor of their following orders from politically motivated editors. Rather, nonevents are a consequence of journalists protecting their own methods of event detection—methods which are wedded to the bureaucrat's methods of formulating events.

Because this study has dealt with beat reporting on a single newspaper, the generality of the findings can be questioned. Moreover, it is not clear whether and to what extent this analysis of nonevents applies to news produced by reporters who do not cover a beat, such as, general assignment reporters and most broadcast journalists. Further research on non-beat reporting and on other news organizations is necessary.

Nevertheless, the available data dealing with whether American newspapers detect occurrences mainly through beats or through general assignment indicates that the beat system is the predominant mode of coverage. Sigal (1974: 119-130) found that on the New York Times and Washington Post reporters largely worked on beats, particularly in government institutions in Washington, and heavily relied on official channels for news. The news organization I studied, which was fairly typical of the smaller news organizations that make up the vast majority of American dailies, located most of its reporters on beats: 69 percent of the paper's reporting staff positions were devoted to full-time beats while 31 percent were full-time general assignment.

The situation is rather complex with regard to broadcast journalism. Few television reporters seem to cover beats in the same sense that their colleagues in the print media do (Epstein, 1973: 135-138). This does not mean, however, that most occurrences are detected and interpreted by general assignment reporters. TV news organizations, both network and local, heavily depend on the print media for their sense of newsworthy events (Epstein, 1973: 141-143; Fishman, 1978). Thus, newspaper reporters, who largely work beats, may indirectly determine what most of the newsworthy events are for television journalists.

## SUMMARY AND CONCLUSIONS

A massive bureaucratic apparatus mediates between happenings in the world and reports of those happenings in the media, between mere occurrences and public events. Recent research on the news media shows that newsworkers detect occurrences primarily through legitimated institutions of the society, which is to say, through such bureaucratically organized agencies as police departments, mortuaries, welfare agencies, congressional committees, and the like. What is known and knowable by the media depends on the information-gathering and information-processing resources of these agencies. Moreover, since reporters mainly "see" events during city council meetings, at White House press conferences, in arrest reports, and through the announcements of public relations officers, news as a form of knowledge is shaped by the contexts in which agencies present and package occurrences for journalists.

Journalists do not simply detect happenings through bureaucracies. They also interpret what they are exposed to by means of schemes of interpretation and schemes of relevance. They employ, and need to employ, virtually the same schemes of interpretation and relevance used by agency officials. While this similarity of perspectives allows journalists to "see" some things as events, it also makes invisible a specific class of occurrences as newsworthy happenings. These become nonevents.

Nonevents are occurrences which cannot be seen as legitimate events under the interpretive schemes of agency officials. Nonevents are occurrences which pay no mind to the idealizations of "proper" bureaucratic procedure embodied in an agency's interpretive schemes. Because reporters adopt the schemes of interpretation and relevance employed within the agencies of their beat, they cannot and will not see as news things which might seriously challenge an agency's idealizations of "what's going on" and "what should be happening."

To a certain extent newswork on a beat is "repair work." In the case of the invisible crank who was seen as sidetracking the normal progression of the budget hearings, both the county officials and the reporters at the press table worked to repair the situation, to restore it to "a right state of affairs," by getting rid of the "crank." The same repair work was apparent in the case of the invisible controversy at city hall. Not reporting both matters was a way of discouraging these and other incidents like them. Beat reporters "clean up" and repair flawed bureaucratic proceedings. Making coherent news stories out of bureaucratic proceedings in this way renders matters which violate or challenge official idealizations invisible in newspapers. Anything outside the "proper" official treatment of the case tends to be ignored in bureaucratic settings and in routine news stories.

Repair work is designed to normalize activities in bureaucratic settings. Beat reporters do not show this repair work and the part they play in doing it because it is one of the methods by which they construct their accounts. Thus, the news story does not show the sense in which it is a repaired version of what happened. Routine news legitimates the existing political order by disseminating bureaucratic idealizations of the world and by filtering out troublesome perceptions of events. It leads the public to assume that the world outside their everyday experience is a proper sphere of bureaucratic (official) control; that everything falls within some agency's jurisdiction; that policy makers, indeed, make the important decisions while administrators merely implement those decisions; and that, with the exception of a few corrupt and incompetent officials, government institutions function smoothly according to rational-legal standards. What readers of routine news see is normalized bureaucratic work, nothing more nor less than the orderly bureaucratic universe as it is meant to be and as it is continually trying to be.

# NOTES

1. The work of Garfinkel (1967), Goffman (1974), Smith (1974a, 1974b), and Zimmerman and Pollner (1970) have been major influences on the studies cited below.

2. For example, in the traditional literature "newsworthiness," "timeliness," or "importance" are sometimes thought to be characteristics in events which enable journalists to decide whether and how to cover them. More often, the assumption is that "newsworthiness," "timeliness," or "importance" are criteria of news selection which journalists apply to particular events. In the latter case, events are assumed to have other intrinsic characteristics (for example, a certain duration, the participation of important persons, drama) which journalists directly translate into their "criteria" of news selection.

3. In a sense, mere occurrences in the collective life of a society are analogous to dreams in the conscious life of the individual: if we do not write, talk, or think about them upon awakening, they are lost to us as meaningful experiences that can be reflected upon and have some bearing on our wakeful existence.

4. The term "phase structure" is my own. However, the idea that schemes of interpretation allow people to see ongoing activities in terms of phases of action or chains of events is a theme that appears throughout the work of Alfred Schutz (1962, 1964, 1966). The concept of "phase structure" also has certain similarities to Tuchman's (1976) and Gitlin's (1980) concept of news as a "frame" (see also Goffman, 1974).

5. This and all other names of specific people, places, and organizations in the research setting are pseudonyms.

6. This distinction between hard and soft news differs from Tuchman's (1973). She claims that the distinguishing characteristic for journalists has to do with the scheduling aspect of the event; that is, an event which demands speedy coverage on the newsworker's part is hard news; an event which can be published at the newsworker's leisure is soft news. However, events themselves cannot demand anything. Rather, it is the way journalists treat events that produces the sense of timeliness. Thus, Tuchman's distinction begs the question of how newsworkers know in the first place whether to treat something as demanding speed. Journalists distinguish hard news from soft news on the basis of whether it is to be written from the angle of its phase structure disposition or from some other nonbureaucratically defined angle. The hardness and softness of news is not inherent in events themselves but in the decisions of newsworkers.

7. This illegitimate quality of nonevents is closely related to Goffman's (1963) notion of "spoiled" social identity. Like the stigmatized person, the stigmatized event is shunned because it possesses attributes which are out of character with the setting in which it is found.

8. This terminology ("morally seen but professionally unnoticed") is patterned after Garfinkel's (1967) characterization of certain essential features in common discourse as "seen but unnoticed" in everyday social settings.

## REFERENCES

BAGDIKIAN, B. H. (1971) The Information Machines. New York: Harper and Row.

BREED, W. (1955) "Social control in the newsroom." Social Forces 33: 326-35.

CROUSE, T. (1974) The Boys on the Bus. New York: Ballantine.

EPSTEIN, E. J. (1973) News from Nowhere. New York: Random House.

FISHMAN, M. (1980) Manufacturing the News. Austin: University of Texas Press.

——— (1978) "Crime waves as ideology." Social Problems 25 (June): 531-543.

GALTUNG, J. and M. RUGE (1973) "Structuring and selecting news," in S. Cohen and J. Young (eds.) The Manufacture of News. Beverly Hills: Sage.

GARFINKEL, H. (1967) Studies in Ethnomethodology. Englewood Cliffs, NJ: Prentice-Hall.

GIEBER, W. (1956) "Across the desk: a study of 16 telegraph editors." Journalism Quarterly 33 (Fall): 423-432.

——— (1964) "News is what newspapermen make it," pp. 173-182 in L. A. Dexter and D. M. White (eds.) People, Society and Mass Communications. New York: Free Press.

GITLIN, T. (1980) The Whole World is Watching. Berkeley: University of California Press.
GOFFMAN, E. (1961) Asylums. Garden City, NY: Doubleday.
_____ (1963) Stigma. Englewood Cliffs, NJ: Prentice-Hall.
_____ (1974) Frame Analysis. New York: Harper and Row.
GOLDENBERG, E. (1975) Making the Papers. Lexington, MA: D. C. Heath.
LANG, K. and G. E. LANG (1953) The unique perspective of television." American Sociological Review 18 (February): 2-12.
_____ (1968) Politics and Television. New York: Quadrangle.
LESTER, M. (1975) "News as practical accomplishment." Ph.D. dissertation, University of California, Santa Barbara.
_____ (1980) "Generating newsworthiness: the interpretive construction of public events." American Sociological Review 45 (December): 984-994.
MOLOTCH, H. and M. LESTER (1973) "Accidents, scandals and routines." The Insurgent Sociologist 3 (Summer): 1-11.
_____ (1974) "News as purposive behavior: the strategic use of routine events, accidents and scandals." American Sociological Review 39 (February): 101-112.
_____ (1975) "Accidental news: the great oil spill." American Journal of Sociology 81 (September): 235-310.
OESTGAARD, E. (1965) "Factors influencing the flow of news." Journal of Peace Research 2: 40-63.
PARK, R. E. (1940) "News as a form of knowledge." American Journal of Sociology 45 (March): 669-686.
ROBINSON, G. J. (1970) "Foreign news selection is non-linear in Yugoslavia's Tanjug agency." Journalism Quarterly 47: 340-51.
ROSHCO, B. (1975) Newsmaking. Chicago: University of Chicago.
ROTH, J. (1963) Timetables. Indianapolis: Bobbs-Merrill.
SCHUTZ, A. (1962) Collected Papers, Vol. I: The Problem of Social Reality. The Hague: M. Nijhoff.
_____ (1964) Collected Papers, Vol. II: Studies in Social Theory. The Hague: M. Nijhoff.
_____ (1966) Collected Papers, Vol. III: Studies in Phenomenological Philosophy. The Hague: M. Nijhoff.
SIGAL, L. V. (1973) Reporters and Officials. Lexington, MA: D. C. Heath.
SIGELMAN, L. (1973) "Reporting the news: an organizational analysis." American Journal of Sociology 79 (July): 132-151.
SMITH, D. (1974a) "Theorizing as ideology," pp. 41-44 in R. Turner (ed.) Ethnomethodology. Baltimore: Penguin.
_____ (1974b) "The social construction of documentary reality." Sociological Inquiry 44, 4: 257-267.
STARK, R. (1962) "Policy and the pros: an organizational analysis of a metropolitan newspaper." Berkeley Journal of Sociology 7: 11-31.
TUCHMAN, G. (1972) "Objectivity as strategic ritual." American Journal of Sociology 77 (January): 660-678.
_____ (1973) "Making news by doing work: routinizing the unexpected." American Journal of Sociology 79, 1: 110-131.
_____ (1976) "Telling stories." Journal of Communication 26, 4: 93-97.
_____ (1977) "The exception proves the rule: the study of routine news practices," pp. 43-62 in P. Hirsch, P. V. Miller, and F. G. Kline (eds.) Strategies for Communication Research. Beverly Hills: Sage.
_____ (1978a) "Television news and the metaphor of myth." Studies in the Anthropology of Visual Communication 5 (Fall): 56-62.
_____ (1978b) Making News: A Study in the Construction of Reality. New York: Free Press.

———— (1978c) "The newspaper as a social movement's resource," pp. 186-215 in G. Tuchman, A. K. Daniels, and J. Benet (eds.) Hearth and Home: Images of Women in the Media. New York: Oxford University.

TUNSTALL, J. (1971) Journalists at Work. London: Constable.

WHITE, D. M. (1964) "The gate-keeper: a case study in the selection of news," pp. 160-172 in L. A. Dexter and D. M. White (eds.) People, Society and Mass Communications. New York: Free Press.

ZIMMERMAN, D. and M. POLLNER (1970) "The everyday world as a phenomenon," pp. 80-103 in J. D. Douglas (ed.) Understanding Everyday Life. Chicago: Aldine.

# Chapter 13

# MASS COMMUNICATOR STUDIES
## Similarity, Difference, and Level of Analysis

### D. Charles Whitney

SOME YEARS AGO the author worked on a morning newspaper on which the reporting of local news was divided traditionally, between a city desk—responsible for gathering, writing, and editing news from the city and county in which the paper was published—and a state desk—charged with production of news from the rest of the state. Early one afternoon, about seven hours before the first deadline of the day, a woman, an apparent suicide, jumped from a bridge into a river that served as a border between the "home" county and an adjacent one. When the police radio report came in, a photographer was dispatched to the scene. No reporter was. The city editor and state editor monitored the police radios waiting to learn which county the woman's body would be recovered from, the "home" county, making it a city desk story, or the adjacent county, making it a state desk story. Three hours later, she came up on the city side.

An organization's policy for allocating newsgathering resources may be arrived at in a number of ways; for newspapers, the major divisions are generally geographical: city desk, state desk, national, international. The decisions for such an allocation, if they could ever be traced within an individual organization, probably would be construable as rational; they make sense in a general sense. That such a decision does not make sense in specific cases is a practical problem for journalists, certainly, but it is also a methodological problem for researchers and one this chapter wishes to address. It is a problem of level of analysis.

A second methodological problem is with the assessment of similarities and differences in research on mass communicators.[1] Defining and finding similarities and differences is at the core of doing any research: where we seek and find similarity or pattern, we interpret it as structure or regularity; more frequently, however, the researcher begins by expecting differences which can be accounted for by some research hypothesis: the variation (differences) in some dependent variable B can be accounted for by variations (differences) in some independent variable A. If these are found and covary as expected, the differences have meaning for the researcher. If not, they are problematic. There are other sorts of similarity-and-difference concerns which are problematic in research on communicators, and several are discussed below. They relate to the initial problem suggested for the chapter, that of level of analysis.

The notions that this essay wishes to explore are relatively simple. They are that the methods by which we have chosen, over the past three decades, to examine the attitudes, practices, and contexts of mass communicators' work by necessity shade researchers from parts of the importance that their studies contain. On the one hand, much of the recent valuable work in the field has been stimulated by shifting level of analysis up by a notch from previous work; on the other, however, a contemporary search for "structure" may leave in its wake a glossing of true and significant differences where none seems apparent.

## LEVELS OF ANALYSIS

Two recent commentaries (Hirsch, 1977; Dimmick, 1978) have argued that integration of mass communicator studies by level of analysis is useful. Hirsch (1977: 13) suggests that a "principle of uniqueness" has impeded communicator study by confusing concepts of internal organization and institutional function. He proposes considering occupational levels, organizational ones, and institutional ones separately. Dimmick (1978), for example, divides the levels of analysis in communicator studies more finely, into eight hierarchical levels, from the intra-individual to the societal, and argues for research across several levels of analysis simultaneously. For present purposes, it is sufficient to point out, as Hirsch does, that often researchers appear not to be aware that they *are* operating at more than one level at a time. Doing so puts researchers at their peril.

## SIMILARITY AND DIFFERENCE

This review arbitrarily dates the history of mass communicator studies from the 1950 publication of David Manning White's pioneering "Mr. Gates" case study of a Peoria, Illinois, telegraph editor. It was the first study to apply Lewin's (1947) concept of a "gate-keeper" to news selection; it chose as a research setting virtually an ideal case for the study of selection, inasmuch as a single, easily observed and interviewed individual actualizes the selection by an entire organization, thus simultaneously operating at two levels of analysis at once. Moreover, the White analysis contained the kernels of several ideas, notably that environmental constraints such as news space, lack of time, and standardization and duplication of content impact on news, that motivated further inquiry by others. White, however, was palpably disappointed by an unanticipated finding that the "gate-keeper's" biases intruded in the selection process. The terminal sentence in White's study (1950: 390) notes: "Through studying his overt reasons for rejecting news stories from the press associations, we see how highly subjective, how based on the 'gate-keeper's' own set of experiences, attitudes and expectations the communication of 'news' really is."

White's surprise at this finding is worthy of note. In the first place, the original gatekeeper study is remarkably atheoretical and ahistoric; its only two footnotes, for example, are to Lewin and to a quotation from Wilbur Schramm noting that enormous numbers of choices must be made in getting a symbol from a sender to a receiver. In such a context, then, and particularly in an era in which "objective" journalism was a norm for journalists and for the researchers studying them, surprise would seem appropriate. Moreover, when one does the first case study of its kind, on one individual, any formal external assessment of similarity or difference, whether it be the question of the representativeness of the gatekeeper or of the institutional function itself, is difficult; the researcher is thrown back on to personal expectations. Here, White recognized that "Mr. Gates" might not be in some senses representative of all newspaper wire editors, but his post hoc assertion of "subjectivity" is relatively unqualified. He presumably would thus expect for other editors that the finding of editors' subjective selection would obtain and be a principal characterization or pattern in news selection, though individual patterns of selection might vary given individual differences in individual editors. Thus a "pattern of idiosyncrasy" might prevail, if the level of analysis were individual behavior.

However, authors of two 1977 articles independently returned to the White study and noted that White's own data contradict a finding of subjective selection as the principal matter of importance in the original gatekeeper study. McCombs and Shaw (1977) and Hirsch (1977) each note that the data should be reinterpreted at a higher level of analysis than White had employed in his interpretation. That higher level is the organization, and specifically at issue are the characteristics of the news "input" and "output" that Mr. Gates dealt with. Both studies noted a remarkable consistency or similarity in the proportions of news in certain content categories presented to the editor, and the proportions he selected as news. White had presented these data but not commented on them. McCombs and Shaw note in reanalyzing White's data that the Spearman rank order correlation coefficient between proportions of news in seven content categories presented to the editor and proportions in the categories that he selected is .64; for a replication of the White study seventeen years later on the same editor (Snider, 1967), the Spearman r rises to .80 (in the interim, the newspaper dropped one wire service).

What led Hirsch and McCombs and Shaw back to the study, a quarter century after its publication? Each notes that White's data make more sense interpreted at a higher level of analysis. Hirsch (1977: 22-23) notes that when the level of analysis is shifted from individual decision about a single transmitted news story to "decision making" about an aggregate ensemble of news, that is, from individual logic or illogic to "organizational logic" or the context in which individual decisions are exercised, the context of relevant data shifts. Hirsch's retrospective look is smoothed by a generation of researchers who have examined news organizations as organizations (see Gieber, 1956; Tuchman, 1972, 1973, 1978, for example). McCombs and Shaw, on the other hand, return to the data for evidence of "agenda-setting;" the White data fit that model's assumptions if proportions of stories in news content categories presented to the editor are taken to be priorities on the "news agenda" and the editor's selection proportions are considered a reflection of a personal news agenda. Since the editor, however, is also in the process of creating a "news agenda" for an ultimate audience, that is, is functioning as an organization, we have an example of agenda-setting one level of analysis higher than usual for the agenda-setting model.

There are, of course, possible confounds that shifting level of analysis on such a data set might introduce. Straightforward observation (such as Bagdikian, 1971: 99-103) indicates that individual news selection decisions are made in linear sequence, as wire copy comes in, and very fast (one observed gatekeeper required two to ten seconds to scan each story, decide whether to use it and order editing changes to be made in those he selected); moreover, given the nature of wire service transmissions and the nature of news production (returning to the organizational level), it is possible that time of transmission, known to be related to probability of selection of an item, so that earlier transmitted items are more likely to be selected (Jones, Troldahl, and Hvistendahl, 1961; Bagdikian, 1971) might also be related to biased probability of inclusion in particular content categories; for example, "international news" might move early, since the United States is near the end of the international day, as might human interest stories, written on a previous day and transmitted at leisure.[2]

To guard against these possibilities, Whitney and Becker (forthcoming) experimentally manipulated proportions of content in two sets of daily "wire files" of 98 news leads each; in one, proportions of content resembled a "normal" wire file, in that disproportionately large numbers of stories concerned international, national, and political events and disproportionately small numbers concerned labor, accidents and disasters, and crime and vice, while in the other, an "abnormal" condition, equal proportions of stories appeared in each of seven content categories. A sample of 46 professional newspaper and television news editors agreed to select 21 stories from each set, with order-of-administration systematically varied. The results can be variously interpreted. On the one hand, selections appear to be idiosyncratic: in the abnormal or balanced condition, only six stories (6.1 percent) were selected by *no* editors, and only seven (7.1 percent) were selected by as many as half, with the most-often selected story chosen by 83 percent of the editors; in the "normal" or unbalanced condition, only *two* stories (2.1 percent) were selected by no editors, but 24 (24.5 percent) were chosen by half the editors, with 78 percent selecting the most favored story. Thus the treatment appears to have introduced some but not an overwhelming amount of structure into the selection task.

By returning to the original selections and examining individual stories, however, a notion of "patterned idiosyncrasy" might be upheld. However, examination of the correlation, in the "normal" condition between proportions of incoming and selected stories in the content categories is revealing, for it shows a strong positive relationship (Pearson r = .71); since incoming proportions in the "abnormal" or balanced condition are invariant, a comparison cannot be computed. If proportions from the "normal" deck are correlated with selections from the "abnormal," however, as an indicator of the degree to which "normal" wire service values impact on selection, the correlation is negative and nonsignificant (Pearson r = −.41). Moreover, when individual editor's proportions of selection in the balanced and unbalanced conditions are compared, they appear virtually unrelated (Pearson r = −.05, n.s.). Taken together, the findings indicate that the priority structure of incoming news, when there is one, cues editors about output priorities, and that the cueing is stronger than a set of internalized "news values" as evidenced by lack of correlations within individuals across treatments. Thus while there are certainly some differences, idiosyncrasy and perhaps "bias" in individual selection, it is less impressive than the similarity manifested across two levels of analysis.

It was early noted that methodology itself affects assessment of similarity and difference even within levels of analysis. In variable analysis, the project concerns the relationship of variation on one variable or set of variables, designated "independent" with variation on some variable or set of variables denoted "dependent." When either the independent or dependent "variable" does not vary, the researcher generally treats the research evidence as problematic, finds some way to make the variables variable again, or ignores the evidence of nonvariation and moves onto some other aspect of the study where variations exist. To do so risks overlooking or undervaluating the meaning of and importance of the evidence.

A content analytic example comes to mind and will be examined although the assumption that content reflects editorial practice in many cases obtains only hazily. In an attempt to discover whether, in April and May of 1973, the then-new format of "Eyewitness News" on WABC-TV made a significant difference in what was reported in the news broadcast, compared with other stations' broadcasts, Dominick, Wurtzel, and Lometti (1975) analyzed two sample weeks of each station's newscasts; they were particularly interested in whether the Eyewitness News (WABC) program featured more violence, more features, more human interest, and more "interaction" than the news on other stations. An analysis of variance on mean minutes devoted to each content category showed statistically significant differences in five of six of their content categories (see Table 13.1).

The point that the article misses, however, is the striking *similarity* among news selection—production structures on the three stations. If minutes devoted to each category are treated as ranks, the average Spearman r for all pairs of stations is .92; the coefficient of concordance for the ranks of the three stations (Kendall's W) is .95. Read this way, the data appear to argue mightily not for differences between the stations but for a standard structure of television news; the differences pale compared with the similarities.[3] This is more than a simple matter of interpretation. It is first a matter of level of analysis. Dominick et al., were seeking differences in the behavior of three organizations. The reanalysis is a step more molar; it looks at structural similarity at a supra-organizational, "institutional" level.

*Why* one would do either sort of analysis depends strongly on the level at which one wishes to operate, and, as will be noted below, particularly upon the theoretical orientation of the researcher. In general, the argument must be made that all researchers would do well, insofar as their evidence will allow them to do so, to heed similarities and differences at a level of analysis one above the focus of their work and to attempt to construe similarities and differences at a level one below their focus. Moreover, a particular problem manifests itself when the research is a variable analytic one: in such studies, the search clearly is for differences, and the object is obtaining statistically significant ones. Hunting for similarities in such approaches is nettlesome, because the research logic demands differences for significant results. One cannot seek similarities, for these require the acceptance of a null hypothesis; for this, no strong rules of evidence, no significance tests, exist.

Another difficulty comes in multivariate analysis. Becker, Beam, and Russial (1978), in seeking correlates of journalistic performance, an institutional concept, through reanalysis of organizational and community data gathered for the New England Daily Newspaper Survey (Ghiglione, 1973),

TABLE 13.1   Total Times Spent on Selected Content Categories (in minutes).

| Category | WABC (n = 10) | WNBC (n = 10) | WCBS (n = 10) | p* |
|---|---|---|---|---|
| Hard news | 270.3 (1) | 243.6 (1) | 245.0 (1) | n.s. |
| Feature | 76.2 (3) | 102.8 (2) | 65.0 (2) | .05 |
| Violence | 76.8 (2) | 33.3 (3) | 51.5 (3) | .05 |
| Humor | 27.2 (5) | 10.4 (4) | 9.6 (4) | .06 |
| Human Interest | 31.8 (4) | 7.8 (5) | 8.5 (5) | .05 |
| Interaction | 1.2 (6) | 1.0 (6) | 6.2 (6) | .01 |

NOTE: *Probability estimate based on an analysis of variance of the means in the above table. Figures in parentheses are column rank orders.

SOURCE: From J. Dominick, A. Wurtzel, and G. Lometti, "Television Journalism versus Show Business: A Content Analysis of Eyewitness News," *Journalism Quarterly* 52: 213-218. Used by permission.

found that only one of eight community variables, median education, was significantly related to the authors' index of performance. Of 21 organizational variables, however, 11 are so related. When circulation, itself related to performance (Pearson r = .24), is dichotomized to seek further differences, few of the variables related to performance are affected; those organizational variables related to "quality" journalistic performance by and large remain related to it regardless of size of newspaper. An attempt to analyze independent contributions of the organization variables in the study, however, proves impossible, because the independent variables are in many cases massively correlated; thus the independent contributions made by, for example, number of full-time news-editorial staff, top editorial salary and large-chain, small-chain, and single-paper ownership in a multiple regression analysis proves impossible because of the statistical problem of multicollinearity.

The problem is that a number of the organizational variables are highly correlated with each other. Under such circumstances, trying to assess in multiple regression analyses the independent effects of any one of them, such as amount of education of recent staff additions, is impossible, since its variation is very closely related to variation on a number of other "performance" correlates, such as number of women on the editorial staff. While multicollinearity is a research problem, it also can be an important finding in its own right, as it defines structure across organizations. In other words, finding a group of organization variables to be strongly related describes the structure of the organization and, more significantly, the institution in terms of those related variables (see also DuBick, 1978).

It was earlier noted that in variable analytic studies, when one is confronted with the possibility that one's variables will not vary, that is, that similarities and not differences might characterize a situation, one can make the variables vary. It is worth reexamining the oft-cited (but never repli-cated) Pool and Shulman (1959) study, "Newsmen's Fantasies, Audiences and Newswriting." They early note that "the author's private fantasies are clearly not the only things that affect the character of what he writes. An experienced professional newsman will have acquired great facility in turn-ing out a standard product for each of the many kinds of routine story of which so much of the news consists."

In short, the "real news" is an organizational product born of routines. That notwithstanding, Pool and Shulman assigned 132 Boston University students, not professional news personnel, to write from factsheets one of four stories, crossbroken by "good news-bad news" and by local and distant events; the students were then asked to name all persons, known and un-known, whom they had thought of while writing and to rate each of these persons on a six-point scale from "very approving" to "very critical" as regarded their thoughts about these persons' approval or disapproval of what they were writing. As expected, students writing "good news" stories pro-duced more approving images (though those writing "bad news" stories also produced images with a mean above the midpoint on the scale, a point missed by the authors).

But the important step came next. To maximize variation and to test an hypothesis that persons holding incongruent images (that is, an approving image on a "bad news" or a critical image on a "good news" one) suggested to Pool and Shulman the trichotomizing of the sample into groups producing "modal," highly supportive and highly critical image groups; data from the 86 modal students (two-thirds of the subjects on whom usable data were collected) were discarded; the remaining 43 students were classified as "congruent," meaning they had critical images on bad news stories or sup-portive images on good news stories, or "incongruent" producers of support-ive images on bad news stories or critical images on good news ones. Interestingly, the classification produces about twice as many incongruent as congruent students. News stories produced by these 43 remaining students were subjected to content analysis ratings by two expert judges and the hypothesis that incongruent images are related to less accurate reporting is supported.

For a number of reasons, the internal validity of the study can be chal-lenged; it is probably more useful, though, to consider the authors' own caveat, at a level of analysis higher than their ingenious experiment, and to suggest that the 86 modal students whose stories were not analyzed since they did not produce highly supportive or critical images might more closely resemble the neutral-valued American journalist of the late 1950s or early 1960s. Further, as Darnton (1975) has suggested, Pool and Shulman ignore the standardizing influences of the newsroom's structure; the immediate reference groups news personnel must deal with, including sources, editors and other reporters; occupational socialization accomplished on-the-job; and the standardized structure of news "story-telling." Each of these, it reasonably can be argued, serve to depress any "natural" differences a group of novice reporters might bring to a newswriting assignment; the similarities will overwhelm any preexisting differences.

## LEVEL OF ANALYSIS AND STRUCTURE

Part, but only part, of the broadening of the study of mass communicators in the past 30 or so years has been marked by upward shifts in level of analysis, from the relatively microscopic "gatekeeper" studies of Pool and Shulman (1959) and White (1950), for example, to "gatekeeping" studies in which the organization becomes the gatekeeper (see Bailey and Lichty, 1972), to institutional studies, and on, in a few cases, to relatively global "media systems" studies (see Donohue, Tichenor, and Olien, 1972). At the most global levels, it is quite possible for an analyst to generalize about individuals or mass communication organizations through cultural, historical, or semiotic analysis, largely by examination of content; to do so is to impute norms, values or ideology to practices (for example, Hall, 1973) or to "organizational adjustment" (McQuail, 1969). Analyses of these sorts are necessarily general (see Dimmick, 1978) both because ascending a hierarchical ladder of analysis level entails generality and because such analysis frequently either assumes homology for a construct at two levels of analysis or, as suggested above, discounts evidence suggesting that other agents at other levels of analysis depress, modify, or eliminate the postulated relationship.

The suggestion that the mapping of concepts at two levels of analysis may require different procedures and definitions is not novel; others within communication studies and particularly in organizational behavior have stressed it in the past; Hirsch (1977: 19), for example, notes that a divergence between "occupational" and "organizational" sociologies is attributable to observations at different levels within the same organization: "What one interprets as arbitrary or politically inspired interference and censorship, the other sees as perfectly reasonable in terms of rationales and logic followed at the higher level of organization with which it is familiar."

In part this is a levels problem, and in part it is a generality-specificity problem. The anecdote at the beginning of the chapter serves as one example: it is "rational" for an organization to allocate its newsgathering resources geographically: doing so facilitates wide coverage, economical communication; that it may lead to individual cases of newsgathering absurdity, to "irrationality" at a lower level of analysis is demonstrable by reference to individual cases. This, however, unfairly pits the general against the specific; similarity and difference must be assessed at the same level of abstraction. To note similarities *across* organizations in casting of the "news net" (Tuchman, 1978; Gans, 1979; Fishman, 1980) and to infer from this and other evidence that these policy considerations introduce an institutional structural bias toward certain types of news may be an abstraction, but it is at a single level of abstraction and touches two levels of analysis.

In addition, specific practices with structural homologies across levels of analysis lend themselves well to cross-level examination. Whitney (1978, 1981) was able to discern variations in editorial resource allocation under increasingly heavy levels of "news load" at the organizational, individual and individual story levels; on busy news days, a radio and wire service newsroom could shift resources around in assigning reporters to stories, while individual reporters and editors on "heavy news days" or at peak periods in more normal days could employ a number of different strategies directly on individual stories or by varying approaches to stories; at the individual news story level, and particularly in one radio newsroom a nearly unidimensional scale for treating a routine story, from "ripping and reading," to superficial editing, to rewriting without new information, to rewriting with information if new information were passively supplied, to active solicitation of additional information, was found. It must be reiterated, however, that research across levels of analysis requires measurement at the same degree of abstraction within levels. A discussion of other concerns with formulating cross-level *hypotheses* is beyond the scope of this chapter; see Dimmick (1978).

## RECENT RESEARCH

The notion that "much news is organizationally 'manufactured,' like spaghetti," (Hirsch, 1977: 15) supplants an older notion that news somehow "reflects" or "mirrors" some social reality, an idea probably always more popular among journalists than the people who study them. In a few places, the "mirror" image was supplanted by the idea that journalists do the mirroring, that "news is what newspapermen make it" (Stewart, 1946; Geiber, 1956).[4] The image that news is "manufactured," however, has become widely and rather rapidly diffused, as the scanning of relatively recent titles of books and articles suggests; the past decade has seen publication of the following: *The Manufacture of News* (Cohen and Young, 1973); *Newsmaking* (Roshco, 1975); *Making the Papers* (Goldenberg, 1975); *Making the News* (Golding and Elliott, 1979); *Making News* (Tuchman, 1978); *Manu-*

*facturing the News* (Fishman, 1980); "The News Factory" (Bantz et al., 1980). The trend may decelerate, however, since the best title-word combinations and permutations appear to have been taken.

The industrial metaphor, however, disguises several important differences in approach. For some, the route to it has been through a literature on formal organizations and administrative behavior. Hirsch (1977) provides a summary of such studies. For others (such as Bantz et al., 1980), the path is through an emphasis on the technology of news production. For the majority of work approaching the problem from these literatures, the methods most frequently have been quantitative, and the emphasis more often than not has been on formal comparisons, on searching for differences to explain structure. Moreover, much of this work has been "administrative" in the broad sense. While little of it has been directly subsidized by media organizations or institutions, the nature of its critique, if any is offered, has been by and large narrow; where a critique is offered, it is by way of noting that media performance could be improved, by degrees, largely within existing institutional frameworks.

There are, however, other trails to the manufacturing metaphor, by way of interpretive and materialist sociologies, and these have increasingly been chosen in recent U.S. work. For these, the idea of "making" news carries rather different meanings. While it does some violence to the differing approaches to characterize them together, a few gross generalizations about these studies (Tuchman, 1978; Fishman, 1980 and this volume; Lester, 1980; Molotch and Lester, 1974; Altheide, 1976; Gitlin, 1978, 1980), can be made. For the interpretive sociologists (Tuchman, Fishman, Lester, Altheide), grounded in phenomenological sociology or ethnomethodology, the "construction" of news is an aspect of a social construction of reality and hence a social construction of news. This construction is an ongoing, practical accomplishment, continuously arrived at through interaction with peers, organization superiors, and news sources. The definitions of news, how occurrences become news events, are so grounded in daily routine, so "normal," that all but their grossest and most formal features are effectively obscured, taken for granted (see Lester, 1980; Fishman in this volume). This central notion is reflected in the research topics these researchers have chosen, such as newsworkers' routines and practices (Tuchman, Fishman, Lester), organizational and extraorganizational response to accidents and scandals (Molotch and Lester, 1974), and coverage of social movements (Tuchman, 1978; Gitlin, 1980).

Research methods are qualitative, largely participant and nonparticipant observation and qualitative content analysis; with such methods, similarity and difference are, perhaps to a greater extent than in quantitative approaches, in the eye of the beholder. Moreover, the maintenance of a single level of analysis is rarely of concern; most of these researchers have worked at the individual-organizational nexus, with an understanding, implicit or explicit, that what occurs at this level is a patterned reflection downward from societal and institutional constraints and, particularly for those following a phenomenological lead (Tuchman, 1978; Lester, 1980) upward from the individual level: "making news" is manifested at the individual level, and within organizations, both from the location of media institutions within a societal power structure and systematically constrained patterns of interaction at the individual-dyadic level. To the degree that these systematic patterns are postulated or demonstrated to exist across levels of analysis, to that degree is "hegemony" postulated or demonstrated to exist. Hall (1973), for example, finds across several layers of society recurring patterns in newspaper selections news photographs that leads him to call their selection "overdetermined" (see also Gitlin, 1978).

At present, there exists no satisfactory critique of the interpretive and materialist sociological approaches to communicator study by students of the empirical organizational or occupational schools. What criticism there has been has focused on the qualitative methods employed and on a lack of explicit predictive power. The interpretive approaches, however, have provided a rich stock of useful findings and do provide a stock of clearly testable hypotheses that those wedded to quantitative approaches can fruitfully employ, with the rigor that comes with a lucid separation of levels of analysis.

## CONCLUSION

This chapter has sought to argue that explicit elaboration of the level of analysis at which a researcher is working is an aid to understanding how the mass communicator works; moreover, examination of what happens at analytical level one above and one below the primary focus of the research may serve to uncover differences and similarities that reinforce original conclusions but likewise may contradict them. Concern with the level of analysis has to date been more identified with quantitative mass communicator research, but this need not and should not remain the case.

## NOTES

1. "Communicator" in this chapter is presumed to cover all levels of analysis unless otherwise specified.

2. However, at the individual-story level and perhaps for some media types, this may not hold true. Whitney (1978) found in observing a radio newsroom that more recent wire service stories routinely replaced "older" equivalents, whether or not they contained added information.

3. It may belabor the point, but in quantitative approaches to structural similarity of news judgment across media, findings of similarity can very heavily depend on how the data are cut. Compare, for example, Sasser and Russell (1972) with Fowler and Showalter (1974). It goes almost without saying, however, that the point is debatable only in some research approaches; in a wide variety of others, representing a wide range of ideological perspectives, high degrees of equivalence, "consonance" or nondifference are postulated. Compare, for example, Ellul (1965), Hall (1973), and Noelle-Neumann (1978).

4. Both were newspaper reporters before they turned to writing about journalists.

# REFERENCES

ALTHEIDE, D. L. (1976) Creating Reality: How TV News Distorts Events. Beverly Hills: Sage.

BAGDIKIAN, B. H. (1971) The Information Machines. New York: Harper and Row.

BAILEY, G. A. and L. LICHTY (1972) "Rough justice on a Saigon street: a gatekeeper study of NBC's Tet execution film." Journalism Quarterly 49: 221-229, 238.

BANTZ, C. R., S. McCORKLE, and R. C. BAADE (1980) "The news factory." Communication Research 7, 1: 45-68.

BECKER, L. B., R. BEAM, and J. RUSSIAL (1978) "Correlates of daily newspaper performance in New England." Journalism Quarterly 55: 100-108.

COHEN, S. and J. YOUNG [eds.] (1973) The Manufacture of News. London: Constable.

DARNTON, R. (1975) "Writing news and telling stories." Daedalus 104, 2 (Spring): 175-194.

DIMMICK, J. (1978) "Levels of analysis in mass media decision-making: a taxonomy and a research strategy." Presented at the Association for Education in Journalism convention, Seattle.

DOMINICK, J., A. WURTZEL, and G. LOMETTI (1975) "Television journalism vs. show business: a content analysis of Eyewitness News." Journalism Quarterly 52: 213-218.

DONOHUE, G., P. J. TICHENOR, and C. N. OLIEN (1972) "Gatekeeping: mass media systems and information control," pp. 41-69 in F. G. Kline and P. Clarke (eds.) Current Perspectives in Mass Communication Research. Beverly Hills: Sage.

DuBICK, M. A. (1978) "The organizational structure of newspapers in relation to their metropolitan environments." Administrative Science Quarterly 23: 418-433.

ELLUL, J. (1965) Propaganda (K. Kellen, trans.). New York: Knopf.

FISHMAN, M. (1980) Manufacturing the News. Austin: University of Texas.

FOWLER, J. S. and S. W. SHOWALTER (1974)."Evening network news selection: a confirmation of news judgment." Journalism Quarterly 51: 712-715.

GANS, H. J. (1979) Deciding What's News. New York: Pantheon.

GHIGLIONE, L. [ed.] (1973) Evaluating the Press: The New England Daily Newspaper Survey. Southbridge, MA: Author.

GIEBER, W. (1956) "Across the desk: a study of 16 telegraph editors." Journalism Quarterly 33: 422-432.

——— (1964) "News is what newspapermen make it," pp. 173-181 in L. A. Dexter and D. M. White (eds.) People, Society and Mass Communications. New York: Free Press.

GITLIN, T. (1978) "Media sociology: the dominant paradigm." Theory and Society 6, 2: 205:53.

——— (1980) The Whole World is Watching. Berkeley: University of California.

GOLDENBERG, E. (1975) Making the Papers. Lexington, MA: D. C. Heath.

GOLDING, P. and P. ELLIOTT (1979) Making the News. London: Longman.

HALL, S. (1973) "The determinations of news photographs," pp. 176-190 in S. Cohen and J. Young (eds.) The Manufacture of News. London: Constable.

HIRSCH, P. M. (1977) "Occupational, organizational and institutional models in mass media research," pp. 13-42 in P. M. Hirsch, P. V. Miller, and F. G. Kline (eds.) Strategies for Communication Research. Beverly Hills: Sage.

JONES, R. L., V. C. TROLDAHL, and J. K. HVISTENDAHL (1961) "News selection patterns from a state Tts wire." Journalism Quarterly 38: 308-312.

LESTER, M. (1980) "Generating newsworthiness: the interpretive construction of public events." American Sociological Review 45 (December): 984-994.

LEWIN, K. (1947) "Channels of group life." Human Relations 1: 143-153.

McCOMBS, M. and D. L. SHAW (1977) "Structuring the 'unseen environment.'" Journal of Communication 26 (Spring): 18-22.

McQUAIL, D. (1969) "Uncertainty about the audience and the organization of mass communications," pp. 75-84 in P. Halmos (ed.) Sociological Review Monograph No. 13: The Sociology of Mass-Media Communicators. Keele: University of Keele.

MOLOTCH, H. and M. LESTER (1974) "Accidents, scandals and routines: resources for insurgent methodology," pp. 53-65 in G. Tuchman (ed.) The TV Establishment. Englewood Cliffs, NJ: Prentice-Hall.

NOELLE-NEUMANN, E. (1973) "Return to the concept of powerful mass media," pp. 65-75 in E. Dennis, D. Gillmor, and A. Ismach (eds.) Enduring issues in mass communication. St. Paul: West.

PATTERSON, T. (1980) The Mass Media Election. New York: Praeger.

POOL, I. and I. SHULMAN (1959) "Newsmen's fantasies, audiences and newswriting." Public Opinion Quarterly 23: 145-158.

ROSHCO, B. (1975) Newsmaking. Chicago: University of Chicago.

SASSER, E. and J. T. RUSSELL (1972) "The fallacy of news judgment." Journalism Quarterly 49: 280-284.

SNIDER, P. (1967) "'Mr. Gates revisited: a 1966 version of the 1949 case study." Journalism Quarterly 44: 419-427.

STEWART, K. (1943) News is What We Make It! Boston: Harcourt Brace Jovanovich.

TUCHMAN, G. (1972) "Objectivity as strategic ritual." American Journal of Sociology 77 (January): 660-679.

——— (1973) "Making news by doing work: routinizing the unexpected." American Journal of Sociology 79 (1): 110-131.

——— (1977) "The exception proves the rule: the study of routine news practice," pp. 43-62 in P. M. Hirsch, P. V. Miller, and F. G. Kline (eds.) Strategies for Communication Research. Beverly Hills: Sage.

——— (1978) Making News: A Study in the Construction of Reality. New York: Free Press.

WHITE, D. M. (1950) "The 'gate-keeper': a case study in the selection of news." Journalism Quarterly 27: 383-396.

WHITNEY, D. C. (1978) "'Information overload' in the newsroom: two case studies." Ph.D. dissertation, University of Minnesota.

——— (1981) "'Information overload' in the newsroom." Journalism Quarterly 58, 1: 69-76, 161.

——— and L. B. BECKER (forthcoming) "'Keeping the gates' for gatekeepers: the effects of wire news." Journalism Quarterly 59 (Spring).

**ABOUT THE CONTRIBUTORS**

ROBERT S. ALLEY is Professor of Humanities and Director of Area Studies Programs at the University of Richmond. He is the author of *Television: Ethics for Hire?*

LEE B. BECKER is Associate Professor of Journalism at Ohio State University. He is coauthor of *Using Mass Communication Theory* and his research interests include mass communication and politics and international communication.

JAY G. BLUMLER is Director of the Centre for Television Research at the University of Leeds, where he also holds a Personal Chair in the Social and Political Aspects of Broadcasting. He is currently completing a cross-national study of the role of broadcasting in the European Community elections of 1979 and is coauthor of *Television in Politics: Its Uses and Influence*, coauthor of *The Challenge of Election Broadcasting*, and coeditor of *The Uses of Mass Communications*, Volume 3 of this series.

MURIEL G. CANTOR is Professor of Sociology at the American University in Washington, D. C. She is the author of *The Hollywood TV Producer: His Work and His Audience* and *Prime-Time Television: Content and Control*, and coeditor of *Varieties of Work Experience*.

PETER CLARKE is Dean of the Annenberg School of Communications at the University of Southern California. He has chaired communication programs at The University of Michigan and at the University of Washington.

DENNIS K. DAVIS is Associate Professor in the Department of Communication at Cleveland State University. He is coauthor of *The Effects of Mass Communication on Political Behavior* and *Mass Communication and Everyday Life: A Perspective on Theory and Effects*.

JAMES S. ETTEMA is Assistant Professor of Journalism and Mass Communication at the University of Minnesota. He is the author of *Working Together: A Study of Cooperation Among Producers, Educators and Researchers to Create Education Television*.

SUSAN H. EVANS is the Director of the Program in Communication and Contemporary Issues at the Annenberg School of Communications at the University of Southern California. She worked in market research before receiving her Ph.D. from the University of Michigan.

MARK FISHMAN is Associate Professor of Sociology at Brooklyn College, City University of New York. He is the author of *Manufacturing the News*.

MICHAEL GUREVITCH is Senior Lecturer in Sociology at The Open University, England, where he was Chairman of the Mass Communication and Society course team. He is coauthor of *The Secularization of Leisure* and *The Challenge of Election Broadcasting,* and coeditor of the forthcoming *Culture, Society and the Media,* based on the Open University course which he chaired.

HORACE M. NEWCOMB is Associate Professor of English at the University of Texas at Austin. He is the author of *TV: The Most Popular Art* and editor of *Television: The Critical View*.

ROBERT PEKURNY is currently serving as a program consultant on the *Happy Days* television series. He is on leave from the Department of Radio-Television-Film at Northwestern University, where he is an assistant professor.

ANNE K. PETERS is Associate Professor of Sociology and Coordinator of the Labor Studies Program at California State University, Dominguez Hills. Her research interests include the artistic labor force and the sexual objectification of women.

RICHARD A. PETERSON is Professor of Sociology at Vanderbilt University. His research on the music industry has helped to develop the "production of culture" perspective within sociology. He recently returned from a year in Washington, D.C., where he consulted on the development of culture indicators.

WALTER W. POWELL is Assistant Professor in the School of Organization and Management and the Department of Sociology at Yale University. His study of decision-making in scholarly publishing houses is forthcoming from the University of Chicago Press. He is currently studying the politics of funding public television.

JOHN P. ROBINSON is Professor of Sociology and Director of the Survey Research Center at the University of Maryland. Among his recent books is *How Americans Use Time: A Social-Psychological Analysis of Everyday Behavior.*

JOHN RYAN is completing a doctoral dissertation entitled "Organization, Task-Environment and Cultural Change: The ASCAP-BMI Controversy" in the Department of Sociology at Vanderbilt University. His research interests include the relationship between organizational form and cultural product and the sociology of the family.

HALUK SAHIN is Associate Professor in the College of Journalism at the University of Maryland. His interests include mass communication theory and international communications.

JOSEPH TUROW is Associate Professor of Communication at Purdue University. He is the author of *Getting Books to Children: An Exploration of Publisher-Market Relations* and *Entertainment, Education and the Hard Sell: Three Decades of Network Children's Television.*

D. CHARLES WHITNEY is Research Assistant Professor in the Institute of Communications Research and Assistant Professor in the Department of Journalism at the University of Illinois. He is coeditor of the Sage *Mass Communication Review Yearbook,* Volumes 3 and 4.